The Protection of Literary Property

Revised Edition

By PHILIP WITTENBERG

THE WRITER, INC., Publishers

Boston

Library of Congress Cataloging in Publication Data

Wittenberg, Philip, 1895-
   The protection of literary property.

   Includes index.
   1. Copyright—United States.   2. Libel and slander
—United States.   3. Censorship—United States.
I. Title
KF2994.W5   1978   346'.73'0482   77-14370
ISBN 0-87116-110-9

Manufactured in the United States of America

Literary property essentially embodies a number of topics. There is the basic concept of property in the original creation of the author, the writer, and the editor. That property is protected through our copyright laws, both domestic and international. It is, of course, like all property, the subject of contract in various forms, including outright sale, lease, license, assignment, in part or in whole. It can be inherited and it can be the subject of devise by will. It has all of the attributes of property.

Literary property has its own peculiar liabilities in that the published word may become the subject of adverse law, including libel, privacy and censorship.

In its wisdom the law presumes that all men know the law. Of course one cannot assume that this is a fact. To make such an assumption would be absurd. But the presumption suffices as a basis for holding persons liable for violation, breach or noncompliance with law and agreements. There is, therefore, an essential need for a work which can serve both for reference and for understanding of the problems arising in the fields of writing and publishing.

Forty years have passed since the first of my books on Literary Property was published. The passage of time and of a much-changed copyright statute, as well as new formulations by the Supreme Court, made revision essential.

This new edition, then, of *The Protection of Literary Property* sets forth the provisions of the Copyright Law passed by Congress in 1976 to take effect on January 1, 1978. Additionally, it deals with many aspects of literary law with regard to libel, privacy and censorship that have been altered by new decisions rendered by the courts. In the international field, with the new Copyright Law, the United States law has been brought more nearly into accord with the Berne Convention, of which we have never been a member country, although we participated in its drafting. The new United States Copyright Law, the first general revision since 1909, has made important changes, not only in the term of copyright, but in the conditions of its being, and hence the need for an up-to-date edition of this book for the use of people confronted with the modern world of publishing and allied fields.

This new edition of *The Protection of Literary Property* was made possible by the cooperation of

JAMES VENIT

for whose research and assistance in the preparation of the material I am deeply indebted.

Philip Wittenberg

New York
January 1, 1978

⚛ CONTENTS

THE PROTECTION OF LITERARY PROPERTY

Chapter 1

THE CONCEPT OF LITERARY PROPERTY—A BRIEF HISTORY

The seeds of law and its processes of germination lie old and deep in a matrix of use and custom. The law of literary property evolved not only from the creative impulse of man, but also from the inhibitions and prohibitions with which writing has ever been involved. From creation for pleasure and aesthetic enjoyment came the notion in acquisitive societies of payment and profit. From autocracy and despotism came prohibition and censorship. All of these commingled to give rise slowly to law governing literary property.

To understand that law one must know its nature and sources. The use of the history of that law is to cast light upon its present statement and interpretation. So contemporary law opens its meanings best when one goes back to the seed. In the manuscripts and their accumulation in ancient libraries, in the universities and abbeys, on the streets of London, in the invention of printing, and in the laws both encouraging it and restricting it which came with the Reformation, in the practices of Stationers' Hall, in the rise of Grub Street, in all of these are intertwined the basis of property in literature and the recurrent attacks and limitations placed upon that property.

As early as 200 B.C., books were burned in China. Though for centuries thereafter a singer might be paid in food and lodging, it was less than two hundred and fifty years ago that

England first gave its authors a copyright. In the interval many forms of protection were struggled for.

During the first century B.C. at Alexandria, then the center of Greek culture, large libraries were in the process of accumulation and building. A great number of scribes were engaged in making copies of existing books, either for themselves or for employers. But the destruction of the learning, the lore, and the poetry collected by the Greeks over centuries was completed when the Moslems conquered Alexandria in the year 642.

In the march toward that culture which was later to be ours, the Roman libraries next appear. Libraries, both public and private, were encouraged in a revival of learning so widespread that books were reproduced in thousands of copies and distributed throughout the provinces as well as in Rome itself. The wealthy householder, with his retinue of educated slaves, caused engrossed copies to be made for himself and had not only his writing slaves, but his reading slaves, so that he could absorb his culture painlessly. Atticus, responding to the demand for many copies of the works of the popular authors, went into the mass publishing business. He had a reader work with a large number of trained slaves who took the dictation directly in book form so that a thousand copies of a small volume of epigrams or poems could be produced in a day. The books thus produced were both plentiful and cheap, selling for as little as what would now be seventy-five cents. "Everyone," says Martial, "has me in his pocket; everyone has me in his hands."

> *Laudat, amat, cantat nostros mea Roma libellos;*
> *Meque sinus omnis, me manus omnis habet.*

Pliny wrote that Regulus ostentatiously mourned for his son and that no one wept like him—"He composes an oration which he is not content with publicly reciting in Rome, but must needs enrich the provinces with a thousand copies of it."

The law had not yet, however, learned to think of property

in letters. Since men had property in things, the publisher owned the parchment and the slaves, the profits went to him. Indignantly Martial wrote:

> *Omnis in hoc gracili xeniorum turba libello*
> *Constabit nummis quatuor empta tibi.*
> *Quatuor est nimium, poterit constare duobus.*
> *Et faciet lucrum bibliopola Tryphon.*
> > (*Epigrammata,* lib. xiii., ep. 3.)

> *Qui tecum cupis esse meos ubicunque libellos.*
> *Et comites longae quaeris habere viae,*
> *Hos eme quos arcet brevibus membrana tabellis:*
> *Scrinia da magnis, me manus una capit.*

and Horace joined in with:

> *Hic meret aera liber Sosiis, hic et mare transit.*
> *Et longum noto scriptori prorogat alvum.*
> > (*Art. Poet.,* 345.)

Although, among others, Terence was able to sell his plays, there was no law that protected the buyer against piracy. There was, as yet, no notion of copyright. This condition which outraged the author continued throughout the days of the manuscript copy. There were books in a steady stream and the booksellers and publishers copied whatever they wished without so much as a by-your-leave to the author; there were some cases where out of moral consideration, or perhaps because the author withheld his manuscript, the publisher paid a price.

With the decline of Rome and the growth of the Church, the production of books entered a new phase. From about 500 A.D. for seven centuries, the reproduction of literary works was in the hands of the Church. Monasteries spread throughout Europe, and in their cells and in the scriptorium monks labored, making copies of books principally for the purposes of the Church. There were no lay writers and there was very little original writing. With the coming of the twelfth and the thirteenth centuries, the great universities appeared and set up groups of copyists to supply the newly risen demand for learning. The lay writer again appeared and new works as well as old were encouraged. Both the university and the monastery were active during this period. But such property as existed was in the copies which they produced, i.e., the physical paper, not the literary material. There were not enough writers or readers, nor was there a sufficient demand for books, nor any system of distribution of sufficient magnitude in existence to bring about a concept of property in literature. The monks lived through the ownership and management of their farms. The scribes of the universities were paid, but their payment was for the labor of copying, not for the originality of writing. The universities, like the monasteries, were still instrumentalities of the Church, but others than churchmen could now find their way into the field of letters. A manuscript trade was built up.

Prior to the invention of printing there were, in Orléans and in Paris alone, tens of thousands of persons employed in the making of copies of manuscripts, all without pay to the authors, although the copies fetched fabulous prices.

The authors were not happy. Marmontel in his *Memoirs* tells of an interview with Bassompierre, a bookseller of Liége. The bookseller had done a right good business in selling Marmontel's works. So much so, that when the author visited his town, the bookseller called upon him to thank him for the services he had rendered the community. Marmontel, like Horace, wanted more than praise; he was angry. "What," he cried. "You first rob me of the fruits of my labors, and then have the effrontery to come and brag about it under my nose!" The bookseller was amazed; he had never given a thought to an author's right to share in the proceeds. "Monsieur," he said, "you forget Liége is a free country and we have nothing to do with you and your privileges."

The minds of authors were fermenting. Just as the Latin poets and dramatists had been unwilling to sing unless they were provided with the necessary bird seed, so the authors of the day were beginning to feel that their works published in large editions ought to yield them more than a meed of praise. The authors of works were unwilling to have them copied without payment. The necessity for some kind of property protection for the author in the form of copyright was forming.

In this connection the most-often-told tale is that of the quarrel between Saint Columba and his teacher, Finnian of Moville. Legend has it that in 567 Saint Columba, sitting up all night, furtively made a copy of Finnian's Psalter, which Finnian had lent him. The good abbot protested and claimed not only the original but also the copy as his property. The violent dispute was carried before King Diarmed, then sitting in Tara's halls. The noble king gave judgment for the abbot, saying: "To every cow her calf, and accordingly to every book its copy." Columba refused to take the verdict and raised a band of followers who fought the king. Columba lost, and went into exile. So ended our first copyright case. The tradition that this was the first case has been voted unworthy of belief, although, as Augustine Birrell put it: "This, in the teeth of the fact that the identical copy of the Psalter in Saint Columba's well-known handwriting was so recently as 1867 in the possession of an Irish baronet and exhibited in the Museum of the Royal Irish Academy at Dublin!"

Almost a thousand years was to elapse after this precedent until, in 1533, we find the first authentic recorded complaint of piracy in English law. When Wynkyn de Worde in 1533 sued for the protection of his right to print a treatise on grammar by Robert Witinton, Wynkyn de Worde obtained a "privilege" for the second edition which prevented further misappropriation, and because Peter Trevers had reprinted it from the edition of 1523, De Worde complained of piracy.

The cow and its generative habits seem to be suggestive to those who write about writing. Many years later, when Dr. Johnson was discussing piracy, Boswell reported, "He said, our judges had not gone deep in the question concerning literary property. I mentioned Lord Monboddo's opinion, that if a man could get a work by heart, he might print it, as by such an act the mind is exercised. *Johnson*: 'No, sir, a man's repeating it no more makes it his property, than a man may sell a cow which he drives home!' I said, printing an abridgment of a work was allowed, which was only cutting the horns and tail off a cow. *Johnson*: 'No, sir, 'tis making cow have a calf.' "

Joshua Bloch tells an interesting story that parallels the Finnian tale. Quoting the proverb "Men do not despise a thief, if he steal to satisfy his soul when he is hungry" (Proverbs 6:30), rabbinical authorities gave it as their legal opinion that one is allowed to copy the text of a book without the knowledge of its owner. Bloch tells the story: "A certain Rabbi Aaron, a respectable gentleman, had passed through the Umbrian town of Perugia. He had with him a collection of fine books, 'a load for a team of mules.' He said that for seven years he had lived at Toledo, which at that time was the capital of Spain, and had brought from there many precious books. He showed to Immanuel and his friends a list of them consisting of about a hundred and eighty titles. The books were hidden and sealed in barrels. As he had to go to Rome he left his books in the care of Immanuel and his friends until his return. He enjoined them that 'no hand shall touch them, but he shall surely be stoned or shot through; for behold, I swear by Him who was and shall be, whether it be man or beast, it shall not live' (cf. Exodus 19:13). But no sooner had the man left the city than Immanuel and his friends opened the barrels and 'as soon as they released the books from their prison they selected the choicest items, ten volumes, and copied their texts, which represented the best works of wisdom and philosophy. About a month later Rabbi Aaron returned from Rome. When he saw what they did with his books he became very angry and wanted to destroy the copies which were made. Immanuel appeased him with a letter written in rhymed prose full of keen wit and humor blended with caustic satire, often bordering on frivolity and want of delicacy of expression. Among other things, he wrote: 'We broke thy barrels of books and thou grewest angry, but when Moses our teacher broke the two tablets he was told: thou didst well to break them.' "

Others who own books might grumble at the copying, but among the Jews it was deemed a blessing to permit the scribes to make copies and their owners would say, "Are books then made [copied] for keepsake? No, let people study from them and make copies of them." But these were all books of the Law and its exegesis.

During the period of the monasteries and the universities, the booksellers were called *stationarii,* a word which was ultimately to yield us Stationers' Hall. The word probably derives from the booksellers adopting a stationary point or booth in the streets as distinguished from the practice of itinerant vendors. They were, in a large sense, brokers, to whom were entrusted illuminated and other manuscripts for sale. They also rented out manuscripts for high prices.

In England the first merchants in books, the stationers, dealt in books imported from abroad and such books as were made in England. The works they were engaged in making and printing were illuminated on parchment and some of them were great, unwieldy works which could scarcely be handled unless they were placed on large lecterns or tables. They were valuable and were frequently chained to their posts. The chief trade was in religious works, including Paternosters, Aves, Creeds, and Amens. Their favorite stations on the streets of London still bear the names Paternoster Row, Amen Corner, and Ave Maria Lane.

The trade in books was becoming of sufficient importance so that those engaged in it felt called upon, for their mutual interest, to form a voluntary association. As early as 1357, in the days of Chaucer and William Langland of England, they formed a Brotherhood of Manuscript Producers. Sometime about 1403 the brotherhood of printers, booksellers, publishers, and the like, under the name of the Craft of Writers of Text-Letters, commonly known as "Limners," was given a charter by the Lord Mayor and the Court of Aldermen of the City of London. They established rules and ordinances "for the good government of their Fellowship."

In or about 1440 printing from blocks was introduced to the western world. Johannes Gutenberg of Mainz, Germany, was the innovator. Block printing had been used in China as early as 868 and printing from movable type had been done in China in about 1040. The 868 book is still in existence.

The art of printing spread from Mainz throughout the Continent to Italy, France, Switzerland, and Spain. The first English printer was William Caxton, who had learned the art on the Continent and moved to Westminster in 1476. He set up a press at The Red Pail in Almanary. He and his successors, Wynkyn de Worde, Richard Pinson, Julian Notary, John Rastall, Thomas Godfrey, et al., were a few of the increasing number of men engaged in printing and publishing. Out of that multiplication of printers there sprang the necessity for a publicly recognized craft of printing. These printers associated themselves with the Brotherhood. In the world of trade associations, this association was known at that time not as the Craft of the Printers, but as the Stationers.

These first printers were and had to be men of great learning and ingenuity. They either wrote or translated most of the material they produced. They built their own presses, cut their own type, made the necessary incidental parts, and bound their own works. There was, as yet, no division of labor among the various artificers whose work contributed to the complete book. The type was cut on wooden blocks and printed on a massive structure of heavy beams, which constituted the press. Since the Continent was the place of origin, many of the first printers went there to study their art and there was an influx of printers into England from abroad. So eagerly were books sought that in 1483 an enactment by Richard III encouraged their importation, and restrictions on aliens were made inapplicable to "any artificer, or merchant stranger, of what nation or country he be, for bringing into this realm, or selling by retail or otherwise, any books written or printed, or for inhabiting within this said realm for the same intent, or any scrivener, alluminor, reader, or printer of such books."

Production exceeded the demand. There was no popular education; there were insufficient readers for the number of books that could be produced, and so these first printers struggled and many of them became bankrupt. In 1533, fifty years after the Statute of Richard, under Henry VIII, the privileges of aliens were wiped out. An act was passed which provided that no persons "resident or inhabitant within this realm shall buy to sell again any printed books brought from any parts out of the King's obeisance ready bound in boards, leather or parchment."

Its preamble restated the grievance which had arisen since the laws of Richard, and set forth

> . . . there hath come to this realm sithen the making of the same, a marvelous number of printed books, and daily doth; and the cause of the making of the same provision seemeth to be, for that there were but few books, and few printers within this realm at that time, which would well exercise and occupy the said science and craft of printing; nevertheless, sithen the making of the said provision, many of this realm, being the King's natural subjects, have given them so diligently to learn and exercise the said craft of printing, that at this day there be within this realm a great number cunning and expert in the said science or craft of printing, as able to exercise the said craft in all points, as any stranger in any other realm or country; and furthermore, where there be a great number of the King's subjects within this realm, which live by the craft and mystery of binding of books, and that there be a great multitude well expert in the same, yet all this notwithstanding, there are divers persons that bring from beyond the sea great plenty of printed books, not only in the Latin tongue, but also in our maternal English tongue, some bound in boards, some in

leather, and some in parchment, and them sell by retail, whereby many of the King's subjects, being binders of books, and having no other faculty wherewith to get their living, be destitute of work and like to be undone, except some reformation herein be had.

There was much more than a simple desire to protect the printer in his living. Books began to appear which challenged the authority of the Church and the King and his lords. Large presses were hard to conceal and the material issuing from the press could be easily controlled by the expedient of licensing the press itself and the printer and by granting privileges therefor.

The earliest privilege granted in England was in 1518 for a Latin sermon by Richard Pace. In 1550 there was granted the first privilege to an author, John Palgrave, but since he was also a printer and publisher, it was much more likely that he received the privilege not as author, but in his capacity as publisher. On May 4, 1556, the Stationers' Company was chartered by Philip and Mary, and on February 1, 1560, they were created by the Lord Mayor one of the liveried companies of the city, then about forty in number.

The very evident purpose of the founding of the Stationers' Company was to prevent the propagation of the Protestant Reformation. After reciting that several seditious and heretical books, "both in rhymes and tracts, were daily printed, renewing and spreading great and detestable heresies against the Catholic doctrine of the Holy Mother Church," the charter provided for the suppression of this evil by constituting ninety-seven named persons an incorporated society of the art of a stationer, and ordered that no person not a member of this society should practice the art of printing. The master and wardens of the society were empowered to search, seize, and burn all prohibited books, and to imprison any person found exercising the art of printing without authority. By decree and statute, the Stationers' Company enjoyed a monopoly which it exercised with despotic zeal. The Catholic Church was fighting for its existence as the state church of England and it imported the methods of the Inquisition.

The notion was that by knowing where and when a printing press was operated and by providing for the licensing of books before they were printed, the attacks upon the Church and upon the heads of the state could be prevented. By organizing the stationers into a small compact company, which they thought could be readily policed, they attempted to stop the Protestant Reformation. This fitted in admirably with the plans of the Stationers' Company, since it gave them a tight hold on the printing industry and kept the profits within a small group.

Since no author could publish his writings except through members of the Stationers' Company, they could control the price they paid and set up a monopoly with all of its trappings and *indicia*. The author could not set his own work in type, since the right to own type was limited to members. Accordingly, the members of the company were able to deal with authors as they wished. The author, it is true, owned the manuscript, but he could get only cold comfort from that. If he wished to communicate it to the public, he could do it only on the printer's terms. The property in literature was not in the writing but in the right to make copies, and the right to make copies belonged to the owner of the press. The right of ownership, not authorship, was respected. The Stationers established a register in which their members could note their ownership of literary property (the first entry showing title to copy was dated 1558) and by custom they respected each other's rights in what they bought from authors. They also registered under special license textbooks and religious works other than newly created original works. The forms of literary property were beginning to emerge but the profits and values inherent in it belonged to the printers, who were also publishers and retailers. It was not to be thought, however, that so lucrative a business as publishing and so important a movement as the Reformation could be stopped by monopoly. Secret presses sprang up.

The Star Chamber Decree of 1637 refers to "a great part of the secret printing in corners" and made provision to penalize "all printing in corners without license." A like provision is found in the order of the Lords and Commons in June, 1643, where we find complaint that "others of sundry other professions, not freed of the *Stationers'* Company, have taken upon them to set up sundry private Printing Presses in corners." Books and pamphlets attacking the Church were imported from abroad, particularly from Holland.

It is a significant fact that the limitation of presses and printing in England and the monopoly they enjoyed caused a physical deterioration in the type which they used and the paper on which they printed. The imported work was far superior in physical quality among other things. Bibles had long been a monopoly with the two universities of Oxford and Cambridge, and the effect of the long monopoly was not only poorly cut type and bad paper, but typographical carelessness. We may find many curious errors in the Bibles of the period. The printers in Charles I's reign had issued an edition of the Bible in which the word "not" had been omitted from the Seventh Commandment and it had thus been made to order a positive instead of a negative injunction. In the Bible of 1653 the printers had permitted to pass uncorrected "Know ye not that the *un*righteous shall inherit the kingdom of God."

The methods of monopoly for the benefit of the Stationers and repression for the benefit of the Church and of the King were failing because the wit of men found methods of circumventing them. So the Star Chamber issued repressive orders in 1556, 1585, 1623, and 1637.

Many years later the Supreme Court of the United States was to say of the Stationers' Company: "They were particularly ruthless and exercised the power of search, confiscation, and imprisonment without interruption from Parliament." (*Holmes v. Hurst.*)

On July 11, 1637, the Star Chamber issued its most famous decree. It ordered:

IMPRIMIS, That no person or persons whatsoeuer shall presume to print, or cause to bee printed, either in the parts beyond the Seas, or in this Realme, or other his Maiesties Dominions, any seditious, scismaticall, or offensive Bookes or Pamphlets, to the scandall of Religion, or the Church, or the Government, or Governours of the Church or State, or Commonwealth, or of any Corporation, or particular person or persons whatsoeuer,

Among other things it provided

That no person or persons whatsoeuer, shall at any time print or cause to be imprinted, any Booke, or Pamphlet whatsoeuer, unlesse the same Booke or Pamphlet, and also all and euery the Titles, Epistles, Prefaces, Proems, Preambles, Introductions, thereunto annexed, or therewith imprinted, shall be first lawfully licensed and authorized onely by such person and persons as are hereafter expressed, and by no other, and shall be also first entered into the Registers Booke of the Company of Stationers; upon paine that every Printer offending therein, shall be forever hereafter disabled to use or exercise the Art of Mysterie of Printing, and receive such further punishment, as by this Court or the high Commission Court respectively as the severall causes shall require, shall be thought fitting.

Among its provisions was that all books were to have imprinted thereon the name and address of the publisher and also the name of the author. This, however, was not in any recognition of any right in the author, it was rather a means of identification for punishment.

Only twenty master printers were provided for and each of those was allowed only two presses. Four founders or casters of type were named and a limit was placed on the number of apprentices allowed to the master printers and master founders of type. Requirement was made for the deposit of a copy of each book in the library of Oxford University.

Then to make sure that no one other than the selected persons printed a book, the decree provided:

> The court doth hereby declare their firme resolution, that if any person or persons, that is not allowed Printer, shall hereafter presume to set up any Presse for printing, or shall worke at any such Presse, or Set, or Compose any Letters to bee wrought by any such Presse; hee, or they so offending, shall from time to time, by the Order of this Court, bee set in the Pillorie, and whipt through the Citie of London, and suffer such other punishment, as this Court shall Order or think fit to inflict upon them, upon Complaint or proofe of such offence or offences, or shall be otherwise punished, as the Court of High Commission shall thinke fit, and is agreeable to their Commission.

Although the principal object of the Star Chamber was the uprooting of heresy, a secondary object was to wipe out the attacks on royal authority and patrician privilege. It was thought that by making it unlawful to buy or keep type or presses that printing could be made too risky a business for the religious reformer, the liberal politician, or the local patriot. Severity of punishment on the one hand, and the hope of being allowed to partake in the monopolistic trust on the other hand, would, it was thought, compel all printers to refrain from publishing any works except those that bore the imprimatur. This particular decree of the Star Chamber seems to have been modeled after a Spanish decree of 1550, which had been re-enforced by order of that notable foe of heresy, Philip II of Spain. It is true that the English law left out the penalties of burning alive or burying alive; public whipping and the pillory were as much as the King's men and the Church thought the inflamed temper of the people of England would stand. Instead of attempting to remove the causes of discontent, the advisers of Charles I thought to destroy criticism. Their decree of 1637 did not long stand, nor did they long live.

For in 1641 the Long Parliament abolished the Court of Star Chamber and brought the head of Strafford to the block. In 1645 Archbishop Long was executed and in 1649 King Charles himself was beheaded. But the Parliament which did this was in some way equally a creature of the times, for after abolishing the Star Chamber it made its own order in January, 1642, that

> It is ordered that the Master and the Wardens of the Company of Stationers shall be required to take especiall Order, that the Printers doe neither print, nor reprint any thing without the name and consent of the Author: And that if any Printer shall notwithstanding print or reprint any thing without the consent and name of the Author, that he shall then be proceeded against, as both Printer and Author thereof, and their names to be certified to this House.

Here again we find an early reference to the author and apparently an order which might help the author, since printers and the members of the Stationers' Company were adjured to publish nothing without consent. This is really the first establishment of a right in the author by law. But the probabilities are that it was not for the sake of the author that the order was made, but rather, again, for the purposes of identifying him for punishment.

Again in March of 1643, the Commons House of Parliament made an order for the regulation of printing: That its Committee for Examinations "have power to appoint such persons as they thinke fit, to search in any house or place where there is iust cause of suspition, That Presses are kept and employed in the printing of scandalous and lying Pamphlets, and that they do demollish and take away such Presses and their materials, . . . and that the Committee or any four of them have power to commit to prison any of the said Printers, or any other persons that do contrive, or publikely or privately vend, sell, or publish any Pamphlet scandalous to his Majesty or the proceedings of both or either Houses of Parliament."

In June, 1643, Parliament issued its most famous order on the subject. Again they confessed that their previous orders for suppressing abuses had failed and that their orders, notwithstanding the diligence of the Stationers' Company to put them in full execution, had taken little or no effect. Its preamble provided:

> WHEREAS divers good Orders have bin lately made by both Houses of Parliament, for suppressing the great late abuses and frequent disorders in Printing many, false forged, scandalous, seditious, libellous, and unlicensed Papers, Pamphlets, and Books to the great defamation of Religion and government. Which orders (notwithstanding the diligence of the Company of *Stationers,* to put them in full execution) have taken little or no effect.

It then discussed conditions in the Stationers' Company and re-established the rights of the members in their copies saying:

> . . . And by reason that divers of the *Stationers* Company and others being Delinquents (contrary to former orders and the constant custome used among the said Company) have taken liberty to Print, Vend and publish, the most profitable vendible Copies of Books, belonging to the Company and other *Stationers,* especially such Agents as are imployed in putting the said Orders in Execution, and that by way of revenge for giveing information against them to the Houses for their Delinquences in Printing, to the great prejudice of the said Company of *Stationers* and Agents, and to their discouragement in this publik service.

And enacted:

> . . . And that no person or persons shall hereafter print, or cause to be reprinted any Book or Books, or part of Book, or Books heretofore allowed of and granted to the said Company of *Stationers* for their relief and maintenance of their poore, without the licence or consent of the Master, Wardens and Assistants of the said Company; Nor any Book or Books lawfully licenced and entred in the Register of the said Company for any particular member thereof, without the licence and consent of the owner or owners thereof.

Unfortunately for those who wish to repress and restrict but fortunately for the world and for authors, John Milton had been unhappily married. When his wife deserted him he answered the insult by writing *The Doctrine and Discipline of Divorce; Restored to the good of both Sexes, from the Bondage of Canon Law, and other Mistakes.* He later wrote a pamphlet entitled *The Judgment of Martin Bucer concerning Divorce.* The first pamphlet was published soon after the Ordinance of 1643 was issued, but without license and without registration. Complaint was made against Milton in a petition of the Stationers to the House of Commons and the matter came before that House and before the Lords in 1644. That proceeding brought forth the most eloquent defense of freedom of the press and of the right of men to write what they must, the famous *Areopagitica; a Speech of John Milton's for the Liberty of Unlicensed Printing To the Parliament of England,* which was published on November 25, 1644, and was issued unlicensed and unregistered. Although the Stationers returned again to the charge, the effect of the pamphlet was such that no punishment was visited upon Milton. Milton did approve that portion of the order "which preserves justly every mans Copy to himselfe." It was such references as these from which there was to grow belief in the notion that there was a property at common law in literature.

Milton was to make further publishing history, for his agreement with Samuel Simmons is one of the first agreements calling for the payment of copy money for an original work. The contract for the publication of *Paradise Lost* was executed on April 27, 1667, and contained provision for a down payment of £5 and £5 more after the sale of the first edition of 1,300 copies and the further promise of two additional sums of £5 after the sale of two more editions of the same size respectively. Frequently one hears the tale that Milton sold all of his rights for £5. Milton was paid the second £5 and in 1680 his widow transferred all her rights in the copyright for £8. Thus over the period of thirteen years the poem brought £18, although twenty had been stipulated. Actually, the publisher does not seem to have had too great a bargain, for the first printing took almost seven years to dispose of, although, in the meantime, the publisher had given it five new title pages in an endeavor to move the sales. Although the poem fetched only £18, the manuscript original of the indenture was subsequently sold for 100 guineas to a national museum to be preserved as a treasure.

After the restoration of the Stuarts, King Charles II urged upon the House of Commons the passing of an act to control the press as necessary to the peace of the kingdom, since the "exorbitant" liberty of the press had been "a great occasion of the late Rebellion, and the schisms in the church." The act which was passed pursuant thereto has been called a marked advance in the recognition of the rights of authors, but its preamble and provisions disclose that it was to serve the same tyrannical powers that were so brashly proclaimed by the Star Chamber. Its preamble discloses its parenthood.

> Whereas the well government and regulating of printers and printing presses is matter of public care and of great concernment, especially considering, that, by the general licentiousness of the late times, many evil-disposed persons have been encouraged to print and sell heretical, schismatical, blasphemous, seditious, and treasonable books, pamphlets, and papers, and still do continue such their unlawful and exorbitant practice to the high dishonor of Almighty God, the endangering the peace of these kingdoms, and raising a disaffection to his most excellent Majesty and his government; for prevention whereof, no surer means can be advised than by reducing and limiting the number of printing-presses, and by ordering and settling the said art of mystery of printing by act of Parliament, in manner as hereinafter is expressed.

Under its terms it was required that at the beginning of every licensed book there be included a certificate of the licenser to the effect that the book contained nothing "contrary to the Christian faith or the doctrine or discipline of the Church of England, or against the state and government of this realm, or contrary to good life or good manners, or otherwise, as the nature and subject of the work shall require." But there was a clause which prohibited any persons from printing or importing, without the consent of the owner, any book which any person had the sole right to print. The owner might be construed to be the author but, since the author could obtain his rights only through registration by a member of the Stationers' Company, the stationers were the principal beneficiaries. One may spell out a property in the author which consisted in his right to withhold from the members of the Stationers' Company the right to sell his works. At best, since he could not print without assigning it to a member, it was a meager form of property.

Decrees of the Star Chamber, which were promulgated to enforce licensing, and the acts of Parliament were alike in one thing. They provided for the licensing of material prior to its publication. That licensing was evidenced by the gracious granting of the Imprimatur. Since more than one person frequently had to pass on a book, title pages were encumbered with the multiplicity of permissions. The Star Chamber Order of 1637 provided:

Item, That all Bookes concerning the common Lawes of this Realme shall be printed by the especiall allowance of the Lords chiefe Iustices, and the Lord chiefe Baron for the time being, or one or more of them, or by their appointment; And that all Books of History, belonging to this State, and present times, or any other Booke of State affaires, shall be licensed by the principall Secretaries of State, or one of them, or by their appointment; And that all Bookes concerning Heraldry, Titles of Honour and Armes, or otherwise concerning the Office of Earle Marshall, shall be licenced by the Earle Marshall, or by his appointment; And further, that all other Books, whether of Diuinitie, Phisicke, Philosophie, Poetry, or whatsoeuer, shall be allowed by the Lord

Arch-Bishop of *Canterbury*, or Bishop of *London* for the time being, or by their appointment, or the Chancellours, or Vice Chancellors of either of the Vniuersities of this Realme for the time being.

Alwayes prouided, that the Chancellour or Vice-Chancellour, of either of the Vniuersities, shall Licence only such Booke or Bookes that are to be Printed within the limits of the Vniuersities respectiuely, but not in London, or elsewhere, not medling either with Bookes of the common Law, or matters of State.

The Imprimatur survived and was found in America as late as 1719 in the Province of Massachusetts Bay.

During the days of the licensing acts and orders, writing was a precarious trade. The author was much more likely to have his ears cropped off than his purse filled. In the latter half of the seventeenth century there came the days of the great booksellers; men such as Thomas Guy who took over from Oxford University the printing of Bibles and put them out in large editions at popular prices, and whose fortune eventually founded Guy's Hospital in London, or John Dunton, founder of the *Athenian Mercury*, the first number of which appeared on March 17, 1690, or Jacob Tonson, John Dryden's publisher, with whom Dryden carried on a bitter feud over the low payment he received from time to time, and who acquired from Brabazon Aylmer a half interest in the original covenant of indenture and the copyright of Milton's poem *Paradise Lost*.

It was Tonson who proposed to his writer friends that he would give them a weekly feast provided that they gave him the refusal of all their productions. This generous proposal was accepted, and the cook's name being Christopher, for brevity called Kit, and his sign being the Cat and Fiddle, they very merrily derived a quaint denomination from puss and her master, and from thence called themselves the Kit-Kat Club. The club became the leading meeting place for the wits and important figures in the political history of the state, as well as in the history of its literature. Each of its members was painted by Sir Godfrey Kneller, a famous artist of his day. The club was one of the most exciting institutions of its time in London and its members exercised considerable authority. Tonson and the club were described in *Faction Displayed* (1705):

> *I am the Touchstone of all modern wit;*
> *Without my stump, in vain you poets writ.*
> *Those only purchase everlasting fame*
> *That in my "Miscellany" plant their name.*
> *I am the founder of your loved Kit-Kat,*
> *A Club that gave direction to the state.*
> *'Twas here we first instructed all our youth*
> *To talk profane and laugh at sacred truth;*
> *We taught them how to toast and rhyme and bite,*
> *To sleep away the day, and drink away the night.*

Tonson not only was the first to make *Paradise Lost* popular, but some years later he traded under the sign of Shakspere's Head and was the first bookseller to throw Shakespeare open to the reading public. In 1709 Tonson produced Rowe's edition in octavo. "Bernard Lintot the elder, who about the same time republished Shakspere's Poems, expresses himself in his advertisement as if Tonson's speculation were an experiment not absolutely certain of success: —'The writings of Mr. Shakspere are in so great esteem that several gentlemen have subscribed to a later edition of his Dramatic Works in six volumes, which makes me hope that this little book will not be unacceptable to the public.'"

It was under these booksellers that the subscription plan of publishing books developed. Two editions would be issued, one at a high price for the nobility and the wealthy friends of the author, and one at a lesser price for others of the public who might care to subscribe. The subscription business flourished, and men like Dryden and Pope, who were among the popular authors of their day, made quite good sums. But the publishers would try as far as possible to buy the copyright outright, and the large profit went to them. Ben Jonson protested against their methods of saving money by "buttering o'er again, once in seven years," antiquated pamphlets and issuing them as new. The system of patrons of literature who guaranteed the subscription series was distasteful and many were the complaints by authors. Later on Dr. Johnson was to write of it: "He that asks for subscriptions soon finds that he has enemies. All who do not encourage him defame him"; and then again: "Now learning is a trade; a man goes to a bookseller and gets what he can. We have done with patronage. In the infancy of learning we find some great men praised for it. This diffused it among others. When it becomes general an author leaves the great and applies to the multitude."

From the time of Shakespeare down to Johnson, the printers and publishers, an undifferentiated trade, were still the real owners of whatever literary property there was. By their methods of registration they were able to acquire whatever works they wanted by setting whatever price they offered with few exceptions. They had even better methods at their command for the acquisition of property. Writers were either gentlemen or inhabitants of what was to be Grub Street. The gentlemen writers, since the lot of the others was so lowly, scorned putting their words in print and distributed them in manuscript copies by hand. Gray, following this tradition, refused to take any payment for his *Elegy*. Edmund Gosse, in his *Gray*, wrote that the poet "had a Quixotic notion that it was beneath a gentleman to take money from a bookseller; a view in which Dodsley [a bookseller] warmly coincided." This was meat and drink to the publishers, for they would obtain a copy of the manuscript (as they did, incidentally, with the *Elegy*) and without a by-your-leave, print it, using either the name of the author or a fictitious name, as they chose, and since by registration they could acquire a monopoly, many a gentleman writer found himself in print against his will.

George Wither in his *The Scholler's Purgatory* (published about 1625), in a curious and lengthy dissertation on the character of dishonest or mere stationers, wrote "that he makes no scruple to put out the right author's name and insert another in the second edition of a booke . . . whether the author be willing, or no, he will publish it, and there shall be contrived on any alsoe according to his owne pleasure, . . . For many of our moderne bookesellers are but needlesse excrements, or rather vermine, . . . yea, since they take upon them to publish bookes contrived, altered and mangled at their own pleasures, without consent of the writers; and to change the name sometymes, both of booke and Author (after they have been ymprinted)."

Sir Thomas Browne (1605–82) discovered that the *Religio Medici* had been published anonymously without his consent. In the preface to a later edition the author states that it was composed for private use, lent to friends, and transcribed until it became "a most depraved copy, and then was surreptitiously printed."

Dryden, in his preface to *The State of Innocence* (1674), gives as his reason for printing it: "I was induced to it in my own defence, many hundred copies of it being dispersed abroad without my knowledge or consent; and every one gathering new faults it became at length a libel against me."

Dryden was one of the first who protested against the differentiation between the gentlemen authors, so-called, and those who wrote for money.

Already authors were seeking a professional relationship to their work and wanting it placed on a plane of property in themselves. In the preface to *All for Love* Dryden said, "We who write, if we want the talent, yet have the excuse that we do it for a poor subsistence: but what can be urged in their defence, who not having the vocation of poverty to scribble, out of mere wantonness take pains to make themselves ridiculous." Dr. Johnson took the same view and wrote of his edition of Shakespeare, "I look upon this as I did upon the *Dictionary;* it is all work, and my inducement to it is not love or desire of fame, but the want of money, which is the only motive to writing that I know of."

For the non-gentleman writers, Grub Street, the Bohemia of its day, developed, and in it there lived the hack writers who doused themselves in gin and who alternated between the degradation of despair and the high time of their life when they were paid a guinea and could eat better than their accustomed slops and dress in better than their accustomed rags. The patron was their refuge. They hung out in the antechambers of the great and sought by fulsome praise and dedication to win an extra guinea, a place at court, or a sinecure which would enable them to live. It was then that there developed the hyperbole and the exaggeration of the long-winded dedication composed in equal parts of servility and flattery. Every holiday, every anniversary, was the occasion for the private laureate, which brought forth Swift's "Directions for Making a Birthday Song," in which he gave the poet appropriate advice.

> *Thus your encomium, to be strong*
> *Must be applied directly wrong:*
> *A tyrant for his mercy praise,*
> *And crown a royal dunce with bays . . .*
> *And as he hears his wit and sense*
> *(To which he never made pretence)*
> *Set out in hyperbolic strains*
> *A guinea shall reward your pains.*
> *For patrons never pay so well*
> *As when they've scarcely learnt to spell.*

Not all patrons were ignorant, not all were vicious. There were learned men and wits among the patrons as well as among the men they patronized but, in general, the position of the writer under patronage was poor. He was a suppliant rather than a man honestly living off the fruits of his labors. He composed too much in the hopes of a precious nod and stood too little on his own feet. The bent knee is an uncomfortable position for writing. Not only poets, but political writers were obliged to seek patrons and found themselves with the turns of events on many sides of the same question. Their opinions went with their patron. They paid their rent the hard way. After the Statute of Anne there would be a change. The recognition of the author's right would slowly give him a sense that what he was selling was property and that he was not the recipient of alms. There would still be a period of conflict with the bookseller replacing the patron; but, in the long run, the author would become a man of property.

Oliver Goldsmith in his *Enquiry into the Present State of Polite Learning in Europe* (1759) said, "Thus the man who, under the patronage of the great, might have done honour to humanity, when only patronized by the bookseller become a thing a little superior to the fellow who works at the press." For Purdon he wrote an epitaph:

> *Here lies poor Ned Purdon, from misery freed,*
> *Who long was a bookseller's hack:*
> *He led such a damnable life in this world*
> *I don't think he'd wish to come back.*

He might have been writing the epitaph for an era. The licensing acts which were still in force toward the end of the seventeenth century expired in 1689 and the powers of the Stationers' Company expired in 1694.

The members of Stationers' Hall, in the meantime, were acquiring the rights in "copy," as it was called, and were recognizing each other's rights more as a method of preventing destructive competition than anything else. The members of the Hall developed a custom or trade recognition of what was called the right of copy. They claimed that this was a common-law right in perpetuity. With the expiration of the licensing act, some enterprising Scotsmen began the printing of books in Edinburgh and imported them into England. The Stationers, believing that this was an infringement of their rights, petitioned Parliament for relief. They wanted a new act that would re-establish in them their rights in copy, which they believed they had acquired in perpetuity. Their petition of 1709 protesting against the infringement of what they deemed to be their copyright ran in part as follows:

> The liberty now set on foot of breaking through this ancient and reasonable usage is no way to be effectually restrained but by an act of Parliament. For by common law a bookseller can recover no more costs than he can prove damage, but it is impossible for him to prove the tenth, nay, perhaps the hundredth part of the damage he suffers, because a thousand counterfeit copies may be dispersed into as many different hands all over the kingdom, and he not be able to prove the sale of ten. Besides, the defendant is always a pauper and so the plaintiff must lose his costs of suit. (No man of substance has been known to offend in this particular nor will any ever appear in it.) Therefore, the only remedy by the common law is to confine a beggar to the rules of the King's Bench or the Fleet, and there he will continue the evil practice with impunity. We, therefore, pray that confiscation of counterfeit copies be one of the penalties to be inflicted on offenders.

In the meantime, sentiment in favor of the author had also come to a head. In 1709 a draft of a copyright law, said to have been written in part by Joseph Addison and in part by Jonathan Swift, was introduced and resulted in the act which became effective on April 10, 1710, known as the Statute of Anne. In that statute, for the first time, the author, as well as the proprietor, is mentioned as among those granted protection. It is entitled "An Act for the Encouragement of Learning by vesting the copies of printed books in the authors or purchasers of such copies during the terms therein mentioned." The preamble declares that "printers, booksellers, and other persons have of late frequently taken the liberty of printing, reprinting, and publishing, or causing to be printed, reprinted, and published, books and other writings, without the consent of the authors or proprietors of such books and writings, to their very great detriment, and too often to the ruin of them and their families"; and that the object of the act is to prevent "such practices for the future, and for the encouragement of learned men to compose and write useful books."

This was the real turning point. Now all references to authors in the provisions of the previous licensing acts and orders of Parliament came to have significance. The notion that the author had always had a common-law right in his property found legal recognition. With that recognition came the realization by the writer that he had something which was his and which he could rightfully, as proprietor, sell. The right alone, of course, would have been useless, unless it could be gainfully employed. Such employment was coming with the extended markets. The separation into publishers and booksellers was about to take place. A market was developing, not only for reprints and translations, but for original works. Pope, Dryden, and Dr. Johnson, among others, could command prices. Bargaining was entering into the market place of letters by men who traded on a more equal basis. The property in the author had been established by law. It did not mean that he had attained Nirvana, for he was still not in an equal position economically or in his power to trade. The booksellers were still united in their organizations and clubs. The author was still a peddler, but he was a peddler whose pack was increasing. We find him asserting himself against the trade which still sought to buy up the copyrights for a flat sum and in perpetuity.

The statute was to create a controversy as to whether or not the booksellers had been successful in obtaining a perpetuity in copyright by their purchase outright of the "copy." It included in its provisions as to the term of copyright not only the new but old books, and provided that

> From the 10th of April, 1710, the author of any book already printed . . . shall have the sole right and liberty of printing such books for the term of twenty-one years to commence from the said 10th day of April and no longer, and that the author of any

book not yet printed, and his assigns, shall have a similar right for fourteen years from first publication and no longer.

The statute contained a proviso for a renewal term of fourteen years in the author if then living.

The booksellers immediately sought to disregard the expiration terms of the statute and endeavored to hold the valuable rights they had been acquiring for centuries by outright purchase. They claimed that they had acquired a common-law title in the property and no statute could deprive them of it and that they continued to own in perpetuity the rights in copy for which they had paid a consideration. They sought by injunction to compel those other publishers, who were rushing into the public domain and seizing property, from enjoying the fruits.

Some of the lower courts took the position that there had been a perpetual copyright at common law. In 1735 an injunction was granted which restrained the publication of *The Whole Duty of Man*, first published in 1657. In 1739 an injunction was granted by Lord Hardwicke against the publication of *Paradise Lost*. The plaintiff was one of the Tonsons who had acquired title, which had been originally conveyed by Milton in 1667. But it was not until 1760 that the question of whether or not there was a perpetual common-law copyright was presented to the Court of King's Bench. The subject matter was Addison's *Spectator*, which had first been published in 1711. But someone with an ax to grind informed the court that the case was collusive and that the defendant was nominal only. The court refused to go on with the case.

An action was brought to recover for the unlicensed publication of Thomson's *Seasons* after the expiration of the statutory period. This was the great case of *Millar* v. *Taylor*, decided in 1769, which later, under the name of *Donaldson* v. *Beckett*, came before the House of Lords. In that case opinions and arguments were made by the greatest lawyers of the day. Donaldson, by the way, is famous for having been the pioneer in selling cheap books. He struck out with the idea of publishing cheap reprints of popular works and extending his business by starting a bookshop in the Strand, London, a step which brought him into competition with the London publishers. He had originally been an Edinburgh man. Johnson called him "a fellow who takes advantage of the state of the law to injure his brethren . . . and supposing he did reduce the price of books, he is no better than Robin Hood, who robbed the rich in order to give to the poor."

Donaldson also left a large fortune to found a hospital in Edinburgh under the name of Donaldson's Hospital.

In *Donaldson* v. *Beckett,* the House of Lords decided that at common law an author of any books or literary composition had the sole right of first printing and publishing the same for sale and that such right had been perpetual, but they further answered the questions before them to the effect that by the Statute of Anne, the sole right of printing and publishing literary property in perpetuity had been taken away. It therefore appears that the Court held that although there had been a common-law copyright in perpetuity, it had been revoked by the copyright act of Anne. It will be noted that the case had not been brought by an author but by a publisher who claimed a perpetual right in an author's work.

Publishers, as monopolists, were not popular. The booksellers were believed to be trying to get a corner on literature. Milton, in the *Areopagitica,* many years before, had written of the "old patentees and monopolizers in the trade of bookselling, men who do not labour in an honest profession to which learning is indetted."

Lord Camden, in moving the judgment of the House of Lords, said: "All our learning will be locked up in the hands of the Tonsons and the Lintons of the age, who will set what price upon it their avarice chooses to demand, till the public become as much their slaves as their own hackney compilers are." But the booksellers, while the case was pending, relying upon their earlier victories holding copyright to be perpetual, had invested large fortunes in copyrights, and they thereupon applied to Parliament for relief against the decision in *Donaldson* v. *Beckett*. They were unsuccessful, and from that decision on we must regard copyright as wholly a creature of statute.

This long battle commencing with the Statute of Anne was not without its repercussions in the United States. The reverberations of the struggle which had led up to the Statute of Anne continued. *Donaldson* v. *Beckett* was decided in 1774. The colonies had no separate copyright statute. As Congress, under the Confederation, had no power to protect literary property, several gentlemen presented a memorial to that body petitioning them to recommend to the several states the enactment of such a law. On May 2, 1783, on the reports of Mr. Williamson, Mr. Izard, and Mr. Madison, Congress passed a resolution which recommended to the several states that they secure to authors or publishers of any books not before printed the copyright of such books for a term of not less than fourteen years.

Noah Webster was anxious to protect his *Spelling Book*. To secure copyright laws in the several states he began a series of journeys throughout the state capitals for the purpose of getting them to adopt such laws. In the autumn of 1782 he went to Philadelphia. On his way, he called on Gov. William Livingston at Trenton and inquired whether or not a copyright law could be obtained in New Jersey. In the following October he went to Hartford and petitioned the Legislature of Connecticut. In January, 1783, he again petitioned the Legislature of Connecticut and, in the same winter, went to Kingston in Ulster County, New York, where the legislature was in session, to present a petition. Through the influence of Gen. Philip Schuyler, in the same winter, New York adopted a copyright law, and the Legislature of Massachusetts enacted a copyright law procured by the agency of the Rev. Timothy Dwight. In

May, 1785, Webster undertook a journey to the middle and southern states. Largely as a result of his lobbying the following copyright acts were passed:

Connecticut, 1783, January Session: An act for the encouragement of literature and genius;

Massachusetts, 1783, March 17: An act for the purpose of securing to authors the exclusive right and benefit of publishing their literary productions for twenty-one years;

Maryland, 1783, April 21: An act respecting literary property;

New Jersey, 1783, May 27: An act for the promotion and encouragement of literature;

New Hampshire, 1783, November 7: An act for the encouragement of literature and genius, and for securing to authors the exclusive right and benefit of publishing their literary productions for twenty years;

Rhode Island, 1783, December Session: An act for the purpose of securing to authors the exclusive right and benefit of publishing their literary productions for twenty-one years;

Pennsylvania, 1784, March 15: An act for the encouragement and promotion of learning by vesting a right to the copies of printed books in the authors or purchasers of such copies during the time therein mentioned;

South Carolina, 1784, March 26: An act for the encouragement of arts and sciences;

Virginia, 1785, October: An act for securing to the authors of literary works an exclusive property therein for a limited time;

North Carolina, 1785, November 19: An act for securing literary property;

Georgia, 1786, February 3: An act for the encouragement of literature and genius;

New York, 1786, April 29: An act to promote literature.

On the adoption of the Federal Constitution in 1789, provision was made for copyright:

The Congress shall have power . . . To promote the Progress of Science and useful Arts, by securing for limited Times to Authors and Inventors the exclusive Right to their respective Writings and Discoveries. (Article I, Sec. 8)

It will be noted that the right granted to Congress was to pass laws granting monopolies for a limited time. Pursuant to the constitutional provision, on May 31, 1790, Congress passed the original copyright act, Laws of the First Congress, Second Session, Chapter 15. It was entitled "AN ACT for the encouragement of learning by securing the copies of maps, charts and books, to the authors and proprietors of such copies, during the times therein mentioned." The act provided for "a term of 14 years and if the author be living at the expiration of the term, an extension for a further term of 14 years, or if not, to his executors, administrators or assigns."

In 1954 the Supreme Court was to say of the law:

"The copyright law, like the patent statutes, makes reward to the owner a secondary consideration." *United States* v. *Paramount Pictures,* 334 U.S. 131, 158, 92 L. ed 1260, 1292, 68 S. Ct. 915. However, it is "intended definitely to grant valuable, enforceable rights to authors, publishers," etc., without burdensome requirements; "to afford greater encouragement to the production of literary (or artistic) works of lasting benefit to the world." *Washingtonian Pub. Co.* v. *Pearson,* 306 U.S. 30, 36, 83 L. ed 470, 473, 59 S. Ct. 397.

The economic philosophy behind the clause empowering Congress to grant patents and copyrights is the conviction that encouragement of individual effort by personal gain is the best way to advance public welfare through the talents of authors and inventors in "Science and useful Arts." Sacrificial days devoted to such creative activities deserve rewards commensurate with the service rendered.

Precisely the same question which had been fought out in England in the case of *Donaldson* v. *Beckett* as to perpetuity in common-law copyright arose in the United States. It was settled by the leading case of *Wharton* v. *Peters* in 1834. The same result was reached as had been reached in England. It was held that common-law copyright in published works does not exist in the United States and that such copyright was wholly statutory. But, more important, it is to be noted that both of these cases assumed that a property right in literature had arisen under the common law through the practices of authors and booksellers, and that such copyright had been confirmed by statute. There could no longer be a question of the existence of literary property as property.

Between 1790 and 1956 some fifty public acts, relating wholly or in part to copyright in the United States, were passed, and there were also passed some nine private copyright acts. The original act, which provided only for the copyright of maps, charts, and books, was supplemented by an act dated April 29, 1802, to extend the benefits to the arts of designing, engraving, and etching, historical and other prints. On February 3, 1831, it was extended to include musical compositions and the term was changed to a first term of twenty-eight years with a renewal term of fourteen years.

On August 8, 1856, the rights of an author or proprietor of dramatic compositions were extended to include the sole right to act, perform, or represent the same during the period of copyright. On March 3, 1865, the act was extended to include photographs and negatives thereof.

At the 41st Congress, on July 8, 1870, the copyright acts then in force were revised, consolidated, and amended, and paintings, drawings, statuaries, and models or designs of works intended to be perfected as a work of the fine arts were included.

On August 1, 1882, manufactures or designs for molded decorative articles, tiles, plaques, or articles of pottery or metal were added.

On March 3, 1891, a general revision was again made. This was the act which, for the first time, established the right of others than citizens or residents of the United States to obtain copyright. The Copyright Act was made to apply to citizens or subjects of a foreign state or nation which permits the citizens of the United States of America the benefit of copyright on substantially the same basis as its own citizens, or when such foreign state or nation is a party to an international agreement which provides for reciprocity and by the terms of which agreement the United States of America may become a party thereto.

Previously, from the time of enactment of the original Copyright Act, only citizens or residents within the United States had been entitled to copyright.

The first Copyright Act provided:

> SEC. 5 *And be it further enacted,* That nothing in this act shall be construed to extend to prohibit the importation or vending, reprinting or publishing within the United States, of any map, chart, book or books, written, printed, or published by any person not a citizen of the United States, in foreign parts or places without the jurisdiction of the United States.

A similar provision was inserted in the revision of February 3, 1831 (Sec. 8), and in the act of July 8, 1870.

It was the act of 1891 which made it possible for the United States to enter into treaties with other countries, giving citizens of the United States protection abroad and, by indirection, it enabled citizens of the United States to take advantage of copyright in all the countries signatory to the Berne Convention by copyrighting in one of them. It contained, however, the much-criticized manufacturing clause passed at the insistence of the trade unions. That clause provided that in the case of a book, photograph, chromo, or lithograph, it should "be printed from type set within the limits of the United States, or from plates made therefrom, or from negatives, or drawings on stone made within the limits of the United States, or from transfers made therefrom." This clause effectively made it impossible for British authors to take copyright by mere publication abroad in like manner as we can and was a barrier to our joining international agreements.

The next general codification, in the Copyright Act of 1909, established the law which remained in effect until January 1,

1978. By that act, the term of copyright was extended for an original period of twenty-eight years, and a renewal period of twenty-eight years.

On October 19, 1976, a new Copyright Act was approved by Congress. The new law represents a substantial revision and modification of the 1909 Act. Among its many changes are the lengthening of the copyright term to a term of the author's life plus an additional fifty years, and the abolition of the renewal term.

Under the new law, which went into effect on January 1, 1978, common-law copyright was abolished for almost all unpublished works, and Congress provided for a term of statutory protection for any works fixed in a tangible medium of expression, whether published or unpublished.

As the invention of the printing press and the revival of learning brought about the gradual march toward the notion of property, so, as new forms of communication and expression by the techniques of our modern civilization are found, new problems of property arise.

One thing is certain: There is an ever-increasing orbit of the field in which literary property exists and is protected.

Chapter 2

⚞ THE NATURE OF LITERARY PROPERTY UNDER THE COMMON LAW

As already noted, the new Copyright Act abolishes the dual system of federal protection for published works and common-law protection for works prior to publication. Essentially this means that under the new law, all works, whether published or not, are protected by statutory copyright as soon as they are "fixed" in a tangible medium of expression. Common-law copyright henceforth exists only for works not so "fixed," such as choreography that has never been filmed or notated, an extemporaneous speech, original works of authorship communicated solely through conversations or live broadcasts, and dramatic sketches or musical compositions improvised from memory without being recorded or written down.

The purpose of this change is to promote national uniformity in copyright law, thereby avoiding the practical difficulties of determining and enforcing an author's rights under the differing laws of the various states, and to facilitate international dealings in copyrighted material.

The new law effects perhaps the most sweeping changes on literary works, since, of the totality of an author's production, only his unrecorded conversations now remain under the protection of the common law. Still, the common-law concepts of literary property are worthy of discussion because of their historical importance and because litigation of disputes arising prior to the effective date of the new law may well involve questions of the common law.

Under the common law, the author, in the very act of creating, created in himself a right of property in the work produced. Out of his labors came a property from which he had the right to exclude others.

In the famous case of *Jeffreys* v. *Boosey*, Erle, J., said:

> The origin of the property is in production. As to works of imagination and reasoning, if not of memory, the author may be said to create; and, in all departments of mind, new books are the product of the labor, skill, and capital of the author. The subject or property is the order of words in the author's composition: not the words themselves, they being analogous to the elements of matter, which are not appropriated unless combined; nor the ideas expressed by those words, they existing in the mind alone, which is not capable of appropriation. The nature of the right of an author in his works is analogous to the rights of ownership in other personal property.

Literary property was similar in this notion of exclusivity, for the essence of property is the right to enjoy it to the exclusion of others. The Supreme Court of New York said:

> . . . "property rights," as has been pointed out are rights which are recognized and protected by the courts by excluding others therefrom.

Literary property does, however, differ from other forms of personal property in that it is intangible and incorporeal. The property is not in the printed matter or the page on which the production is embodied, nor is it in the means of communication to others. It is rather in the expression that property inheres. As Sir William Blackstone said:

> The identity of a literary composition consists entirely in the sentiment and the language: the same conceptions, clothed in the same words, must necessarily be the same composition; and what-

ever method be taken of exhibiting that composition to the ear or the eye of another, by recital, by writing, or by printing, in any number of copies, or at any period of time, it is always the identical work of the author which is so exhibited; and no man (it hath been thought) can have a right to exhibit it, especially for profit, without the author's consent.

The property itself was incorporeal and intangible, but fixed nevertheless in the form and content which the author had selected for expression. The words, phrases, basic ideas, characters, situations, and incidents might all have had prior existence and have been common to others. When an author made his own arrangement of them, they became vested with a special right of property, so that he might thereafter claim his work to the exclusion of others. The notion of exclusivity is incorporated in the Constitution, which grants to Congress the right to pass laws giving authors the exclusive right to their writings. At the moment of creation the property inhered, and from that moment on the dominion over the work lay with the author. He might determine when, where, and to whom it should be divulged and by what means of communication it was to be conveyed.

Under the new law this concept of the author's proprietary right inhering from the moment of creation retains its vitality, provided that it is accompanied by "fixation," but the protection afforded is no longer that of the common law, but rather that of statutory copyright.

Under common law, this right remained with the author until he performed some act by which the law deemed that he had waived his exclusive right, or it might remain in him as an exclusive right for a limited term, if he chose to take advantage of statutory copyright. Under the new law, this choice no longer exists, since there is automatic statutory protection for a fixed term from the moment of creation. As a result, the perpetual protection for unpublished works that existed under common law has been lost.

It was publication without a claim of statutory copyright, or some other form of dedication to the public, which divested the author of his common-law right in the work.

The property existed not in the paper or other physical embodiment, but in the expression. The making of copies did not in and of itself divest the author of his right. It was only when he distributed the copies to the public that his right was lost. There might be a restricted publication which did not indicate an intention to dedicate the work to the public. So for instance, if a teacher distributed notes to a class, but with the understanding that the students would not make or give copies thereof and that the notes would be used solely for the purposes of the classroom, that was not a dedication to the public generally.

What constituted publication was a question that gave the courts much concern. The Supreme Court adopted as its own the following criterion for determining the matter: "It is a fundamental rule that to constitute publication there must be such a dissemination of the work of art itself among the public as to justify the belief that it took place with the intention of rendering such work common property."

The publication, to be effective, was to be a general publication. A limited publication which communicated the contents of a manuscript to a definite group and for a limited purpose, and without the right of diffusion, reproduction, distribution, or sale, was considered a "limited publication," which did not result in the loss of the author's common-law right to his manuscript.

An early American case contains a very clear statement of the conditions which rendered a publication limited in nature:

> The distinction between a public circulation of written copies, and a restricted or private communication of their contents, was, for some purposes, recognized before the use of printing. . . . But, except under special and unusual circumstances, an author who then parted with a manuscript copy gave to it the most public circulation of which it was capable. Now, the parting by an author

with manuscript copies of his unprinted composition is ordinarily regarded as an act of mere private circulation. . . . Printed copies may also be circulated privately. Their circulation is thus private when they are delivered to a few ascertained persons only, who receive them under conditions expressly or impliedly precluding any ulterior diffusion of the knowledge of their contents. Such a case occurs when a small first edition of a book, printed with a notice on the title page that it is for private circulation, is gratuitously distributed by the author among particular persons.

One of the older authorities on the law of property in intellectual production summed up the common-law rights of the author in an unpublished book in this manner:

He has the right to exclude all persons from its enjoyment; and, when he chooses to do so, any use of the property without his consent is a violation of his own rights. He may admit one or more persons to its use, to the exclusion of all others; and, in doing so, he may restrict the use which shall be made of it. He may give a copy of his manuscript to another person, without parting with his literary property in it. He may circulate copies among his friends, for their own personal enjoyment, without giving them or others the right to publish such copies.

From this it is evident that in determining whether a publication was general or special, the test was whether there was or was not such a surrender as permitted the absolute and unqualified enjoyment of the subject matter by the public or the members thereof to whom it might have been committed.

The law on this subject was epitomized as follows:

A general publication consists in such a disclosure, communication, circulation, exhibition, or distribution of the subject of copyright, tendered or given to one or more members of the general public, as implies an abandonment of the right to copyright or its dedication to the public. Prior to such publication, a person entitled to copyright may restrict the use or enjoyment of such subject to definitely selected individuals or a limited, ascertained class, or he may expressly or by implication confine the enjoyment of such subject to some occasion or definite purpose. A publication under such restrictions is a limited publication, and no rights inconsistent with or adverse to such restrictions are surrendered. Restrictions imposed upon the use prior to publication protect the copyright. Such restrictions imposed after publication cannot affect the public rights acquired by reason of the fact of publication.

As can be seen, under our old copyright law, a determination of whether or not general publication had occurred was of vital importance, since the author's exclusive control over his property turned on that question. Under the new law, the question of publication is less urgent, since statutory copyright is protected for five years, even in the case of general publication without notice. Moreover, copyright protection for the full term may be secured, even after general publication, if registration is made within five years and a reasonable effort is made to add notice to already distributed copies, or if no more than a relatively small number of copies has been distributed.

As central as the concept of publication was to copyright law, it became, nevertheless, increasingly obscure and artificial in the light of new technologies. To cope with the legal consequences of a concept that had lost much of its meaning, the courts gave "publication" a number of diverse interpretations. To rectify this situation, the new law imposes a single federal definition which preempts state law:

> "Publication" is the distribution of copies or phonorecords of a work to the public by sale or other transfer of ownership or by rental, lease or lending. The offering to distribute copies of phonorecords to a group of persons for purposes of further distribution, public performance, or public display, constitutes publication. A public performance or display of a work does not itself constitute publication.

Prior to the effective date of the new law, letters, diaries, and personal manuscripts were entitled to protection under the common law. So, if one wrote a letter, the property in the paper and envelope would pass to the recipient, but the property in the writing would belong to the sender or his heirs, who alone had the right to publish and copyright the letters, whether or not a copy of the letter had been retained. The same was true for personal writings. Thus anyone owning letters of someone else had, generally, to seek and obtain permission from the writer prior to publication. Such is the case under the new law as well, although the protection is statutory, and not from the common law.

Under the law, the world claims for its own the words in the dictionary, characteristics of men, the history of man, geographical places, and all the wealth of incident and plot and things past which are the common heritage. The ideas which men have thought, even though recorded, are free. The engineer discovering a new formula for the building of bridges, the surgeon finding a new technique for operations, the mathematician finding a new concretion for abstraction, cannot claim their ideas are theirs to the exclusion of other persons. All are free to use them, but the synthesis in words which the author creates is property. In that, and only that, can he claim exclusivity. He has no property in the idea itself. He has none in common characters. He has none in historic events or persons. His property is confined to his creation, which lies in the selection of the word, its combination with others, and the expression which he thereby achieves. Everything else lies in what is known as the "public domain," from which all may take. When an author has by his labor produced such a new work he may claim it for his own solely by virtue of his toil. The labor need not be of a literary nature. It may lack artistic result. If original toil results in a writing, the author may claim it for his own. So, for instance, if a man should walk through the streets of a city and note the name of every one of its inhabitants and record it, he would acquire material of which he would be the owner. The compiler of a street directory has literary property therein. Literary style has no bearing on whether or not he has created property.

An interesting case was one in which Mary Baker Eddy's executors sued to restrain an auctioneer of manuscripts from publishing for advertising purposes certain autographed letters written by Mrs. Eddy. They were written in her own hand "during one of the most interesting periods of her career, that is, just after the publication of her *Science and Health, with Key to the Scriptures.*" The answer to the suit set forth that the letters had no attribute of literature. The court said: "No sound distinction in this regard can be made between that which has literary merit and that which is without it. Such a distinction could not be drawn with any certainty. While extremes might be discovered, compositions near the dividing line would be subject to no fixed criterion at any given moment, and scarcely anything is more fluctuating than the literary taste of the general public. Even those counted as experts in literature differ widely in opinion both in the same and in successive generations as to the relative merits of different authors. The basic principle on which the right of the author is sustained, even as to writings confessedly literature, is not their literary quality, but the fact that they are the product of labor."

Even gibberish might have property inherent in it. Some of the writings of Gertrude Stein may be incomprehensible, but to the law they are comprehensible enough to be property. Judge Learned Hand said:

Suppose someone devised a set of words or symbols to form a new abstract speech, with inflections, but as yet with no meaning, a kind of blank Esperanto. . . . Mathematics has its symbols, indeed a language of its own, Peanese, understood by only a few people in the world. Suppose a mathematician were to devise a new set of compressed and more abstract symbols, and left them for some conventional meaning to be filled in. . . .

Not all words communicate ideas; some are mere spontaneous ejaculations. Some are used for their sound alone, like nursery jingles, or the rhymes of children in their play. Might not someone, with a gift for catching syllables, devise others? There has of late been prose written avowedly senseless but designed by its sound alone to produce an emotion. Conceivably there may arise a poet who strings together words without rational sequence—perhaps even coined syllables—through whose beauty, cadence, meter, and rhyme he may seek to make poetry. Music is not normally a representative art, yet it is a "writing." There are meaningless rhymes— e.g. "Barbara Celarent," which boys use in their logic, or to remember their paradigms or the rules of grammar. . . .

I can see no reason why words should not be [writings] because they communicate nothing. They may have their uses for all that, aesthetic or practical, and they may be the production of high ingenuity, or even genius.

Alfred Korzbyski claimed copyright of a model or relief diagram which he said illustrated and formulated certain scientific information, i.e., illustrated thought processes. Regarding this, Judge Augustus N. Hand said:

It may be reasonably contended that complainant's system of symbols, though unaccompanied by any explanation, resembles a table of logarithms, or the text of a book in the language of a savage tribe, known only to the author. It can hardly be doubted that such matters may be copyrighted, even without any accompanying explanation or comment. Certainly both would be books.

Although, as a result of the new law, all of an author's written productions are protected by statute, his unrecorded conversations still fall under the common law. Mary Hemingway, widow of Ernest Hemingway, brought an action against Random House and A. E. Hotchner, author of the book entitled *Papa Hemingway*. Mr. Hotchner had been an intimate friend of both Hemingways up to 1961 when Ernest Hemingway died. The book was a biographical study, chronologically limited to the period from 1948, when Hotchner first met Hemingway, up to his death thirteen years later. It was intended as a presentation from the vantage of the friendship, camaraderie, and personal experiences that the younger Hotchner shared with (what the court characterized as) the literary giant.

Mrs. Hemingway claimed that the material incorporated in the book was based upon the language, expressions, comments, and communications of Ernest Hemingway, which were subject to a common-law copyright, and that therefore the right of first publication of such material belonged to his estate. The court noted that this claim of common-law copyright was that primarily relied on by Mrs. Hemingway, and said:

> Such copyright, which is separate and distinct from the protection afforded by the statutory copyright law, is simply the right which the author or proprietor of an unpublished literary work has to first publication of such work, or his alternative right to withhold it from publication for so long as he is disposed.

Hotchner maintained that the conversations were not necessarily verbatim but were his renditions of notes which he kept and recorded during the years of his friendship, and the court went on to say:

> We are dealing here with a possible limitation upon "speech," an area pregnant with social and historical implications striking at the very fundamentals of our political structure. The free and unfettered exchange of ideas and information of all types has been a hallowed tradition that has served to nourish an informed and alert citizenry. The intellectual benefits derived from access to the intimate articulations and experiences of figures of note and achievement are emphatically demonstrated by the enduring fame and inspirational stimulus of the works of recorders such as Plutarch, Boswell, and Carlyle. That the restrictive action here sought would serve in large measure to frustrate the continued availability of such hitherto permissible material is not without significance. Social cost and the public interest may be considered. (Cf. *University of Notre Dame* v. *Twentieth Century-Fox Film Corp.*, 22 A. D. 2d 452 15 N.Y. 2d 940.) Conversation is a media of expression of unique character. Because of its several nature any conversational exchange necessarily reflects the various participants thereto not only with respect to the different contributions of each, but also in so far as each party acts as a catalyst in evoking the thoughts and expressions of the other. The articulations of each are to some extent indelibly colored by the intangible influences

of the subjective responses engendered by the particular other. Conversation cannot be catalogued as merely the cumulative product of separated and unrelated individual efforts, but, on the contrary, it is rather a synthesized whole that is indivisibly welded by the interaction of the parties involved. As a participant in the conversations, the defendant Hotchner would be as much an architect thereof as any of the other participants. In this case, where most of the quoted conversations took place between the defendant author and the subject of the work, such conversations necessarily reflect a duality that defies dissection or divisibility. In light of the interaction which renders conversation indivisible, it is difficult to see how conversation can be held to constitute the sort of individual intellectual production to which protection is afforded by way of a common-law copyright.

It was the finding of the court that Mrs. Hemingway had failed to establish any right to a common-law copyright. Her application for an injunction was denied.

One of the more interesting suits for the infringement of common-law copyright was brought by the widow of Lee Harvey Oswald, the accused assassin of President Kennedy. She sought just compensation for letters, a diary, and other materials seized by government agents and published by the Warren Commission in the report of its investigation of the assassination. The suit by Oswald's widow, then Mrs. Porter, posed the question of whether recovery could be had for the diminution of the value of Oswald's writings because of their publication in the Warren Commission study. The court decided the question in the negative, holding that 28 U.S.C. 1398, which makes the government liable for its copyright infringements, did not apply to common-law copyrights, but only to writings "protected under the copyright laws of the United States." As a result Mrs. Porter was unable to recover an estimated $15,000 in damages. Under the new law, which provides federal statutory protection for unpublished writings, the result, were such a case to arise today, would presumably be different.

An interesting case which well illustrates the point that common-law copyright could not be divested by indirection arose out of the publication of a story, *A Murder, a Mystery, and a Marriage*, written by Samuel L. Clemens in 1876, under his pen name of Mark Twain. In the year of its writing he offered the manuscript to William Dean Howells, editor of *The Atlantic Monthly*, for publication. Twain had in mind an unusual publication. He proposed that other writers of the period, such as Bret Harte and Howells himself, be enlisted, each to write his own final chapter to the work; so for the mystery set up in the first few chapters, each author would produce his own ending as an addition to Twain's. For one reason or another, including the reluctance of famous writers to dance to Twain's music, the scheme came to nothing. When Mark Twain died in 1910, the manuscript was not found among his effects and had never been published anywhere by anyone. In 1945, Lew D. Feldman bought the original manuscript at an auction sale in New York City. It had been in the possession, during his life, of Dr. James Brentano Clemens, who was no kin of Mark Twain. How Dr. Clemens came to have the writing is not known. Mr. Feldman sought permission from Mark Twain's trustees to publish the work, but permission was refused. He then went ahead with the publication, and suit was brought to restrain him. The court found that the circumstances under which the manuscript left the possession of the author, without intention on his part that it be published, were such that Mr. Feldman could not have bought publication rights. It said that the common-law copyright or right of first publication was a right different from that of ownership of the physical paper.

Decision with regard to whether or not publication by the author was intended was technical, for each decision stood on its own fact. Hovsep Pushman enjoyed an international reputation as an artist for his execution of still-life subjects in color. In 1930 he completed a painting entitled "When Autumn is

Here," and turned it over to Grand Central Art Galleries for sale. It did not appear that he had made any reservation with regard to reproduction rights. But Pushman never expressly authorized the gallery to sell the rights to reproduce, nor did he forbid it. A purchaser through the gallery sold the reproduction rights to the New York Graphic Society, Inc. The court held that the common-law copyright which was involved was sometimes called the right of first publication, and that there was no question but that it was a different and independent right from the usual right of ownership of an article of personal property. It quoted Lord Mansfield as saying it was "a property in notion, and has no corporeal tangible substance." It held that while it was true that there was under the common law a right to sell the corporeal embodiment of an author's work while reserving the right to reproduce, nevertheless an unrestricted sale of the physical embodiment would carry with it the right to reproduce. The distinction should here be noted that in the Mark Twain case there had been no proof that Twain himself had parted with the manuscript in any unrestricted fashion.

In neither case was any significance given to Section 27 of the old copyright law which provided, in part, that "the copyright is distinct from the property in the material object copyrighted, and the sale or conveyance, by gift or otherwise, of the material object shall not of itself constitute a transfer of the copyright. . . ."

Of course, this section applied only to the statutory copyright and material copyrighted under it. It had, however, some bearing by way of reasoning on the subject, since it pointed to the distinction between conception and embodiment.

A case which illustrates the abandonment of common-law rights and dedication to the public arose out of the publication by Aaron Hirsch of a story published by him in a newspaper of which he was the founder, publisher, and editor. The paper enjoyed second-class mailing privilege, which imports regular issue at stated intervals and a publication for dissemination of information of a public character or devotion to literature. Mr. Hirsch's administrator brought action when Twentieth Century-Fox Film Corp. used the story. He contended that there was no dedication, urging that the paper as such went to only a limited public and therefore there was a limited public use, relying upon a case in which the court had said:

> There must be found an intent to abandon or the property is not lost; and while, of course, as in other cases, intent may be inferred when the facts are shown, yet the facts must be adequate to support the finding.

The court held that the admitted facts demonstrated an unqualified act of publication by printing and offering for sale; that there could be no question of the intent under the facts adduced.

The production of a play was not such publication as took the work out of common-law copyright. The leading case on this subject in this country was *Palmer* v. *DeWitt*, decided in New York in 1872. The drama there involved was called *Play*. It had been presented on the stage in London and in the City of New York. An injunction was sought against a distribution of books of the play, printed by one who had obtained no license from the author. The court held the permission to act a play at a public theatre does not amount to the abandonment by the author of his title to it, or a dedication of it to the public, and that therefore the printing and selling of copies was a violation of the author's rights and of his assignee's as the sole proprietor of the right to print and publish the work within the United States. Lectures and plays, the court said, "are not, by their public delivery or performance, in the presence of all who choose to attend, so dedicated to the public that they can be printed and published without the author's permission. It does not give to the hearer any title to the manuscript or a copy of it, or a right to the use of a copy. The manuscript and the right of the author therein are still within the protection of the law, the same as if they had never been communicated to the public in any form."

Under the old copyright statute, provision was made for a form of copyright in works not reproduced for sale. Section 12 provided in part:

> Works Not Reproduced for Sale.—Copyright may also be had of the works of an author, of which copies are not reproduced for sale, by the deposit, with claim of copyright, of one complete copy of such work if it be a lecture or similar production or a dramatic, musical, or dramatico-musical composition; . . .

It should be noted that the right to obtain such a copyright was restricted to dramatic, musical, or dramatico-musical compositions. Books were not given this protection, but motion pictures were. Such copyright, however, was not an unmixed blessing, for it was held that if one took advantage of this section, one lost the perpetual right which inhered in a common-law copyright. It is only statutory copyright which has a limited term. The common-law copyright discussed herein was a right in perpetuity just as much as such rights exist in tangible personal property. A right in a watch lasts as long as the watch. But the right in literary property lasted forever under the common law, or until one took advantage of statutory copyright, at which point the statutory term of years affixed.

The limitation to the statutory period of copyright for works deposited under Section 12 was decided in a criminal case involving Groucho and Chico Marx. They were convicted of infringing and aiding and abetting the infringement of a copyrighted dramatic composition. It appeared that two brothers, Garrett and Carroll Graham, had submitted a radio script entitled "The Hollywood Adventures of Mr. Dibble and Mr. Dabble" to an agent. The agent sent a copy to Groucho Marx, who expressed an interest in the script. Thereafter the Graham brothers had a conference in Hollywood with the Marxes, who were informed at that time that the script had been copyrighted. A year later the Marx brothers made arrangements for a broadcast, and in 1936 they did broadcast a lengthy program, which included in somewhat altered but plainly recognizable form the Graham material. The Marx brothers testified that they had forgotten the Graham composition, and that if it was pirated, it was by accident and not design. Among their defenses was the contention that Section 12 was unconstitutional since Congress had power to grant copyright only for a limited time, and that since Congress had failed to provide for the term of copyrights secured under this section, it had exceeded constitutional authority.

The court held that the time of twenty-eight years expressed in the statute applied to the copyright under this section as much as to published copyright. Although works not reproduced for sale were generally regarded as unpublished, the court held that the date of deposit of copies in the Register's office was sufficient as the date on which to commence the running of the statutory term, thus destroying the common-law copyright in perpetuity in such works.

One may contrast what happened when one filed under Section 12 of the old copyright statute with the result reached in the case of Mark Twain's *A Murder, a Mystery and a Marriage*.

When Eugene O'Neill wrote his earliest works, he registered them for copyright under Section 12. They included *A Wife for a Life, Abortion, The Movie Man*, and *The Sniper*, which were copyrighted, respectively, on August 15, 1913; May 19, 1914; July 1, 1914; and March 13, 1915. Copyright on all of these works had expired by 1943. These plays were never produced or published with O'Neill's permission, principally because he thought them unworthy of publication. The plays were not lost, but rather they were suppressed by him as the works of his youth. He thought so little of them that he did not even renew the copyright. Perhaps he thought that the copyright under this section was merely for registration and did not impair his common-law perpetual copyright. The apparent flaw in the copyright was discovered. A publishing house named New Fathoms Press, Ltd., in New York, procured copies and had Lawrence Gellert write an introduction. They published the plays under the title *Lost Plays of Eugene O'Neill*, and advertised them blatantly as:

> The dean of American playwrights' *very first* play. Also four other of O'Neill's earliest plays, all believed destroyed 40 years ago. A rare collector's item. Never before published.

In his preface Mr. Gellert said of the book:

> . . . the uncovering of this important group of O'Neill's "firsts" is an outstanding publishing event.

Unfortunately for Mr. O'Neill, who did not agree with this conclusion, he thought there was nothing he could do to stop publication. Reviewers were outraged and laid his failure to defend himself to his poor health at the time, but nothing was done. O'Neill had to grin and bear the unauthorized publication.

Had the new copyright law been in effect when O'Neill first copyrighted his unpublished plays, this would not have been the case since the copyright term would have continued until fifty years after Mr. O'Neill's death without any need for renewal.

In the Mark Twain situation, since there was no proof that the works had ever left the author's hands with the intention that anyone could reproduce them, the work was protected against unauthorized publication.

The situation created both as to the shortening of the time of protection and the very right to have exclusive control under the old statute was such as to raise a grave doubt as to whether a play or other material not reproduced for sale should be deposited under the old copyright act. Since literary property was the exclusive monopolistic property of the author at common law, he would lose as well as gain through statutory copyright under the old law. Under the new law, such quandaries no longer exist. The Copyright Act now provides for automatic statutory protection of unpublished works, and common-law copyright has been preempted. In the process, of course, the author has lost the copyright in perpetuity conferred by the common law. But this is compensated for, to some extent, by the lengthening of the term of copyright protection to fifty years after the author's death.

Like all other personal property, literary property under the common law could be disposed of by gift or assignment, and on the death of the author would pass by his will, or in the case of intestacy, to those entitled to take under the law. Special questions arose, as in the case of letters or other material which have historical value after the death of the author, in view of the fact that common-law literary property had perpetual existence, and therefore it was necessary to obtain permission from those who qualified as assignees, executors, administrators, beneficiaries, or descendants. Since this could often mean a search for an innumerable class of people, it raised special difficulties for the historian or biographer. Under the new law, similar problems are avoided, provided the author has been dead for more than fifty years.

Chapter 3

⚜ STATUTORY COPYRIGHT

The law, which until January 1, 1978, had been our copyright law, had been passed in 1909, and although recodified in 1947, it had undergone little change. With the passage of time, new techniques for capturing and communicating printed matter, visual images, and recorded sounds came into use, and these technological advances created new methods for the reproduction and dissemination of copyrighted works. In addition, the business relations between authors and users evolved in new ways, and experiences in the field of international copyright law further indicated the shortcomings of our law.

By 1955, when the United States became a member of the Universal Copyright Convention, the movement for the general revision of our copyright law had begun. The first legislative hearings were held in the House in 1965, and in 1976 the bill for the general revision of the United States copyright laws was finally signed. This new law went into effect on January 1, 1978, and confers upon any person who complies with the provisions of the statute the exclusive right:

(1) to reproduce the copyrighted work in copies or phonorecords;
(2) to prepare derivative works based upon the copyrighted work;
(3) to distribute copies or phonorecords of the copyrighted work to the public by sale or other transfer of ownership, or by rental, lease, or lending.

(4) in the case of literary, musical, dramatic, and choreographic works, pantomimes, and motion pictures and other audiovisual works, to perform the copyrighted work publicly; and

(5) in the case of literary, musical, dramatic and choreographic works, pantomimes, and pictorial, graphic, or sculptural works, including the individual images of a motion picture or other audiovisual work, to display the copyrighted work publicly.

The new statutory provisions effect many changes in the old law. Under the 1909 Act, the essence of copyright was the publication with notice. The new law, however, abandons the notion that an author must do anything to obtain his copyright: unpublished works are protected automatically from the moment of their creation, and even works published without notice receive an automatic five-year period of protection. In addition, the new law has lengthened the original period of copyright protection, abandoned the renewal provisions of the old act, liberalized the requirements for notice of copyright, and recognized the inalienable right of the author to terminate any grant of copyright after thirty-five years. The new law also includes new and detailed provisions on mechanical rights, required by the development of new technologies, which limit the author's exclusive rights, and abandons some, but not all, of the obstacles to United States participation in the Berne Convention.

However, enactment into law of the new statute does not mean that all of the provisions of the 1909 Act can be ignored. Under provisions of the new law, the old law will remain in effect for works under statutory copyright prior to January 1, 1978, as well as for works whose renewal term was subsisting between December 31, 1976 and December 31, 1977, or whose registration for renewal had been made between those dates. These provisions, and the fact that determination of whether works have entered the public domain prior to the effective date of the new law can only be determined with reference to the old law, will extend the 1909 Act's control, in applicable cases, for another seventy-five years. Moreover, since the new law retains the old law's provisions of originality, the 1909 Act will continue to be referred to and thus will remain of more than merely historical interest. For these reasons, the discussion that follows will refer to the relevant, parallel provisions of the old law, as it considers the new law.

Provisions of the New Law

§ 106. Exclusive rights in copyrighted works.

Subject to sections 107 through 118, the owner of copyright under this title has the exclusive rights to do and to authorize any of the following:

(1) to reproduce the copyrighted work in copies or phonorecords;

(2) to prepare derivative works based upon the copyrighted work;

(3) to distribute copies or phonorecords of the copyrighted work to the public by sale or other transfer of ownership, or by rental, lease, or lending;

(4) in the case of literary, musical, dramatic, and choreographic works, pantomimes, and motion pictures and other audiovisual works, to perform the copyrighted work publicly; and

(5) in the case of literary, musical, dramatic, and choreographic works, pantomimes, and pictorial, graphic, or sculptural works, including the individual images of a motion picture or other audiovisual work, to display the copyrighted work publicly.

Provisions of the Old Law

§ 1. Exclusive rights as to copyrighted works.

Any person entitled thereto, upon complying with the provisions of this title, shall have the exclusive right:

(a) To print, reprint, publish, copy, and vend the copyrighted work;

(b) To translate the copyrighted work into other languages or dialects, or make any other version thereof, if it be a literary work; to dramatize it if it be a nondramatic work; to convert it into a novel or other nondramatic work if it be a drama; to arrange or adapt it if it be a musical work; to complete, execute, and finish it if it be a model or design for a work of art;

(c) To deliver, authorize the delivery of, read, or present the copyrighted work in public for profit if it be a lecture, sermon, address or similar production, or other nondramatic literary work; to make or procure the making of any transcription or record thereof by or from which, in whole or in part, it may in any manner or by any method be exhibited, delivered, presented, produced, or reproduced; and to play or perform it in public for profit, and to exhibit, represent, produce, or reproduce it in any manner or by any method whatsoever. The damages for the infringement by broadcast of any work referred to in this subsection shall not exceed the sum of $100 where the infringing broadcaster shows that he was not aware that he was infringing and that such infringement could not have been reasonably foreseen; and

(d) To perform or represent the copyrighted work publicly if it be a drama or, if it be a dramatic work and not reproduced in copies for sale, to vend any manuscript or any record whatsoever thereof; to make or to procure the making of any transcription or record thereof by or from which, in whole or in part, it may in any manner or by any method be exhibited, performed, represented, produced, or reproduced; and to exhibit, perform, represent, produce, or reproduce it in any manner or by any method whatsoever; and

(e) To perform the copyrighted work publicly for profit if it be a musical composition; and for the purpose of public performance for profit, and for the purposes set forth in subsection (a) hereof, to make any arrangement or setting of it or of the melody of it in any system of notation or any form of record in which the thought of an author may be recorded and from which it may be read or reproduced * * *

WHO MAY SECURE STATUTORY COPYRIGHT

Under the new law, protection for unpublished works is afforded to all persons without regard to citizenship and nationality, and for published works if:

(1) on the date of first publication, one or more of the authors is a national or domiciliary of the United States, or is a national, domiciliary, or sovereign authority of a foreign nation that is a party to a copyright treaty to which the United States is also a party, or is a stateless person, wherever that person may be domiciled; or

(2) the work is first published in the United States or in a foreign nation that, on the date of first publication, is a party to the Universal Copyright Convention; or

(3) the work is first published by the United Nations or any of its specialized agencies, or by the Organization of American States; or

(4) the work comes within the scope of a Presidential proclamation. * * *

The existence of reciprocal conditions between the United States and any other nation, which is a precondition of the granting of copyright to an alien, under subsection (4) is determined by the President of the United States in proclamations made by him from time to time. A consideration of the reciprocal conditions is discussed in the chapter on international copyright.

Under the old law, and thus for works copyrighted prior to January 1, 1978, or renewed, or in their renewal term, between December 31, 1976 and December 31, 1977, copyright protection is afforded to the following:

a. The author or proprietor of any work made the subject of copyright by this title, or his executors, administrators, or assigns.

b. Alien authors or proprietors domiciled within the United States at the time of the first publication of their work.

c. Aliens who are citizens or subjects of a foreign state or nation which by treaty, convention, or agreement of law gives to citizens of the United States the benefit of copyright on substantially the same basis as its own citizens.

d. Aliens who are citizens or subjects of a country which is party to an international agreement which provides for reciprocity in the granting of copyright, by the terms of which agreement the United States may at its pleasure become a party thereto.

As can be seen, the old law did not explicitly provide protection for stateless persons, and this presented an interesting problem which was adjudicated in connection with Adolph Hitler's book *Mein Kampf*.

Hitler, who had a mystic concept of himself as a German, although he was Austrian born, had described himself as a *Staatenloser Deutscher* in his application for registration of the first volume of *Mein Kampf*. The application for the second volume described him as a citizen of Austria. For various reasons Hitler had been willing to have only bowdlerized versions of *Mein Kampf* translated, so that in each country where he permitted translation, such a version was produced. Stackpole Sons, Inc., published the first complete translation in English. The American owners of a version entitled *My Battle*, Houghton Mifflin Company, sued, claiming infringement. The defense was set up that since Hitler did not qualify under the copyright statute, his work was not protected. The Circuit Court of Appeals held that authors who were not citizens or subjects of any country came within the privilege granted to all authors under Section 8(9) of the old law. Among other things the court said:

> Any other result than this would be unfortunate for it would mean that stateless aliens cannot be secure even in their literary property. True, the problem of statelessness has only become acute of late years, but it promises to become increasingly more difficult as time goes on. The rule contended for by the defendants would mean that the United States, contrary to its general policy and tradition, is putting another obstacle in the way of survival of homeless refugees, of whom many have been students and scholars and writers.

The court thereby created a class of aliens outside the statute who were entitled to the protection of the Copyright Law. The new Act, by extending protection to stateless persons, accepts the logic of the *Mein Kampf* decision, although with none of the grim irony that history was to bring to bear on that decisión. The relevant sections of the new and old laws follow:

Provisions of the New Law	Provisions of the Old Law

§ 104. Subject matter of Copyright: National origin.

(a) UNPUBLISHED WORKS.—The works specified by sections 102 and 103, while unpublished, are subject to protection under this title without regard to the nationality or domicile of the author.

(b) PUBLISHED WORKS.—The works specified by sections 102 and 103, when published, are subject to protection under this title if—

(1) on the date of first publication, one or more of the authors is a national, or domiciliary, or sovereign authority of a foreign nation that is a party to a copyright treaty to which the United States is also a party, or is a stateless person, wherever that person may be domiciled; or

(2) the work is first published in the United States or in a foreign nation that on the date of first publication, is a party to the Universal Copyright Convention; or

(3) the work is first published by the United Nations or any of its specialized agencies, or by the Organization of American States; or

(4) the work comes within the scope of a Presidential proclamation. Whenever the President finds that a particular foreign nation extends, to works by authors who are nationals or domiciliaries of the United States or to works that are first published in the United States, copyright protection on substantially the same basis as that on which the foreign nation extends protection to the

§ 9. Authors or proprietors, entitled: aliens.

The author or proprietor of any work made the subject of copyright by this title, or his executors, administrators, or assigns, shall have copyright for such work under the conditions and for the terms specified in this title: *Provided, however,* That the copyright secured by this title shall extend to the work of an author or proprietor who is a citizen or subject of a foreign state or nation only under conditions described in subsections (a), (b), or (c) below:

(a) When an alien author or proprietor shall be domiciled within the United States at the time of the first publication of his work; or

(b) When the foreign state or nation of which such author or proprietor is a citizen or subject grants, either by treaty, convention, agreement, or law, to citizens of the United States the benefit of copyright on substantially the same basis as to its own citizens, or copyright protection, substantially equal to the protection secured to such foreign author under this title or by treaty; or when such foreign state or nation is a party to an international agreement which provides for reciprocity in the granting of copyright, by the terms of which agreement the United States may, at its pleasure, become a party thereto.

The existence of the reciprocal conditions aforesaid shall be determined by the President of the works of its own nationals and domiciliaries and works first published in that nation, the President may by proclamation extend protection under this title to works of which one or more of the authors is, on the date of first publication, a national, domiciliary, or sovereign authority of that nation, or which was first published in that nation. The President may revise, suspend, or revoke any such proclamation or impose any conditions or limitations on protection under a proclamation.

United States, by proclamation made from time to time, as the purposes of this title may require: *Provided*, That whenever the President shall find that the authors, copyright owners, or proprietors of works first produced or published abroad and subject to copyright or to renewal of copyright under the laws of the United States, including works subject to ad interim copyright, are or may have been temporarily unable to comply with the conditions and formalities prescribed with respect to such works by the copyright laws of the United States, because of the disruption or suspension of facilities essential for such compliance, he may by proclamation grant such extension of time as he may deem appropriate for the fulfillment of such conditions or formalities by authors, copyright owners, or proprietors who are citizens of the United States or who are nationals of countries which accord substantially equal treatment in this respect to authors, copyright owners, or proprietors who are citizens of the United States: *Provided further*, That no liability shall attach under this title for lawful uses made or acts done prior to the effective date of such proclamation in connection with such works, or in respect to the continuance for one year subsequent to such date of any business undertaking or enterprise lawfully undertaken prior to such date involving expenditure or contractual obligation in connection with the exploitation, production, reproduction, circulation, or performance of any such work.

The President may at any time terminate any proclamation authorized herein or any part thereof or suspend or extend its operation for such period or periods of time as in his judgment the interests of the United States may require.

(c) When the Universal Copyright Convention, signed at Geneva on September 6, 1952, shall be in force between the United States of America and the foreign state or nation of which such author is a citizen or subject, or in which the work was first published. Any work to which copyright is extended pursuant to this subsection shall be exempt from the following provisions of this title: (1) The requirement in section 1(e) that a foreign state or nation must grant to United States citizens mechanical reproduction rights similar to those specified therein; (2) the obligatory deposit requirements of the first sentence of section 13; (3) the provisions of sections 14, 16, 17, and 18; (4) the import prohibitions of section 107, to the extent that they are related to the manufacturing requirements of section 16; and (5) the requirements of sections 19 and 20: *Provided, however,* That such exemptions shall apply only if from the time of first publication all the copies of the work published with the authority of the author or other copyright proprietor shall bear the symbol © accompanied by the name of the copyright proprietor and the year of first publication placed in such manner and location as to give reasonable notice of claim of copyright.

Upon the coming into force of the Universal Copyright Convention in a foreign state or nation as hereinbefore provided, every book or periodical of a citizen or subject thereof in which ad interim copyright was subsisting on the effective date of said coming into force shall have copyright for twenty-eight years from the date of first publication abroad without the necessity of complying with the further formalities specified in section 23 of this title.

The provisions of this subsection shall not be extended to works of an author who is a citizen of, or domiciled in the United States of America regardless of place of first publication, or to works first published in the United States.

THE AUTHOR

The word "author" has generally been given a broad construction under the old law, and this will continue to be the case with the new statute as well. Originally, and in terms of the Constitution, it probably meant one who produced literary writings. Congress and the courts have since included all forms of writing, printing, engraving, etching, photography, mapmaking, sculpture, and to these have been added choreography and pantomime, by the new Act. In keeping with the original notion of an author, protection was at first denied to the writer of advertising matter. In the modern view such a writer is an author and advertising comes within the protection of statute.

The word "author," by the terms of both the new and old statutes, includes an employer in the case of works made for hire. Therefore, a motion picture company hiring an author at a weekly salary to write for it might become the author for statutory purposes of procuring copyright in its own name, as it might also when it hires a film-maker to direct a film. This is illustrated in a case decided in 1975 involving D. W. Griffith's film, *The Birth of a Nation*. The original copyright had been obtained by the Epoch Production Company, as the employer for hire, in 1915 and had been renewed in 1942. In a suit for infringement brought by Epoch, it was held that Epoch had no right to the renewal of the copyright because it could not prove that it was the employer of a work made for hire.

The Birth of a Nation had been based on Thomas Dixon's novel *The Clansman*, copyrighted in 1904, and this copyright had been granted to the Majestic Motion Picture Company which planned to make a film of the novel. However, Majestic was unable to complete its contractual obligations with Dixon, even as the film was being made, and in 1915, after *Birth* had been completed, another corporation, Epoch, was established to do so. The court found that there was insufficient evidence to prove that the scenario for the film, written by Griffith and Frank E. Woods, and produced and directed by Griffith, had been undertaken as a work for hire. Said the court:

> The evidence does not indicate whether Majestic and/or Epoch simply supplied capital for the production of the picture, whether they commissioned Griffith independently to produce the film, whether they "hired" Griffith as employee to do the work, and most important, whether they could have exercised the requisite power to control or supervise Griffith's work, which is the hallmark of "an employment for hire."

As a result it was held that Epoch's renewal of the copyright was invalid and thus that no compensable infringement had occurred.

In the past, motion picture companies hired writers and composers who were paid weekly salaries. More recently, these companies have adopted the practice of retaining individuals not on a weekly salaried basis, but to produce specific works for individual films. In the case of *Leonard Bernstein* v. *Uni-*

versal Pictures, it was held that the work-for-hire doctrine under the old statute applied where the creator of the work is an independent contractor. In such a situation, the court found, the ownership of the copyright rests with the party who commissioned the work, absent a contrary indication of contractual intent.

The new law incorporates this decision with regard to the ownership of works made for hire but makes it possible for those in Mr. Bernstein's position to obtain copyright by express contractual provision.

§ 201. Ownership of copyright

(a) INITIAL OWNERSHIP.—Copyright in a work protected under this title vests initially in the author or authors of the work. The authors of a joint work are coowners of copyright in the work.

(b) WORKS MADE FOR HIRE.—In the case of a work made for hire, the employer or other person for whom the work was prepared is considered the author for purposes of this title, and, unless the parties have expressly agreed otherwise in a written instrument signed by them, owns all of the rights comprised in the copyright.

Under the section on definitions, the new law defines a work made for hire as follows:

(1) a work prepared by an employee within the scope of his or her employment; or

(2) a work specially ordered or commissioned for use as a contribution to a collective work, as a part of a motion picture or other audiovisual work, as a translation, as a supplementary work, as a compilation, as an instructional text, as a test, as answer material for a test, or as an atlas, if the parties expressly agree in a written instrument signed by them that the work shall be considered a work made for hire. For the purpose of the foregoing sentence, a "supplementary work" is a work prepared for publication as a secondary adjunct to a work by another author for the purpose of introducing, concluding, illustrating, explaining, revising, commenting upon, or assisting in the use of the other work, such as forewords, afterwords, pictorial illustrations, maps, charts, tables, editorial notes, musical arrangements, answer material for

tests, bibliographies, appendixes, indexes, and an "instructional text" is a literary, pictorial, or graphic work prepared for publication and with the purpose of use in systematic instructional activities.

Individual contributions by authors of works, not specially commissioned, to collective works, such as anthologies of poems, essays, stories and the like, are not considered as works for hire under section 201 (c) of the new law. Copyright in the individual contribution and copyright in the collective work as a whole are separate and distinct, and the author of the contribution is the first owner of copyright to it.

(c) CONTRIBUTIONS TO COLLECTIVE WORKS.—Copyright in each separate contribution to a collective work is distinct from copyright in the collective work as a whole, and vests initially in the author of the contribution. In the absence of express transfer of the copyright or of any rights under it, the owner of the copyright in the collective work is presumed to have acquired only the privilege of reproducing and distributing the contribution as part of that particular collective work, any revision of that collective work, and any later collective work in the same series.

The right of ghost writers to be called authors is in some doubt. In an English case, where a ghost wrote a celebrity's book and the form of expression was his, it was held that the ghost was the sole author and entitled to the copyright. In the case of a collaboration, either or both the principal and the ghost might be entitled to copyright.

A New York decision has cast some doubt upon the legal morality, and therefore the validity, of ghost-writing contracts.

It was alleged in an action against Milton Berle that he had requested Anita Roddy-Eden to write a serious novel to be published under Milton Berle's name as sole author. Thereafter he breached the contract, and Roddy-Eden sued for damages. The court said that the contract obviously was a scheme concocted and devised deliberately to foist a fraud on the public, and since no contract could arise out of an immoral or unlawful consideration, the contract was unenforceable and void. This, of course, goes counter to the accepted practice, so widely diffused, of ghost writing.

Frederick Spencer Oliver wrote a book which he claimed to have been dictated to him by a deceased person's spirit; he described himself as the "amanuensis" to whom it was dictated by Phylos the Tibetan, a spirit. The court held that since he wished to impress on the purchasers of the book that he, a mortal being, was not the author, he could not change his position for the purposes of benefitting by the law and claim that he was the author.

WHAT IS ENTITLED TO COPYRIGHT

To the classification of works copyrightable under the old law, the new law has added choreographic works and pantomime. The statute has also adopted broad language to provide copyright protection for works which may take their form from, or be "fixed" in technologies at present unknown, but which may at some future time be developed. A work is "fixed," according to the new law, when its embodiment in a copy or phonorecord is sufficiently permanent or stable to permit it to be perceived, reproduced, or otherwise communicated for a period of more than transitory duration. The parallel provisions of the new and old laws are as follows:

Provisions of the New Law

§ 102. Subject matter of copyright: In general

(a) Copyright protection subsists, in accordance with this title, in original works of authorship fixed in any tangible medium of expression, now known or later developed, from which they can be perceived, reproduced, or otherwise communi-

Provisions of the Old Law

§ 5. Classification of works for registration

The application for registration shall specify to which of the following classes the work in which copyright is claimed belongs:

(a) Books, including composite and cyclopedic works, directories, gazetteers, and other compilations.

cated, either directly or with the aid of a machine or device. Works of authorship include the following categories:

(1) literary works;

(2) musical works, including any accompanying words;

(3) dramatic works, including any accompanying music;

(4) pantomimes and choreographic works;

(5) pictorial, graphic, and sculptural works;

(6) motion pictures and other audiovisual works; and

(7) sound recordings.

§ 103. Subject matter of copyright: Compilations and derivative works.

(a) The subject matter of copyright as specified by section 102 includes compilations and derivative works, but protection for a work employing preexisting material in which copyright subsists does not extend to any part of the work in which such material has been used unlawfully.

(b) The copyright in a compilation or derivative work extends only to the material contributed by the author of such work, as distinguished from the preexisting material employed in the work, and does not imply any exclusive right in the preexisting material. The copyright in such work is independent of, and does not affect or enlarge the scope, duration, ownership, or subsistence of, any copyright protection in the preexisting material.

(b) Periodicals, including newspapers.

(c) Lectures, sermons, addresses (prepared for oral delivery).

(d) Dramatic or dramatico-musical compositions.

(e) Musical compositions.

(f) Maps.

(g) Works of art; models or designs for works of art.

(h) Reproductions of a work of art.

(i) Drawings or plastic works of a scientific or technical character.

(j) Photographs.

(k) Prints and pictorial illustrations including prints or labels used for articles of merchandise.

(l) Motion-picture photoplays.

(m) Motion pictures other than photoplays.

The seven categories of copyrightable works under the new law are meant to be illustrative, and do not exhaust the scope of "original works of authorship" protected by the law. Nor in applying for copyright should mere error in classification invalidate a copyright properly obtained with notice. There might, for instance, be confusion between dramatical musical works and musical compositions with words. Such a confusion in registration for copyright would not be fatal.

Within the classifications of the old act, copyrightable works were defined as follows:

A. Books have been defined by the Supreme Court as follows, "It is the intellectual production of the author which the copyright protects and not the particular form which such production ultimately takes, and the word 'book' as used in the statute is not to be understood in its technical sense of a bound volume, but any species of publication which the author selects to embody his literary product."

B. A poem or song without music is a book within the law. Scenarios, stories, or synopses of motion pictures are classified as books. A literary composition explaining a game or other text matter of original character thereto is described as a book. Any original writing, describing an idea, system, plan, or method, if it is published as a book.

Generally, works of fiction, nonfiction, poems, compilations, directories, catalogues, information in tabular form and similar text matter published as books, pamphlets, leaflets, cards, single pages, and the like, were included within "books." Thus, under the old law, owners of the copyright for the *Readers' Guide to Periodical Literature* were able to bring a suit for infringement against a company which had copied verbatim past issues of the *Guide*. The suit was unsuccessful, not because the material was not copyrightable, but because no copyright had been obtained for the issues in question.

C. Periodicals include works such as newspapers, magazines, reviews, bulletins, and serial publications which appear at intervals of less than a year. A periodical has been described by the courts as:

"a publication appearing at stated intervals, each number of which contains a variety of original articles by different authors"; and "books are not turned into periodicals by number and sequence where each volume is complete in itself and betrays no inward need of more—though further adventures may be promised at the end."

D. Within the classification of lectures or similar productions are included lectures, sermons, addresses, monologues, recording scripts, and scripts for television and radio programs. These may be either published or unpublished. When published they may be copyrighted as books and registration secured for them.

E. Under drama or dramatic works are included works dramatic in character, such as plays, dramatic scripts designed for radio or television broadcasts, pantomimes, ballets, musical comedies, and operas. Dialogue, it has been held, is not necessary. Justice Holmes said:

> Action can tell a story, display all the most vivid relations between men, and depict every kind of human emotion without the aid of a word. . . . It would be impossible to deny the title of drama to pantomime as played by masters of the art.

F. Under musical compositions there are included all musical compositions, with or without words, as well as new versions of musical compositions, such as adaptations, arrangements, and editings, but such editings should be of a substantial enough class so that it may be characterized as the writing of an author.

G. Compilations or abridgments, adaptations, arrangements, dramatizations, translations, or other versions of works in the public domain or of copyrighted works when produced with the consent of the proprietor of the copyright in such works, or works republished with new matter, are new works subject to copyright.

The new law encompasses all of the above-mentioned works, adding, as has already been noted, pantomimes and choreographic works, even if they do not tell a story. Moreover, the law contains many definitions which are useful in any consideration of either the present, or previous law.

§ 101. Definitions

As used in this title, the following terms and their variant forms mean the following:

An "anonymous work" is a work on the copies or phonorecords of which no natural person is identified as author.

"Audiovisual works" are works that consist of a series of related images which are intrinsically intended to be shown by the use of machines or devices such as projectors, viewers, or electronic equipment, together with accompanying sounds, if any, regardless of the nature of the material objects, such as films or tapes, in which the works are embodied.

The "best edition" of a work is the edition, published in the United States at any time before the date of deposit, that the Library of Congress determines to be most suitable for its purposes.

A person's "children" are that person's immediate offspring, whether legitimate or not, and any children legally adopted by that person.

A "collective work" is a work, such as a periodical issue, anthology, or encyclopedia, in which a number of contributions, constituting separate and independent works in themselves, are assembled into a collective whole.

A "compilation" is a work formed by the collection and assembling of preexisting materials or of data that are selected, coordinated, or arranged in such a way that the resulting work as a whole constitutes an original work of authorship. The term "compilation" includes collective works.

"Copies" are material objects, other than phonorecords, in which a work is fixed by any method now known or later developed, and from which the work can be perceived, reproduced, or otherwise communicated, either directly or with the aid of a machine or device. The term "copies" includes the material object, other than a phonorecord, in which the work is first fixed.

"Copyright owner", with respect to any one of the exclusive rights comprised in a copyright, refers to the owner of that particular right.

A work is "created" when it is fixed in a copy or phonorecord for the first time; where a work is prepared over a period of time, the portion of it that has been fixed at any particular time constitutes the work as of that time, and where the work has been prepared in different versions, each version constitutes a separate work.

A "derivative work" is a work based upon one or more preexisting works, such as a translation, musical arrangement, dramatization, fictionalization, motion picture version, sound recording, art reproduction, abridgment, condensation, or any other form in which a work may be recast, transformed, or adapted. A work consisting of editorial revisions, annotations, elaborations, or other modifications which, as a whole, represent an original work of authorship, is a "derivative work".

A "device", "machine", or "process" is one now known or later developed.

To "display" a work means to show a copy of it, either directly or by means of a film, slide, television image, or any other device or process or, in the case of a motion picture or other audiovisual work, to show individual images nonsequentially.

A work is "fixed" in a tangible medium of expression when its embodiment in a copy or phonorecord, by or under the authority of the author, is sufficiently permanent or stable to permit it to be perceived, reproduced, or otherwise communicated for a period of more than transitory duration. A work consisting of sounds, images, or both, that are being transmitted, is "fixed" for purposes of this title if a fixation of the work is being made simultaneously with its transmission.

The terms "including" and "such as" are illustrative and not limitative.

A "joint work" is a work prepared by two or more authors with the intention that their contributions be merged into inseparable or interdependent parts of a unitary whole.

"Literary works" are works, other than audiovisual works, expressed in words, numbers, or other verbal or numerical symbols or indicia, regardless of the nature of the material objects, such as books, periodicals, manuscripts, phonorecords, film, tapes, disks, or cards, in which they are embodied.

"Motion pictures" are audiovisual works consisting of a series of related images which, when shown in succession, impart an impression of motion, together with accompanying sounds, if any.

To "perform" a work means to recite, render, play, dance, or act it, either directly or by means of any device or process or, in the case of a motion picture or other audiovisual work, to show its images in any sequence or to make the sounds accompanying it audible.

"Phonorecords" are material objects in which sounds, other than those accompanying a motion picture or other audiovisual work, are fixed by any method now known or later developed, and from which the sounds can be perceived, reproduced, or otherwise communicated, either directly or with the aid of a machine or device. The term "phonorecords" includes the material object in which the sounds are first fixed.

"Pictorial, graphic, and sculptural works" include two-dimensional and three-dimensional works of fine, graphic, and applied art, photographs, prints and art reproductions, maps, globes, charts, technical drawings, diagrams, and models. Such works shall include works of artistic craftsmanship insofar as their form but not their mechanical or utilitarian aspects are concerned; the design of a useful article, as defined in this section, shall be considered a pictorial, graphic, or sculptural work only if, and only to the extent that, such design incorporates pictorial, graphic, or sculptural features that can be identified separately from, and are capable of existing independently of, the utilitarian aspects of the article.

A "pseudonymous work" is a work on the copies or phonorecords of which the author is identified under a fictitious name.

"Publication" is the distribution of copies or phonorecords of a work to the public by sale or other transfer of ownership, or by rental, lease, or lending. The offering to distribute copies or phonorecords to a group of persons for purposes of further distribution, public performance, or public display, constitutes publication. A public performance or display of a work does not of itself constitute publication.

To perform or display a work "publicly" means—

(1) to perform or display it at a place open to the public or at any place where a substantial number of persons outside of a normal circle of a family and its social acquaintances is gathered; or

(2) to transmit or otherwise communicate a performance or display of the work to a place specified by clause (1) or to the public, by means of any device or process, whether the members of the public capable of receiving the performance or display receive it in the same place or in separate places and at the same time or at different times.

"Sound recordings" are works that result from the fixation of a series of musical, spoken, or other sounds, but not including the sounds accompanying a motion picture or other audiovisual work, regardless of the nature of the material objects, such as disks, tapes, or other phonorecords, in which they are embodied.

"State" includes the District of Columbia and the Commonwealth of Puerto Rico, and any territories to which this title is made applicable by an Act of Congress.

A "transfer of copyright ownership" is an assignment, mortgage, exclusive license, or any other conveyance, alienation, or hypothecation of a copyright or of any of the exclusive rights comprised in a copyright, whether or not it is limited in time or place of effect, but not including a nonexclusive license.

A "transmission program" is a body of material that, as an aggregate, has been produced for the sole purpose of transmission to the public in sequence and as a unit.

To "transmit" a performance or display is to communicate it by any device or process whereby images or sounds are received beyond the place from which they are sent.

The "United States", when used in a geographical sense, comprises the several States, the District of Columbia and the Commonwealth of Puerto Rico, and the organized territories under the jurisdiction of the United States Government.

A "useful article" is an article having an intrinsic utilitarian function that is not merely to portray the appearance of the article or to convey information. An article that is normally a part of a useful article is considered a "useful article".

The author's "widow" or "widower" is the author's surviving spouse under the law of the author's domicile at the time of his or her death, whether or not the spouse has later remarried.

A "work of the United States Government" is a work prepared by an officer or employee of the United States Government as part of that person's official duties.

A "work made for hire" is—

(1) a work prepared by an employee within the scope of his or her employment: or

(2) a work specially ordered or commissioned for use as a contribution to a collective work, as a part of a motion picture or other audiovisual work, as a translation, as a supplementary work, as a compilation, as an instructional text, as a test, as answer material for a test, or as an atlas, if the parties expressly agree in a written instrument signed by them that the work shall be considered a work made for hire. For the purpose of the foregoing sentence, a "supplementary work" is a work prepared for publication as a secondary

adjunct to a work by another author for the purpose of introducing, concluding, illustrating, explaining, revising, commenting
upon, or assisting in the use of the other work, such as forewords, afterwords, pictorial illustrations, maps, charts, tables,
editorial notes, musical arrangements, answer material for tests,
bibliographies, appendixes, and indexes, and an "instructional
text" is a literary, pictorial, or graphic work prepared for publication and with the purpose of use in systematic instructional
activities.

WHAT IS NOT ENTITLED TO COPYRIGHT

Under the old law, no copyright protection existed for any
publication of the United States Government, or any reprint
thereof, with the exception of certain publications made by the
Postmaster General on behalf of the United States.

The parallel provision of the new law similarly prohibits
copyright of any work of the United States Government, and
expands this provision to include unpublished as well as published works. A limited exception is made for the National Technical Information Service which operates as a clearinghouse
for the collection and dissemination of scientific, technical, and
engineering information. As under the old law, works of the
United States Postal Service, such as designs for stamps, are
copyrightable.

§ 105. Subject matter of copyright: United States Government works

Copyright protection under this title is not available for any
work of the United States Government, but the United States
Government is not precluded from receiving and holding copyrights
transferred to it by assignment, bequest, or otherwise.

A work of the United States Government is defined as one
"prepared by an officer or employee of the United States Government as part of that person's official duties."

Court decisions interpreting the old statute have held that for government publications to be non-copyrightable, "they must not only be printed at the cost and direction of the United States, but they should also be authorized expositions on matters of governmental interest by governmental authority." Thus, in a case involving speeches by Admiral Hyman Rickover, it was held that the Admiral's speeches were not government publications for purposes of the old statute because they were not delivered as part of the Admiral's official duties, even though they had been reproduced and disseminated to the Navy.

Conversely, publication by the government of copyrighted material does not destroy the owner's copyright even if such material is printed without notice of copyright. This was affirmed in two recent cases involving the report of the Warren Commission and the social critic and comedian, Lenny Bruce.

In 1963, a Dallas citizen and amateur film buff, Abraham Zapruder, happened to be filming President John F. Kennedy's motorcade when the President was struck and killed by an assassin's bullets. Zapruder subsequently sold both the films and his copyright to *Life* Magazine, which proceeded to copyright the material and publish frames from the film sequence in several articles on the assassination. Subsequently, a professor of philosophy at Haverford College wrote a book about the assassination and included, as illustrations, charcoal drawings which admittedly had been copied from frames of the Zapruder film. When Time, Inc., the parent company of *Life*, sued for infringement of its copyright, the defense was set up that publication of the film in the report of the Warren Commission, which had been charged with investigating the assassination and publishing its findings, without notice of copyright, had destroyed *Life*'s right to exclusive use of the material. Although the court eventually held that there had been no infringement under the doctrine of "fair use," it did affirm that publication by the government of stills taken from the Zapruder film without notice of copyright did not divest *Life* of its ownership of the copyright.

A similar result occurred in litigation involving Lenny Bruce and a film, *Dirtymouth*, which was made after his death. Here the court found that the film had made extensive use of material which had previously been copyrighted and published in one book by Bruce himself, and in another about him published after his death. The defense argued that this material was in the public domain because much of it had been printed in court transcripts produced during the obscenity trials that marked the final stages of Bruce's career. The court held that the original copyrighted material did not enter the public domain because of its publication in court transcripts. As the court observed:

> To hold that such originally copyrighted material becomes somehow dedicated by use in the courts would permit the unravelling of the fabric of copyright protection. If defendant's theory was accepted, James Joyce's *Ulysses*, for example, would lie within the public domain merely because the United States prosecuted the book.

Inasmuch as the new law does not purport to change the rules of originality established by the courts under the old copyright law, copyright also will not lie for the following under the new law as under the old:

B. Compilations, abridgements, adaptations, arrangements, dramatizations, translations, or other versions of copyrighted works produced without the consent of the copyright proprietor.

C. Works in the public domain, including:

1. Works in which the copyright term has expired.

2. Works in which a defective copyright subsists.

3. Works which have been published with no claim of copyright prior to the effective date of the new law, which includes works which were published without copyright notice as required prior to January 1, 1978.

4. Works published abroad without claim of copyright or protection under treaty, convention, or agreement.

5. Works produced abroad prior to the enactment of the Law of 1891 permitting copyright for aliens.

D. Ideas, systems, plans, or methods which become common property on publication, subject only to the fact that the particular expression and the original writing are protectible. Such copyright would not, however, establish any right in and to the idea, plan, or system therein embodied.

E. Works designed for recording information which do not in themselves convey information; such as time cards, graph paper, account books, diaries, checks, score cards, address books, report forms, order forms and similar forms.

F. Slogans, column headings, simple check lists, phrases, or clauses.

G. Works containing only information which is common property, such as standard calendars, height and weight charts, tape measures, rulers and tables of figures taken from statutes or other common sources.

H. Works not "fixed" in a tangible medium of expression such as choreography that has never been filmed or notated, extemporaneous speeches, original works of authorship communicated solely through conversations or live broadcasts, dramatic sketches or musical compositions improvised from memory without being recorded or written down also are not subject to statutory copyright. For these works, common-law copyright still exists.

In reference to the items listed under (E), it should be noted that scoring sheets for standardized intelligence and achievement tests may be protected by copyright. This was held in a suit involving Harcourt Brace and World, Inc., which sought to protect such sheets designed to be scored by scanning and used for the Stanford Achievement Test and the Otis-Lennon Mental Ability Test. The decision that such score sheets are protectible is but another indication of the breadth with which courts have construed "writings" under the copyright law.

COMBINATIONS OF COPYRIGHTABLE AND NON-COPYRIGHTABLE MATERIAL

When a work consists of material, some of which is copyrightable and some of which is not, a copyright may nevertheless be obtained to protect the material which is copyrightable, under both the old and new law. So a book in the public domain to which there has been added a new preface may be copyrighted, but the copyright will be effective only as to the preface. A book that contains information which is in the public domain may be copyrighted even though the information therein contained will not be copyrighted, for no one can have an exclusive right thereto. Two persons may independently create a new version, such as a play out of a novel, or a motion picture out of a novel, and where the novel is in the public domain each new version will be separately entitled to copyright.

LIMITATIONS ON EXCLUSIVE RIGHTS

The development of new technologies continually creates new modes of expression and new means of disseminating information, thus at once affording new opportunities for an author's creativity, while creating new means for infringing on that creativity. So it was with the development of radio, television, and phonorecording, and so it has been with the development of photocopying and cable television.

Although the new copyright law generally affords an author or proprietor easier access to, and thus more secure copyright protection for, the five exclusive rights—reproduction, adaptation, publication, performance, and display—delineated by the new statute, the new law also diminishes his rights by providing for express limitations on exclusivity in other areas. Most notably for literary property, these limitations involve the use of photocopying, both by libraries and archives and by class-room teachers.

Under the 1909 Act, of course, no reference was made to the mechanical reproduction by photocopying of printed copy-righted works. In the leading case, *Williams and Wilkens Company* v. *United States*, in which the publisher of medical textbooks sued the Department of Health, Education and Welfare, the National Institutes of Health, and the National Library of Medicine for infringement resulting from the photocopying of some of its texts, it was held that such photocopying, where it was not for commercial purposes and was intended to aid in the dissemination of information to medical researchers, did not constitute an actionable infringement.

Adopting the spirit of the *Williams-Wilkens* decision, the new law provides that under certain conditions it is not an infringement of copyright for a library or archives to reproduce or distribute not more than one copy of a work. The conditions under which such photocopying is not an infringement are set forth in Section 108 of the new law:

§ 108. Limitations on exclusive rights: Reproduction by libraries and archives

(a) Notwithstanding the provisions of section 106, it is not an infringement of copyright for a library or archives, or any of its employees acting within the scope of their employment, to re-produce no more than one copy or phonorecord of a work, or to distribute such copy or phonorecord, under the conditions specified by this section if—

(1) the reproduction or distribution is made without any purpose of direct or indirect commercial advantage;

(2) the collections of the library or archives are (i) open to the public, or (ii) available not only to researchers affiliated with the library or archives or with the institution of which it is a part, but also to other persons doing research in a specialized field; and

(3) the reproduction or distribution of the work includes a notice of copyright. * * *

Archival reproduction is permitted for replacement of damaged copies, articles and small excerpts, and out of print works. The statute further provides for periodic five-year review of these provisions to determine if the intended balance between the needs of users and the rights of authors has been achieved.

The author's exclusive rights to his property are further limited by the provisions set forth in the new law which would permit the making of multiple copies for classroom use, under the doctrine of fair use, which has been incorporated in the Act.

§ 107. Limitations on exclusive rights: Fair use

Notwithstanding the provisions of section 106, the fair use of a copyrighted work, including such use by reproduction in copies or phonorecords or by any other means specified by that section, for purposes such as criticism, comment, news reporting, teaching (including multiple copies for classroom use), scholarship, or research, is not an infringement of copyright. * * *

Although not specifically included in the text of the law, guidelines, resulting from negotiations between representatives of educators, publishers, and authors, are set forth in an accompanying report and suggest the following limitations for the making of copies for classroom use:

1) teachers are permitted to make, for use in research or preparation, a single copy of a chapter from a book, an article from a periodical or newspaper, and a short story, short essay or short poem whether or not from a collective work;

2) multiple classroom copying cannot exceed the number of pupils in the class;

3) copies must include a notice of copyright;

4) copying must meet standards of brevity, spontaneity, and non-cumulative effect.

The cumulative effect standard would limit classroom copying to:

i) only one course in the school for which the copies are made;

ii) not more than one short poem, article, or essay per author, or three excerpts from the same collective work, during one class term;

    iii) not more than nine instances of such multiple copying per term.

Further limitations on the exclusivity of the author's rights have been incorporated in the sections of the new law dealing with secondary transmissions via cable television, although here the author or copyright proprietor will be compensated for the loss of exclusive control by the payment of royalties.

Prior to the adoption of the new law, the Supreme Court had exempted the owners and operators of cable television systems from liability for copyright infringement, holding that these secondary transmissions were not "performances" for purposes of the 1909 Act. The new law puts an end to this exemption and provides for the compulsory licensing of cable television systems and public broadcast systems, in addition to the licensing already required for jukebox operators under the old law. To insure that copyright owners will be properly remunerated for the use of their materials, the statute provides for the establishment of a Copyright Royalty Tribunal.

HOW COPYRIGHT IS OBTAINED

The law has always justified its requirement that notice of copyright be published with the author's work for three reasons: notice informs the public as to whether material is copyrighted or not; it identifies the copyright owner; and it shows the date of publication. However, formal notice requirements also give rise to arbitrary or unjust forfeitures which may result from unintentional or relatively unimportant omissions or errors in providing notice.

Under the old law, statutory copyright could only be secured by publication with notice. Under the new law, all works now receive federal copyright protection from the date of creation. However, notice still plays an important part in the obtaining of copyright protection for published works, despite the fact that the new law has departed from the more stringent notice requirements of the 1909 Act. Under the new law, failure to provide proper notice of copyright is not fatal and will not automatically result in the work's falling into the public domain as was the case under the old law, since the new law allows a five-year grace period for works published without proper notice of copyright. Still, notice is ultimately required to obtain copyright protection for published works. Moreover, although copyright is obtained by publication with notice within five years, protection against infringement of the copyright can only be secured by compliance with the provisions of the statute governing registration and deposit. Clearly then, it is advisable for notice to be given with publication, and for this to be done properly, the formal provisions of the statute should be followed.

Provisions of the New Law

§ 401. Notice of copyright: Visually perceptible copies.

(a) GENERAL REQUIREMENT.— Whenever a work protected under this title is published in the United States or elsewhere by authority of the copyright owner, a notice of copyright as provided by this section shall be placed on all publicly distributed copies from which the work can be visually perceived, either directly or with the aid of a machine or device.

(b) FORM OF NOTICE.—The notice appearing on the copies shall consist of the following three elements:

(1) the symbol © (the letter C in a circle), or the word "Copyright", or the abbreviation "Copr."; and

Provisions of the Old Law

§ 10. Publication of work with notice.

Any person entitled thereto by this title may secure copyright for his work by publication thereof with the notice of copyright required by this title; and such notice shall be affixed to each copy thereof published or offered for sale in the United States by authority of the copyright proprietor, except in the case of books seeking ad interim protection under section 22 of this title.

§ 19. Notice; Form.

The notice of copyright required by section 10 of this title shall consist either of the word "Copyright", the abbreviation "Copr.", or the symbol ©, accompanied by the

(2) the year of first publication of the work; in the case of compilations or derivative works incorporating previously published material, the year date of first publication of the compilation or derivative work is sufficient. The year date may be omitted where a pictorial, graphic, or sculptural work, with accompanying text matter, if any, is reproduced in or on greeting cards, postcards, stationery, jewelry, dolls, toys, or any useful articles; and

(3) the name of the owner of copyright in the work, or an abbreviation by which the name can be recognized, or a generally known alternative designation of the owner.

name of the copyright proprietor, and if the work be a printed literary, musical, or dramatic work, the notice shall include also the year in which the copyright was secured by publication. * * *

Under both the new and old laws, the notice required consists of either the word "Copyright," or the abbreviation "Copr.," or the symbol © accompanied by the name of the copyright proprietor, and, in the case of printed literary, musical, or dramatic material, the year in which copyright was secured by publication. The letter C in a circle is also the symbol required by the Universal Copyright Convention, and since it has legally been added to both new and old statutes, it suffices.

The name of the copyright proprietor may be:

    a. The author;

    b. A person to whom the author has transferred all of his rights in the work;

    c. An employer in the case of a work made for hire;

    d. Joint authors or collaborators;

    e. The literary name of the author;

    f. The name of the corporate proprietor;

    g. The name of the partnership proprietor;

    h. A lawful trade name;

    i. A membership corporation;

    j. An unincorporated association.

The year in the notice should be the actual year of first publication. Under the old law, a mistake as to the year of publication could result in the forfeiture of copyright. Since the initial term of protection ran for twenty-eight years from publication, notice of the date of publication alerted the public to the amount of time remaining, after which the work would fall into the public domain if not renewed. Thus, where the notice contained a year date subsequent to the year in which the work was published, the public would be misled into belief that the copyright term ran from the later year, and therefore, such notice was fatally defective. On the other hand, antedating publication in the notice did not affect the public adversely and therefore was not a fatal defect. Confusion sometimes occurred when the book was published for the Christmas trade and the copyright notice was dated the following year. This common error would result in the loss of copyright.

Since the copyright term under the new law is the author's life plus fifty years, notice of the date of publication no longer serves the same function when the author's identity is known. Where the author is not known, as in the case of pseudonymous or anonymous works, or where the work was done for hire, statutory notice does serve a function since the copyright term is computed at seventy-five years from publication, or one hundred years from creation, whichever is less.

In the case of serial publication, where a work is copyrighted over a period that spans two annual dates, the first year is the year date which should be used when the work is published in book form. The date may be included in any recognized form of number, Roman or Arabic. Roman dates are sometimes used in reprints on the assumption that the public cannot read them and therefore will not readily be apprised of the age of the reprinted work.

Where works are compilations, the year date, if the works are by the same author, need only be the year date of the publication of the compilation. Previous copyright years on work included need not be listed. This was true of the old law as well.

One important difference between the new and old laws concerns collective works. Under the old law, where works separately copyrighted by various authors were included in an anthology, a single copyright notice for the entire work did not comply with the statute. This is changed by the new law which provides that although separate contributions to a collective work may bear their own notice of copyright, a single notice applicable to the collective work as a whole will protect the copyrights of the individual contributors. If the contributions have not been previously published, a single notice will still protect the individual author's rights. Where the individual works do not bear their own notice, however, innocent infringers will not be penalized.

It has often been the practice of commercial publishers when publishing or republishing government works to add some new material, either by way of introduction or illustration and then to include a general copyright notice in the name of the publisher. In this way the public is misled into believing that the bulk of the material is protected and therefore not free for general use. To prevent this practice the new law has added a section which requires that when works consist preponderantly of government material, the copyright notice must identify those parts of the work for which copyright is claimed.

Under the old statute, for books published in the United States where ad interim copyright had been obtained, the year date and the notice were that of the first publication abroad. Ad interim copyright no longer exists for works published after January 1, 1978. The new law, moreover, differs from the old in that it requires notice whenever the work is published "in the United States or elsewhere by authority of the copyright owner." This makes notice requirements applicable to copies distributed to the public anywhere in the world, regardless of where and when the work was first published.

Under the old law, books, short stories, poems, and certain other types of work had to be published with notice of copyright before they were eligible for statutory copyright, while musical compositions, dramas, works of art, drawings and plastic works of a scientific or technical character, photographs, motion pictures, and works prepared for oral delivery could all be copyrighted before publication. Under the new law, all works come under statutory protection from the time of their creation, creation being used in a technical sense to mean the point at which they are fixed in a tangible medium, although unpublished works may be registered for copyright.

PLACE OF NOTICE

The new law has more liberal notice provisions than the old and only requires that notice be placed so as to give reasonable notice of copyright.

Provisions of the New Law

§ 401 ° ° °

(c) POSITION OF NOTICE.—The notice shall be affixed to the copies in such manner and location as to give reasonable notice of the claim of copyright. The Register of Copyrights shall prescribe by regulation, as examples, specific methods of affixation and positions of the notice on various types of works that will satisfy this requirement, but these specifications shall not be considered exhaustive.

Provisions of the Old Law

§ 20. **Same; place of application of; one notice in each volume or number of newspaper or periodical.**

The notice of copyright shall be applied, in the case of a book or other printed publication, upon its title page or the page immediately following, or if a periodical either upon the title page or upon the first page of text of each separate number or under the title heading, or if a musical work either upon its title page or the first page of music. * * *

Under the old law, the courts had frequently ruled that in the absence of strict compliance with the notice provisions, copyright was defective and could not be enforced. Although all works published after January 1, 1978, benefit from the more liberal notice provisions of the new law, it is possible that problems may arise in regard to works published before that date. For such works, the following discussion is still pertinent:

- the title page has been defined by the courts as "the page devoted in whole or in part, especially to the title."
- notice on any other page, including the back cover of a pamphlet no matter how prominent, is ineffective.
- where there is no title page, a copyright notice on the front cover, or on the page following may suffice, but is dangerous practice.

In one case involving a portfolio, under the old statute, the court said that the title page was the outside of the cover because there was sufficient printed matter on the outside ordinarily to constitute a title page. The court held that a copyright notice on the first leaf following the cover did not meet the requirements of the statute, since a page intervened between the title page and the page bearing the copyright notice. Where it appeared that only the cover would be the title page and the notice of the copyright appeared on page three of the book, the court held the copyright notice defective. From these examples, all of which resulted in abandonment and the loss of statutory protection, the virtues of the new law's simplified provision that notice simply be "reasonably" placed are apparent.

OMISSION OF NOTICE FROM COPIES

Significant changes in the old law have been made in regard to the omission of notice. Under the new law, outright omission of a copyright notice, whether intentional or unintentional, whether involving only a few, or all the published copies, does not automatically throw the work into the public domain. Instead the statute provides three conditions under which statutory protection will not be lost. These exceptions are as follows:

§ 405. Notice of copyright: Omission of notice

(a) EFFECT OF OMISSION ON COPYRIGHT.—The omission of the copyright notice prescribed by sections 401 through 403 from copies or phonorecords publicly distributed by authority of the copyright owner does not invalidate the copyright in a work if—

(1) the notice has been omitted from no more than a relatively small number of copies or phonorecords distributed to the public; or

(2) registration for the work has been made before or is made within five years after the publication without notice, and a reasonable effort is made to add notice to all copies or phonorecords that are distributed to the public in the United States after the omission has been discovered; or

(3) the notice has been omitted in violation of an express requirement in writing that, as a condition of the copyright owner's authorization of the public distribution of copies or phonorecords, they bear the prescribed notice.

Under the old law, exceptions for the omission of notice were made only when the omission was accidental, and only where a particular copy or limited number of copies had omitted notice.

The new law provides far greater protection against forfeiture, and it is conceivable for an entire edition of a work to be printed without copyright notice, and for statutory protection to still be retained, provided registration of the work occurs within five years, and a reasonable effort is made to add notice to the distributed copies. The key here, of course, is the court's interpretation of what constitutes a reasonable effort, for if courts construe this strictly, the practical result of widespread publication without notice of copyright under the new statute will be rendered the same as under the old.

Under both new and old statutes, innocent infringers are protected against liability where they have relied on the omission of notice.

The provisions of the old law did not protect the copyright proprietor if notice was defective, as, for instance, if no name of the copyright owner or no date was included, or if the symbol or word "copyright" was not used, or another word, such as "registered" inserted in its place. Such is no longer the case under the new law. Where the person named in the copyright notice is not the actual copyright owner, the validity and ownership of the copyright are not affected. If either the name of the copyright owner or the date of publication is omitted altogether, notice is treated as omitted and the provisions of section 405 are brought into play. Where the year of publication has been antedated, the new law, like the old, computes any period from the date in the notice. Where the year date published in the notice is more than one year later than the actual year of publication, the work is considered to have been published without notice. Under the old law this would result in the forfeit of copyright. Under the new law, the mistake may be either excused or corrected in accordance with the provisions of section 405 discussed above. The section of the new law treating errors in name or date follows:

§ 406. Notice of copyright: Error in name or date

(a) Error in Name.—Where the person named in the copyright notice on copies or phonorecords publicly distributed by authority of the copyright owner is not the owner of copyright, the validity and ownership of the copyright are not affected. In such a case, however, any person who innocently begins an undertaking that infringes the copyright has a complete defense to any action for such infringement if such person proves that he or she was misled by the notice and began the undertaking in good faith under a purported transfer or license from the person named therein, unless before the undertaking was begun—

(1) registration for the work had been made in the name of the owner of copyright; or

(2) a document executed by the person named in the notice and showing the ownership of the copyright had been recorded. The person named in the notice is liable to account to the copyright owner for all receipts from transfers or licenses purportedly made under the copyright by the person named in the notice.

(b) Error in Date.—When the year date in the notice on copies or phonorecords distributed by authority of the copyright owner is earlier than the year in which publication first occurred, any period computed from the year of first publication under section 302 is to be computed from the year in the notice. Where the year date is more than one year later than the year in which publication first occurred, the work is considered to have been published without any notice and is governed by the provisions of section 405.

(c) OMISSION OF NAME OR DATE.—Where copies or phonorecords publicly distributed by authority of the copyright owner contain no name or no date that could reasonably be considered a part of the notice, the work is considered to have been published without any notice and is governed by the provisions of section 405.

REGISTRATION AND DEPOSIT

A major change effected by the new law is that there are now statutory provisions for two types of deposit. The first, deposit with the Library of Congress of two copies of the best edition, is mandatory within three months of publication, but is not a prerequisite to enforcement of the copyright. The second, deposit of two copies of the best edition with the Copyright Office, accompanying registration, although not mandatory, is required before the copyright owner can enforce his copyright against an infringer. For the first type of deposit, the new law provides that the Register of Copyrights of the Library of Congress may demand deposit, and provides for a series of fines to enforce this demand.

§ 407. Deposit of copies or phonorecords for Library of Congress

(a) Except as provided by subsection (c), and subject to the provisions of subsection (e), the owner of copyright or of the exclusive right of publication in a work published with notice of copyright in the United States shall deposit, within three months after the date of such publication—

(1) two complete copies of the best edition; or

(2) if the work is a sound recording, two complete phonorecords of the best edition, together with any printed or other visually perceptible material published with such phonorecords.

Neither the deposit requirements of this subsection nor the acquisition provisions of subsection (e) are conditions of copyright protection.

(b) The required copies or phonorecords shall be deposited in the Copyright Office for the use or disposition of the Library of Congress. The Register of Copyrights shall, when requested by the depositor and upon payment of the fee prescribed by section 708, issue a receipt for the deposit. ***

(d) At any time after publication of a work as provided by subsection (a), the Register of Copyrights may make written demand for the required deposit on any of the persons obligated to make the deposit under subsection (a). Unless deposit is made within three months after the demand is received, the person or persons on whom the demand was made are liable—

(1) to a fine of not more than $250 for each work; and

(2) to pay into a specially designated fund in the Library of Congress the total retail price of the copies or phonorecords demanded, or, if no retail price has been fixed, the reasonable cost of the Library of Congress of acquiring them; and

(3) to pay a fine of $2,500, in addition to any fine or liability imposed under clauses (1) and (2), if such person willfully or repeatedly fails or refuses to comply with such a demand. ***

The intent of these provisions is to avoid cases under the old law in which the deposit requirements were repeatedly and intentionally ignored. Under the new law, failure to deposit copies does not result in forfeiture of copyright. Under the old law, failure to comply with a formal demand for deposit and registration, which were combined, resulted in total loss of copyright. However, registration and deposit may occur at the same time, and the effect of the new law's mandatory deposit provision is to encourage registration as well.

Under both the new and old statutes, registration is not required for the acquisition of copyright itself since copyright vests from the creation of the work under the new law, or was obtained by publication with notice under the old law. Section 408(a) of the new law makes explicit the permissive nature of registration by providing that:

At any time during the subsistence of copyright in any published or unpublished work, the owner of copyright or of any exclusive right in the work may obtain registration of the copyright claim by delivering to the Copyright Office the deposit specified by this section, together with the application and fee specified by sections 409 and 708.

However, under the new law, as under the old, registration is necessary to enforce copyright in a suit against an infringer. Moreover, under the new law, no statutory damages or attorney's fees will be awarded unless registration occurs within three months of publication of the work. The relevant sections of the new law are as follows:

§ 411. Registration as prerequisite to infringement suit

(a) Subject to the provisions of subsection (b), no action for infringement of the copyright in any work shall be instituted until registration of the copyright claim has been made in accordance with this title. In any case, however, where the deposit, application, and fee required for registration have been delivered to the Copyright Office in proper form and registration has been refused, the applicant is entitled to institute an action for infringement if notice thereof, with a copy of the complaint, is served on the Register of Copyrights. The Register may, at his or her option, become a party to the action with respect to the issue of registrability of the copyright claim by entering an appearance within sixty days after such service, but the Register's failure to become a party shall not deprive the court of jurisdiction to determine that issue.

§ 412. Registration as prerequisite to certain remedies for infringement

In any action under this title, other than an action instituted under section 411(b), no award of statutory damages or of attorney's fees, as provided by sections 504 and 505, shall be made for—

(1) any infringement of copyright in an unpublished work commenced before the effective date of its registration; or

(2) any infringement of copyright commenced after first publication of the work and before the effective date of its registration, unless such registration is made within three months after the first publication of the work.

As with the old statute, the decision of the Register of Copyrights as to whether or not material submitted adequately complies with the law is reviewable by the courts. Thus the Register's decision is not final. Nevertheless, it is wise to comply fully with the requirements of the statute, rather than to await a test in the courts and possible invalidity. Section 408(b) of the new statute provides that the material for deposit for copyright registration shall include:

> (1) in the case of an unpublished work, one complete copy or phonorecord;
> (2) in the case of a published work, two complete copies or phonorecords of the best edition;
> (3) in the case of a work first published outside the United States, one complete copy or phonorecord as so published;
> (4) in the case of a contribution to a collective work, one complete copy or phonorecord of the best edition of the collective work.***

It should be noted that this deposit requirement may be met independently of the mandatory requirement that two complete copies of the best edition be deposited with the Library of Congress. The latter is not a prerequisite for enforcement of copyright, per se, but exists for the convenience of the Library of Congress. However, copies deposited for the Library of Congress may be used to satisfy the deposit provisions for registration, if they are accompanied by the prescribed application and fee. These provisions and the separation of deposit with the Library of Congress from deposit accompanying registration with the Copyright Office are somewhat more complex than the unitary system under the old law which provided that a person entitled to copyright might obtain registration by depositing two complete copies of the best edition of the work in the Office of the Register of Copyrights after copyright had been secured by publication, or one complete copy of the best edition if the work had been published in a foreign country and the author was an alien.

However, because deposit with the Library of Congress also satisfies the deposit requirement of registration, the net effect of the new law's provisions is to provide strong incentives for registration and deposit within three months of publication. These incentives are provided in two ways. First, failure to deposit copies with the Library of Congress within three months of publication makes the copyright holder liable to fines, and the ability to combine deposit with the Library and registration with the Copyright Office facilitates the latter. Second, failure to register within three months of publication results in the copyright owner's forfeiture of any right to statutory damages and attorney's fees in a suit for infringement.

These new provisions remedy some of the deficiencies of the earlier Act but in effect make the registration and deposit requirements more stringent.

Although under the old act it was required that copies be deposited promptly, courts had held that a mere failure in making deposit of copies did not cause forfeiture of the copyright in view of the fact that the act nowhere defined "promptly."

Thus in *The Washingtonian* case, an issue of that magazine had been published in December, 1931, containing material written by Drew Pearson and Robert S. Allen. Copyright was claimed by printing the required notice. Fourteen months later, in February, 1933, copies were deposited and a certificate of registration secured. In August, 1932, Liveright published a book containing in part the material written by Pearson and Allen. The Supreme Court held that delay in the deposit of copies did not destroy the right to sue after publication with notice.

As a matter of practice the Copyright Office under the old law has accepted works for registration, under the prompt deposit clause, as much as twenty-seven years after publication with notice. Under the new law such tardiness in deposit would result in the copyright owner's loss of statutory damages and attorney's fees and the provisions in the new law to this effect, therefore, encourage deposit and registration within three months of publication.

The language of both the new and old laws requires that two complete copies of the best edition be deposited, so where a work is simultaneously published in paper and cloth, the cloth volumes should be deposited. An interesting question arises where a limited edition is produced for sale at the same time as a general trade edition, since the limited edition is obviously the best and deposit of it would be required. Similarly, as in the case of Samuel Eliot Morison's famous biography of Christopher Columbus, where one edition was produced at $5 and simultaneously another at $10, it is obvious that the $10 edition would be the best copy. It would not only have been the best copy, it would have been the only copy containing the entire work, and the entire work must be submitted, not a mere outline or epitome.

Where material for serialization was set up in what appeared to be page-proof form, and bound into books containing a proper copyright notice, and in addition each page contained a separate notice of copyright and a release date, the bound volumes were held to be entitled to copyright as a book, under the old law, and since this was the only edition of the book available, it was the best edition entitled to copyright.

Registration of unpublished works under the new law, as with registration of unpublished works eligible for statutory copyright under the old law, is accomplished by depositing one complete copy of the work with the Copyright Office. There is no deposit requirement for unpublished works with the Library of Congress. However, unlike the old law which required that a work registered in unpublished form be reregistered when published, the new law does not require a second registration for the published edition unless it contains sufficient added material to be considered a derivative work or a compilation.

MANUFACTURE IN THE UNITED STATES

Sections 16, 17, and 18 of the old copyright law required that all books, periodicals, etc., except works of foreign origin in languages other than English submitted for copyright, be manufactured in the United States. For many years this clause stood in the way of our adhering to the Berne Convention or to any other proposed international agreement, since the Berne Convention had at its very root the notion of international protection without the imposition of such terms on copyright. Prior to our adherence to the Universal Copyright Convention, we amended our law so as to make unnecessary manufacture in the United States to nationals of countries similarly belonging to the UCC.

However, until adoption of the new law, the manufacturing clause still applied to books copyrighted in the United States in the first instance by citizens and residents of this country, and to books and periodicals in the English language manufactured and first published outside the United States in the following three classes:

1. The works of authors who were United States citizens or domiciliaries.
2. Works which could have qualified for protection under our law by virtue of the UCC, but which did not qualify for the exemption from the manufacturing clause because of failure to use the notice of copyright provided for in the Convention.
3. Works by authors who were citizens of countries with which the United States had established copyright relations, but who were not citizens of a country party to the UCC and who did not first publish the work in a country party to the Convention.

By manufacture was meant printing from type set within the limits of the United States, either by hand or with the aid of any typesetting machine or from plates made within the United States, from type set therein, or by lithographing process or photoengraving process wholly made in the United States. Further, the printing of the text and binding of the book had to be performed within the United States, and these requirements extended to the illustrations of a book by whatever process produced.

The new statute provides for substantial changes, and after July 1, 1982, the manufacturing clause will be eliminated from our copyright law entirely. Until then, under the new law, foreign nationals will no longer be required to have their works manufactured in the United States unless they are also domiciliaries of this country. Further, United States nationals are not required to comply with the manufacturing provision if they are domiciled outside the United States for a continuous period of at least one year preceding the date of importation or distribution of the work in the United States, or if, in the case of a work made for hire, the employer is not a national or domiciliary of the United States or a domestic corporation or enterprise. However, until July 1, 1982, when the manufacturing clause ceases to have any effect, the new law still discriminates against nationals or domiciliaries of the United States by requiring manufacture in this country, or in Canada, of works consisting predominately of non-dramatic literary material that is in English.

§ 601. Manufacture, importation, and public distribution of certain copies

(a) Prior to July 1, 1982, and except as provided by subsection (b), the importation into or public distribution in the United States of copies of a work consisting preponderantly of nondramatic literary material that is in the English language and is protected under this title is prohibited unless the portions consisting of such material have been manufactured in the United States or Canada.

(b) The provisions of subsection (a) do not apply—

(1) where, on the date when importation is sought or public distribution in the United States is made, the author of any substantial part of such material is neither a national nor a

domiciliary of the United States or, if such author is a national
of the United States, he or she has been domiciled outside the
United States for a continuous period of at least one year immediately preceding that date; in the case of a work made for
hire, the exemption provided by this clause does not apply
unless a substantial part of the work was prepared for an
employer or other person who is not a national or domiciliary
of the United States or a domestic corporation or enterprise;

    (2) where the United States Customs Service is presented with
an import statement issued under the seal of the Copyright
Office, in which case a total of no more than two thousand copies
of any one such work shall be allowed entry; the import statement shall be issued upon request to the copyright owner or to
a person designated by such owner at the time of registration for
the work under section 408 or at any time thereafter.***

Exempted from the manufacturing requirement are dramatic,
musical, pictorial, or graphic works, foreign-language, bilingual,
or multi-lingual works, as well as material in the public domain.
In addition, while the manufacturing clause still applies, it will
be possible under the new law, to import and distribute 2,000
copies of non-dramatic literary material in English where the
United States Customs Service is presented with an import
statement issued under the seal of the Copyright Office.

Under the old law protection of an ad interim copyright for
a period of five years from the date of first publication abroad
could be procured by registering a claim to ad interim copyright within six months of the date of first publication outside
the United States. If such application were not filed, the work
fell into the public domain and there was no valid copyright
subsisting in the United States.

If within that period of five years, an edition was manufactured and published in the United States in accordance with
the provisions of the manufacturing clause, then a full twenty-
eight-year term of copyright could be obtained by filing an
application for registration of that edition before the end of
the five-year period. Under these provisions of the old law, the

date of publication abroad, not the date of first publication in the United States, governed. A mistake in printing in the notice of the first publication date in the United States and disregarding the first publication date abroad resulted in invalidating the copyright. Copies that were imported for the purpose of obtaining ad interim copyright were not required to contain the notice of copyright. During the five-year period the ad interim copyright holder was permitted to import 1,500 copies of the work in which the ad interim copyright was claimed. For that purpose the Copyright Office would issue an import statement to be presented to the customs office at the port of entry. If less than 1,500 copies were imported in one shipment, the Copyright Office would issue successive import statements for the balance. Importation by the copyright holder of more than 1,500 copies invalidated the ad interim copyright, and with the fall of the ad interim copyright all rights to a full term of twenty-eight years also fell.

The new law does not provide for the acquisition of ad interim copyright for works published outside of the United States after January 1, 1978. Ad interim copyright, as provided for under the old law as described above, remains in effect for any work in which ad interim copyright was subsisting, or was capable of being secured on December 31, 1977, and copyright protection is extended to endure for the appropriate new terms established by the new Copyright Act.

THE TERM OF COPYRIGHT

The 1976 Act effects substantial changes in the law by lengthening the original term of copyright and abolishing the renewal term for works created after January 1, 1978.

Under the Act, the copyright term for works created after January 1, 1978 is fixed at a term lasting for the author's life plus an additional fifty years after his or her death. For works made for hire, and for anonymous and pseudonymous works, the term is seventy-five years from publication or one hundred years from creation, whichever is shorter. In the case of joint authors, the fifty-year period is measured from the death of the last surviving joint author.

§ 302. Duration of copyright: Works created on or after January 1, 1978

(a) IN GENERAL.—Copyright in a work created on or after January 1, 1978, subsists from its creation and, except as provided by the following subsections, endures for a term consisting of the life of the author and fifty years after the author's death.

(b) JOINT WORKS.—In the case of a joint work prepared by two or more authors who did not work for hire, the copyright endures for a term consisting of the life of the last surviving author and fifty years after such last surviving author's death.

(c) ANONYMOUS WORKS, PSEUDONYMOUS WORKS, AND WORKS MADE FOR HIRE.—In the case of an anonymous work, a pseudonymous work, or a work made for hire, the copyright endures for a term of seventy-five years from the year of its first publication, or a term of one hundred years from the year of its creation, whichever expires first. If, before the end of such term, the identity of one or more of the authors of an anonymous or pseudonymous work is revealed in the records of a registration made for that work under subsections (a) or (d) of section 408, or in the records provided by this subsection, the copyright in the work endures for the term specified by subsection (a) or (b), based on the life of the author or authors whose identity has been revealed.

There are several cogent reasons for this change. First, given the increase in life expectancy, the fifty-six-year term (twenty-eight years plus a renewal term of twenty-eight years) of the old statute is insufficient to insure that the author and his dependents will receive fair economic benefits from his work. Many authors have seen their works fall into the public domain during their lifetimes. Second, a short copyright term discriminates against serious works of literature whose value is not always recognized until after the passage of a considerable amount of time. Third, extension of the term eliminates the burden of renewal and use of the author's death provides a generally easy and fixed way to compute the coypright term. Finally, a large majority of the world's nations have adopted the same copyright term, and conformity with international practice facilitates international copyright relations as well as minimizes the likelihood of retaliatory legislation directed at American authors.

For works already in their first term of statutory copyright under the old law, prior to January 1, 1978, the original twenty-eight year copyright term will remain in effect, to be followed by a renewal period of forty-seven years, thus providing seventy-five years of protection from the original date of copyright. Renewal registration is required during the twenty-eighth year of the copyright. Copyrights in their first term before January 1, 1978, must be renewed by the appropriate persons in order to benefit from the renewal period. Copyrights, either already in their renewal period between December 31, 1976 and December 31, 1977, or for which renewal registration has already been made between those dates, are automatically extended to the maximum seventy-five year period.

§ 304. Duration of copyright: Subsisting copyrights

(a) Copyrights in Their First Term on January 1, 1978.— Any copyright, the first term of which is subsisting on January 1, 1978, shall endure for twenty-eight years from the date it was originally secured: *Provided*, That in the case of any posthumous work or of any periodical, cyclopedic, or other composite work upon which the copyright was originally secured by the proprietor thereof, or of any work copyrighted by a corporate body (otherwise than as assignee or licensee of the individual author) or by an employer for whom such work is made for hire, the proprietor of such copyright shall be entitled to a renewal and extension of the copyright in such work for the further term of forty-seven years when application for such renewal and extension shall have been made to the Copyright Office and duly registered therein within one year prior to the expiration of the original term of copyright: *And provided further*, That in the case of any other copyrighted work, including a contribution by an individual author to a periodical or to a cyclopedic or other composite work, the author of such work, if still living, or the widow, widower, or children of the author, if the author be not living, or if such author, widow, widower, or children be not living, then the author's executors, or in the absence of a will, his or her next of kin shall be entitled to a renewal and extension of the copyright in such work for a further term of forty-seven years when application for such renewal and extension shall have been made to the Copyright Office and duly registered therein within one year prior to the expiration of the original term of copyright: *And provided further,* That in default of the registration of such application for renewal and extension, the copyright in any work shall terminate at the expiration of twenty-eight years from the date copyright was originally secured.

(b) COPYRIGHTS IN THEIR RENEWAL TERM OR REGISTERED FOR RENEWAL BEFORE JANUARY 1, 1978.—The duration of any copyright, the renewal term of which is subsisting at any time between December 31, 1976, and December 31, 1977, inclusive, or for which renewal registration is made between December 31, 1976, and December 31, 1977, inclusive, is extended to endure for a term of seventy-five years from the date copyright was originally secured.

Failure to register for renewal for works in their first term of copyright on January 1, 1978 results in the work's falling into the public domain after the expiration of its twenty-eight year term.

Any work which entered the public domain prior to January 1, 1978, is, of course, not protected by the statute. Since works may have entered the public domain because of failure to comply with the 1909 Act's notice and renewal provisions, these continue to be of importance beyond the expiration date of the old law. Similarly, the old law's concepts of publication must continue to be consulted since under the old law, publication without notice of copyright throws the work into the public domain, and publication with notice starts the statutory period running.

Under the 1909 Act, the original term of copyright ran for

twenty-eight years after the first date of publication with notice, with a renewal period of another twenty-eight years. First publication was defined as the earliest date when copies were placed on sale, sold, or publicly distributed by the proprietor of the copyright or under his authority. Unauthorized sale by a bookseller did not constitute distribution where books were shipped for distribution and an authorized release date had been set, nor did the exhibition of sample copies by a salesman constitute placing on sale. The words "publicly distributed," however, did not cover material which was not sold, including house organs, advertising books distributed free, throw-away newspapers, and the like.

RENEWAL

The renewal term of twenty-eight years which existed under the old law has been abolished, and there is no longer a renewal term for any works created after January 1, 1978. Works already in their renewal term, or which have already been registered for renewal between December 31, 1976 and December 31, 1977, have their renewals extended so that the total of the copyright for both original and renewal terms equals seventy-five years. However, registration for a renewal period of forty-seven years is required by the 1976 Act for all works in their first term of copyright prior to January 1, 1978. Failure to renew will result in the work's falling into the public domain. As provided by the new law, the right to renew belongs to

1. the author, if living;
2. the widow, widower, or children of the author if he is not living, or if these are not living;
3. the author's executors, or in the absence of a will;
4. his next of kin.

This class is the same as that in which renewal rights vested under the old law, and is intended to be construed similarly. Thus the phrase "widow, widower, or children," is conjunctive and they take collectively, not in the order of their naming. Similarly, even though the widow of an author has remarried prior to the renewal date, she is still for purposes of the new act, his widow, and has a right to renew. As with the old law, children of the author include not only legitimate children, but also illegitimate children, who have an equal right to take with the widow and legitimate issue. In the absence of a will naming an executor, the next of kin have a right to renew as an indivisible class. Should one of them renew, he would hold it in trust for the benefit of all the next of kin. While an executor has a right to renew, administrators are not named in the statute and have no such right. An employer, who is an author within the statute in the case of a work made for hire, has the right of renewal. Since the new law with its renewal provisions for all works in their first term of copyright prior to January 1, 1978, in effect continues the life of the renewal provisions of the old law, until all such works have either been renewed or fallen into the public domain, the above provisions are still of some importance. The last of these mentioned has given rise to some interesting litigation, which conceivably may also arise under the 1976 Act.

Theodore M. Tobani was a music arranger for Carl Fischer. His wife predeceased him before the time for renewal of copyright in works arranged by him was reached. In the last year of the term, a son, Joseph Tobani, renewed copyright in the works. Carl Fischer, Inc., claimed that it, as an employer for hire, was entitled to the renewals but failed to make timely application for renewal. The court held that the son, Joseph Tobani, had no right to a renewal of the copyright. Fischer sued to compel the son to assign his renewals. The court held that Fischer could not recover. The result thus reached was that the person entitled to renewal did not make timely application, while the person who did make timely application was not entitled to do so. Thereupon the work fell into the public domain.

Another interesting case, decided in 1975, was presented when the son of Bela Bartok, the composer, and Boosey & Hawkes, Inc., the music publisher and proprietor of the initial copyright to Bartok's "Concerto for Orchestra," both claimed the right to renew the copyright. The concerto had been performed during the composer's life, but was not copyrighted until six months after Bartok's death by Boosey & Hawkes. The latter claimed that the concerto was a posthumous work and that as such, it was entitled to renew the copyright. The Circuit Court, in reversing the District Court, held that the work was not posthumous and that the renewal rights therefore fell to Peter Bartok as the author's surviving kin. The 1976 Act adopts the Circuit Court's interpretation of what constitutes a posthumous work.

The renewal in copyrighted work contributed to magazines, anthologies, etc., was frequently lost to authors by their failure to make application for renewal. It is, therefore, important for such contributors to keep a list of their contributions for works already under their first copyright term prior to January 1, 1978, so that they can make timely application for renewal of these works under the new law. Failure to apply for renewal will result in the works falling into the public domain.

ASSIGNMENT OF COPYRIGHT

Copyright secured under the new law may be assigned, granted, or mortgaged by an instrument in writing, signed by the proprietor of the copyright, or may be bequeathed by will, as was the case under the old law. Under the old law, only the balance of the then subsisting term passed. The beneficiary under the will did not obtain the right to renew for the additional term unless he was also one of the class named in the statute.

Under the old law, copyright was indivisible, and unless an assignment conveyed all of the copyright and the rights incident thereto, it was treated not as an assignment of the copyright, but rather as a license.

The 1976 Act provides that copyright is no longer indivisible, and it is now possible for an author to assign any one of the bundle of rights separately. The owner of any exclusive right under the Act is treated as a copyright owner.

§ 201. * * *

(d) TRANSFER OF OWNERSHIP.—

(1) The ownership of a copyright may be transferred in whole or in part by any means of conveyance or by operation of law, and may be bequeathed by will or pass as personal property by the applicable laws of intestate succession.

(2) Any of the exclusive rights comprised in a copyright, including any subdivision of any of the rights specified by section 106, may be transferred as provided by clause (1) and owned separately. The owner of any particular exclusive right is entitled, to the extent of that right, to all of the protection and remedies accorded to the copyright owner by this title.

When an assignment has been duly made in writing, it may be recorded in the Copyright Office, and after it has been recorded, the assignee may substitute his name for that of the assignor in the statutory notice of copyright.

Under the 1909 Act, the author could contract to assign his or her renewal rights. However, the 1976 Act permits the author or his or her heirs to terminate such assignment for works in their first term of copyright prior to the effective date of the new law. The rationale underlying this provision is that the extended renewal term of forty-seven years is a completely new property right, which the author, as beneficiary of the Act, should have an opportunity of enjoying.

TERMINATION OF ASSIGNMENT

In order to protect authors against unremunerative transfers of copyright, the 1976 Act contains a provision permitting the author or his or her heirs to terminate any transfer of copyright with notice. Such termination is to be effective after thirty-five years of the original transfer, or, in the case of a grant of the right of publication, at the end of thirty-five years from the date of publication, or forty years from the execution of the grant, whichever is shorter. Termination may be effected at any time during a five-year period from the thirty-five or forty-year period.

§ 203. Termination of transfers and licenses granted by the author

(a) CONDITIONS FOR TERMINATION.—In the case of any work other than a work made for hire, the exclusive or nonexclusive grant of a transfer or license of copyright or of any right under a copyright, executed by the author on or after January 1, 1978, otherwise than by will, is subject to termination under the following conditions:

(1) In the case of a grant executed by one author, termination of the grant may be effected by that author or, if the author is dead, by the person or persons who, under clause (2) of this subsection, own and are entitled to exercise a total of more than one-half of that author's termination interest. . . .

(2) Where an author is dead, his or her termination interest is owned, and may be exercised, by his widow or her widower and his or her children or grandchildren ***

(3) Termination of the grant may be effected at any time during a period of five years beginning at the end of thirty-five years from the date of execution of the grant; or, if the grant covers the right of publication of the work, the period begins at the end of thirty-five years from the date of publication of the work under the grant or at the end of forty years from the date of execution of the grant, whichever term ends earlier.

(4) The termination shall be effected by serving an advance notice in writing, signed by the number and proportion of owners of termination interests required under clauses (1) and (2) of this subsection, or by their duly authorized agents, upon the grantee or the grantee's successor in title. ***

For the termination to be effective, advance notice must be served in writing on the grantee. A copy of the notice is to be recorded in the Copyright Office before the effective date of termination as a condition to its taking effect. Termination of the grant may be effected notwithstanding any agreement to the contrary, including an agreement to make a will or a future grant.

The underlying purpose of this provision is to protect authors who have transferred their copyrights at a time when the true value of their work was not known. To some extent, it also compensates the author for the loss of some of his exclusive rights under other provisions of the statute. The provision may also be used to prevent dissemination of the work in a manner that displeases the author. However, termination does not apply to a derivative work prepared earlier which may continue to be utilized under the provisions of the terminated grant.

In 1940, Lillian Hellman signed a contract with Samuel Goldwyn Inc., in which she granted Goldwyn "all motion picture rights . . . throughout the world" in her play, *The Little Foxes.* Included among these exclusive rights were rights

> To make, exhibit, and market everywhere motion pictures, trailers, sound records (in connection with motion pictures), and stills based upon or adapted from the Property, using any devices which are now or hereafter known or used.

Although Miss Hellman reserved for herself exclusive right to television rights "direct from living actors," the rights granted to Goldwyn encompassed "the right to televise (by broadcast, wire, or any other means or methods) motion pictures, sound or silent based in whole or in part on the property."

More than twenty years later, Goldwyn licensed CBS to show the movie it had made of *The Little Foxes* on television and Miss Hellman sued for breach of contract. In finding that Goldwyn had not breached the terms of its contract with Miss Hellman, the court observed:

> While it may be logical to assume that, had the development of television as a medium been foreseen when the contract herein was

made, appellant would have sought greater remuneration for her grant of television rights, the rights of the parties must be governed by the intent of the parties as evidenced by the terms in the contract when made.

Under the termination provisions of the Act, even if the necessary thirty-five-year period had elapsed and the proper notice had been served, the result would be the same, inasmuch as Goldwyn's film was a derivative work prepared prior to notice of termination. However, under the 1976 Act, with the proper notice and time interval, Miss Hellman would be able to revoke her grant of exclusive film rights to Goldwyn, thereby terminating Goldwyn's right to make any new movies of *The Little Foxes* or to sue the owner of any new film version of *The Little Foxes* for infringement.

THE TERM IN UNPUBLISHED WORKS

The 1976 Act abolishes the perpetual common-law copyright in almost all unpublished works and provides the same period of statutory protection for all works created after January 1, 1978, whether published or not.

§ 301. Preemption with respect to other laws

(a) On and after January 1, 1978, all legal or equitable rights that are equivalent to any of the exclusive rights within the general scope of copyright as specified by section 106 in works of authorship that are fixed in a tangible medium of expression and come within the subject matter of copyright as specified by sections 102 and 103, whether created before or after that date and whether published or unpublished, are governed exclusively by this title. Thereafter, no person is entitled to any such right or equivalent right in any such work under the common law or statutes of any State.

(b) Nothing in this title annuls or limits any rights or remedies under the common law or statutes of any State with respect to—

(1) subject matter that does not come within the subject mat-

ter of copyright as specified by sections 102 and 103, including work of authorship not fixed in any tangible medium of expression;***

Common-law copyright, however, is retained for any cause of action arising before the effective date of the statute, and for any works not "fixed" in a tangible medium of expression. These include extemporaneous speeches, and dramatic sketches or musical compositions improvised from memory without being recorded or written down, and choreography that has never been filmed or notated.

For unpublished works created but not copyrighted before January 1, 1978, the 1976 Act similarly provides automatic statutory protection for the appropriate term of the author's life plus fifty years, or in the case of works for hire, and anonymous and pseudonymous works which remain unpublished, one hundred years from the time of their creation. No protection for unpublished works is to expire before December 31, 2002.

§ 303. Duration of copyright: Works created but not published or copyrighted before January 1, 1978

Copyright in a work created before January 1, 1978, but not theretofore in the public domain or copyrighted, subsists from January 1, 1978, and endures for the term provided by section 302. In no case, however, shall the term of copyright in such a work expire before December 31, 2002; and, if the work is published on or before December 31, 2002, the term of copyright shall not expire before December 31, 2027.

Under the old law, statutory copyright for a term of twenty-eight years was permitted for unpublished works not reproduced for sale, such as lectures, dramatic, musical, or dramatico-musical works. However the old law required renewal upon the expiration of the first copyright term. Thus, when Eugene O'Neill failed to renew his copyright in unpublished dramatic work copyrighted under the old law, some publishers discovered the failure to renew and thereupon flamboyantly advertised their publication of the work as the newly discovered, hitherto unpublished work of the great dramatist. It was a work which O'Neill did not want to have published or reproduced, one of the works of his early youth which he wished to forget. Since, however, he had failed to renew his unpublished copyright, the work was in the public domain and could be so utilized. Under the new law, unpublished works which are copyrighted after January 1, 1978 do not have to be renewed and remain protected for fifty years after the author's death.

Chapter 4

~~ INTERNATIONAL COPYRIGHT

International protection of the literary property of United States citizens presents a highly complex situation. It depends upon conventions, treaties or agreements to which the United States is a party. There are three major international Conventions, the Berne, the Buenos Aires and the Universal Copyright (UCC). We are members of the Universal Copyright Convention and the Buenos Aires. We are not a member of the Berne, but we enter it through the back door by copyrighting in a country which is a member.

The problems are rendered more difficult of definition because in each country copyright is subject to the domestic law of the country and to the vagaries of its judicial system.

Our first federal statute on copyright was adopted in 1790, but it was not until 1891, with the passage of the Chace Act, that we granted protection to foreigners and made it possible for foreigners to obtain copyright in the United States.

The first move toward international copyright in the English-speaking countries was through a law passed July 31, 1838, in England, entitled "An Act for Securing to Authors, in Certain Cases, the Benefit of International Copyright" (which act provided for the deposit at Stationers' Hall of a copy of each foreign work to be protected, and the title thereof to be entered on the Register of Stationers' Hall).

Under this act, the Queen was empowered by an Order in Council to direct:

that the authors of books which shall after a future time to be specified in such Order in Council be published in any foreign country to be specified in such Order in Council, their executors, administrators and assigns, shall have the sole liberty of printing and reprinting such books within the United Kingdom of Great Britain and Ireland and every other part of the British Dominion . . .

Six years later an act known as "The International Copyright Act" was passed, extending the benefits of the British copyright acts to works first published in any foreign country, provided, however, that protection has been secured by such country for similar works of British subjects first published in England. Pursuant thereto, England made treaties with other countries, including France, but was unable to make any with the United States, for our laws still failed to make provision for such international protection.

THE BERNE COPYRIGHT UNION

In 1878 the Association Littéraire et Artistique Internationale was founded in Paris. Victor Hugo was its president. It planned to replace treaties then in existence by an international copyright convention. Pursuant thereto, it held meetings in Rome in 1882, and in 1883, 1884, and 1885 conventions were held at Berne, Switzerland. There were seventeen countries represented at these conferences, including the United States. The Berne Convention went into effect on September 5, 1887, but was not signed by the United States delegate. The United States required certain formalities, including notice of copyright on the publication of works, and the Berne Convention had no requirements for formalities.

Essentially, the Berne Convention provided protection for unpublished works of citizens of a Convention state and for all works first published in a Convention state. Authors of a country not belonging to the Union could secure rights granted by that Convention provided that their works were first or simultaneously published in a country which was a member of the Berne Union.

Under the revised Berne Convention protection is automatic upon the creation of the work. Formalities of all kinds were abolished, and the authors of each country became, for copyright purposes, members of a worldwide literary commonwealth. Although our new Copyright Act, which for the first time in our history provides for automatic statutory copyright protection from the creation of the work, brings our law more nearly in line with the Berne Convention, such was not the case prior to the adoption of the new law.

Since the Berne Convention is not only a treaty, but a uniform statute, our adherence to it, prior to January 1, 1978, would, to an extent, have overruled our own then existing copyright law, insofar as it conflicted with the Berne Convention. Our Constitution, in Article VI, provides:

> This Constitution, and the Laws of the United States which shall be made in pursuance thereof; and all Treaties made, or which shall be made under the Authority of the United States, shall be the supreme Law of the Land; and the Judges in every State shall be bound thereby, any Thing in the Constitution or Laws of any State to the contrary notwithstanding.

Adherence to Berne might, therefore, make that treaty the supreme law of the United States governing copyright. Since the Convention contains provisions for uniformity as to the works of persons protected, the period of protection, the mode of calculation of the period, a presumption as to ownership, as well as certain provisions governing the right of translation, the right of public performances of dramatic, musical, and dramatico-musical works, rights of adaptation and moral rights, confusion would have resulted, since the provisions of Berne would automatically have superseded our conflicting domestic law.

At the Berlin Convention held in 1908, every effort was made to procure the adherence of the United States to the Berne Union. There were representatives of fifteen countries which adhered to the Convention and nineteen non-Union countries, including the United States. We had already passed a law providing for international copyright under certain conditions, but we had added to the obstacles for our adherence the provisions of the manufacturing clause. We had a voice at that Convention but no vote. In addition to the self-executing clauses of the Berne Convention, provision was made for regulation by law of the country in which the right was claimed, so that one must look not only to the Convention for its statutory provisions, but to the laws and decisions of the respective countries which adhere to it for its enforcement.

In 1914 a fourth conference was held at Berne, and at this time a retaliatory clause against the United States and our practices of obtaining protection in the countries of the Berne Union by copyrighting in one country of that union, principally England or Canada, was adopted. It provided that "when a country, not belonging to the Union, does not protect the work of authors of the country of the Union, then that country may restrict the protection of works of authors of the country which discriminates against the works of authors of the Berne Convention countries."

In 1928 a Moral Rights Clause was added to the Berne Convention, Article VI, which provided, "independently of the author's copyright, and even after assignment of the said copyright, the author shall retain the right to claim authorship of the work, as well as the right to object to every deformation, mutilation, or other modification of the said work which may be prejudicial to his honor or to his reputation."

The rights under this clause were left for enforcement to the specific countries in which the question was raised. Since citizens of the United States frequently attempt to copyright in the Berne Union by copyrighting in Canada, it should be noted that the Canadian law specifically contains a Moral Rights Clause as follows:

> Independently of the author's copyright, and even after the assignment, either wholly or partially, of the said copyright, the author shall have the right to claim authorship of the work, as well as the right to restrain any distortion, mutilation or other modification of the said work which would be prejudicial to his honour or reputation.

Works copyrighted in Canada, therefore, would be subject to this clause, which becomes of importance to United States authors and publishers.

Under the Moral Rights Clause the author has the following rights:

A. He has the right to control publication or presentation of his work, including, among other things, whether the work shall be published, and the author has the right to modify the work and to withdraw it from circulation.

B. Where a work reflects a changed philosophy, the author has the right to require that the work be changed so that it reflects his present philosophy and to regulate the form of its use.

C. The author has the right to have his name on the work and to prevent an alteration in the use of his name, and to prevent the use of his name in connection with the work of others.

It should be noted that Moral Rights cannot be sold or assigned. Under the Moral Rights Doctrine plays or novels cannot be changed in their tenor from tragedy to melodrama, nor can moving pictures be changed to incorporate scenes which the author thinks harmful to his reputation, such as, for instance, interpolating pictures of nude women, or pictures of degradation not contemplated by the author. The Moral Rights Doctrine has not been contained in any of the statutes of the United States, and there has been some feeling, even in Europe, that the courts have gone too far in enforcing it.

In the Shostakovich case against Twentieth Century-Fox Film Corporation an attempt was made on the part of the Russian composers whose work was used in the motion picture, *The Iron Curtain*, to prevent its use. They claimed that since the picture was anti-Russian the use of their names and their music would be harmful to them. The court said:

> The wrong which is alleged here is the use of plaintiffs' music in a moving picture whose theme is objectionable to them in that it is unsympathetic to their political ideology. The logical development of this theory leads inescapably to the Doctrine of Moral Rights (53 Harv. L. Rev. 554). There is no charge of distortion of the compositions nor any claim that they have not been faithfully reproduced. Conceivably, under the doctrine of Moral Right, the court could, in a proper case, prevent the use of a composition or work, in the public domain, in such a manner as would be violative of the author's rights. The application of the doctrine presents much difficulty, however. With reference to that which is in the public domain there arises a conflict between the moral right and the well-established rights of others to use such works. So, too, there arises the question of the norm by which the use of such work is to be tested to determine whether or not the author's moral right as an author has been violated. Is the standard to be good taste, artistic worth, political beliefs, moral concepts, or what is it to be? In the present state of our law the very existence of the right is not clear, the relative position of the rights thereunder with reference to the rights of others is not defined nor has the nature of the proper remedy been determined.

In France, on the other hand, a dissimilar finding was had when Igor Stravinsky sued Warner Bros. over the production of a motion picture entitled *The Firebird*. Warner Bros. had obtained from the publishers of Stravinsky's work the right to synchronize portions of the "Firebird Suite" in the motion picture. The music was played for only four minutes. Part of the music was used as the motif of the "Infernal Dance" at the end of the ballet. Stravinsky claimed that this use of the music served as the motif of seduction. The court held that the pub lisher of Stravinsky's work did not have the right to authorize such use of Stravinsky's work and that it was a violation of the moral rights of the author.

It should be noted that the moral rights provisions of the Berne Convention have been somewhat revised to limit some of the author's exclusive rights by providing for compulsory licensing, a change which is similar to the licensing provisions of our new law.

The Copyright Act of 1976 has brought United States law more nearly into accord with the Berne Convention than at anytime previous. The adoption of the new term of life plus fifty years follows the minimum term of the Convention. Anonymous and pseudonymous works, protected by the Berne Convention, are given similar protection under the new law, and our law now provides, as does the Convention, for automatic statutory protection from the creation of the work. Finally, the elimination of the manufacturing clause after July 1, 1982, removes one of the most significant obstacles to our adherence to the Berne Convention.

However, although the new law has moved in the direction of compliance with the Berne Convention, it has not fully arrived at Berne's standard that copyright protection shall not be subject to any formalities. For although the securing of copyright in this country is virtually automatic, there still remain notice requirements upon publication, and it is still necessary to register the copyright in order to enforce it against an infringer. More importantly, the new law, like the old, does not adopt a moral rights provision. Even though the 1971 Paris revision of the Convention has provided for compulsory licensing, similar to provisions in our new law, and has thereby weakened one aspect of the moral rights doctrine, since the author is no longer given exclusive control of all aspects of the dissemination of his work, the Convention still retains other elements of the moral rights doctrine. Thus the new Act's failure to provide statutory protection for those moral rights still recognized by the Berne Convention may preclude United States adherence to the Convention.

Members of the Berne Union countries are Argentina, Australia, Austria, Bahamas, Belgium, Benin, Brazil, Bulgaria, Cameroon, Canada, Chad, Chile, Congo, Cyprus, Czechoslovakia, Denmark, Fiji, Finland, France, Gabon, German Democratic Republic, Germany, Federal Republic, Greece, Holy See, Hungary, Iceland, India, Ireland, Israel, Italy, Ivory Coast, Japan, Lebanon, Libyan Arab Republic, Liechtenstein, Luxembourg, Madagascar, Mali, Malta, Mauritania, Mexico, Monaco, Morocco, Netherlands, New Zealand, Niger, Norway, Pakistan, Philippines, Poland, Portugal, Rumania, Senegal, South Africa, Spain, Sri Lanka, Surinam, Sweden, Switzerland, Thailand, Togo, Tunisia, Turkey, United Kingdom, Upper Volta, Uruguay, Yugoslavia, and Zaire.

Since not all these countries are signatory to the five separate conventions, Berne-Berlin, Berne-Rome, Berne-Brussels, Berne-Stockholm, and Berne-Paris, specific details with regard to each country cannot be given and reference should be had to the Bureau de l'Union, at Berne, Switzerland.

The provision for enforcement of rights under the laws of the several countries of the Union and by their courts has created a situation in which the United States does not fare too well. Protection is granted on simultaneous publication, but in the Netherlands at least, publication has been held to be more than merely placing on sale. The courts there have felt that publication requires some actual work in connection with the literary material and have refused to enforce copyrights obtained through the back door.

Canada provided a retaliatory provision in its law aimed at our manufacturing clause, and from time to time other countries have refused enforcement on various grounds. Therefore it was desirable for us that we adhere to some international convention, provided that we were willing to make some compromise in our desire for formalities and registration and provided we were willing to sacrifice in part the manufacturing provisions of our Copyright Law.

THE UNIVERSAL COPYRIGHT CONVENTION

The United Nations had adopted in its Universal Declaration of Human Rights:

> Everyone has the right freely to participate in the cultural life of the community, to enjoy the arts and to share in scientific advancement and its benefits.
>
> Everyone has the right to the protection of the moral and material interests resulting from any scientific, literary or artistic production of which he is the author.

Meetings were held under the leadership of UNESCO commencing in 1947. Finally, in 1951, a draft of a convention was reached. At an intergovernmental conference at Geneva, Switzerland, the Convention and three related protocols were signed under date of September 6, 1952. The Convention consists of a preamble and twenty-one articles. The Preamble follows:

> The contracting States,
> Moved by the desire to assure in all countries copyright protection of literary, scientific and artistic works,
> Convinced that a system of copyright protection appropriate to all nations of the world and expressed in a universal convention, additional to, and without impairing international systems already in force, will ensure respect for the rights of the individual and encourage the development of literature, the sciences and the arts,
> Persuaded that such a universal copyright system will facilitate a wider dissemination of works of the human mind and increase international understanding, . . .

Unlike Berne, the Universal Copyright Convention is not self-enacting legislation. The protection given by it is what is called "national" protection; that is, citizens of each state of the Union enjoy in the other states the rights accorded by that state to its citizens. Since the rights must be determined by domestic legislation, each member country is required to have an effective copyright system. There is no definition or enumeration of works protected, such as had been contained in the Berne Convention. All such details are left to the several countries. In deference to the wishes of the United States, a form of copyright notice, which consists of the symbol ©, was required to be inserted in published works, and contains the name of the copyright proprietor and the year of first publication in such a way as to give reasonable notice of the claim of copyright. Compliance with formalities as a condition of copyright, such as deposit, registration, manufacture, publication, etc., is waived. This, however, must not be taken too literally, since copyright and enforcement thereof are divisible, and copyright may be obtained even in the United States without registration or deposit, but enforcement still requires compliance with formalities. Each contracting state has the right to impose conditions prerequisite to judicial relief, provided that such conditions are equally applicable to nationals of the state in which protection is claimed.

In addition, a concession was made to the United States in that any contracting state was allowed to regard as its own national any person domiciled therein. This permits us to require of foreigners domiciled in the United States the same formalities and other requirements as are imposed on our own citizens. Under the Convention, the duration of copyright in the several contracting states is governed by the law where protection is claimed. It may be either (1) not less than twenty-five years after the death of the author, or (2) if the term be governed from the date of first publication, not less than twenty-five years from that date. We meet the Convention's requirement by our new law, which sets the term at fifty years from the author's death.

The protection of the right of translation is concurrent with the duration of copyright, but is subject to a compulsory license after seven years from first publication if no authorized translation has been published in the national language, and subject to the provision that the license may be granted only to a national of the state in which application is made and on proper payment.

When the Universal Copyright Convention came before the 83rd Congress, the Committee on Foreign Relations submitted a report which it prefaced as follows:

> The Universal Copyright Convention would correct the unsatisfactory and burdensome basis upon which American citizens must now rely to protect their works from piracy abroad, and at the same time simplify their task of obtaining it. Through this new multilateral agreement, the United States would also strengthen its affiliation with the remainder of the free world in the interchange of ideas, and demonstrate its desire to grant protection on a reciprocal basis to the citizens of other contracting states.

In order to enable us to enter into the Universal Copyright Convention we amended our law so as to provide for a notice of copyright uniform with that adopted by the Convention, and we made changes in the manufacturing clause so as to make it inapplicable to citizens of the contracting states who publish with notice.

THE BUENOS AIRES COPYRIGHT CONVENTION

The United States is also a member of the Buenos Aires Copyright Convention, together with the following countries: Argentina, Bolivia, Brazil, Chile, Colombia, Costa Rica, Dominican Republic, Ecuador, Guatemala, Haiti, Honduras, Mexico, Nicaragua, Panama, Paraguay, Peru, and Uruguay. This convention is open to adherence only by countries of the Western Hemisphere, excluding Canada.

Under this Convention, copyright obtained under any one contracting state in conformity with its laws gives copyright in all the other states without the necessity of complying with any other formality, providing that there appears in the work a statement which indicates the reservation of the property right. A notice in the form provided for registering American copyright is adequate. The copyright thus obtained gives the exclusive power to the author, or his assigns, to publish, translate, and reproduce in any form, wholly or in part. The authors of the several states enjoy in the signatory countries the protection of the laws of the country, except that the term of protection cannot exceed the term of the country of origin.

In addition to these conventions, the United States has copyright treaties with some fifty-three countries. These treaties all, more or less, confer upon the nationals of the contracting countries rights enjoyed by local citizens or domiciliaries. Reference, of course, must be made to each treaty for the coverage of, among other things, films and musical rights.

Although we have adhered to the Universal Copyright Convention and have not adhered to the Berne Copyright Union, it is still advisable to publish with a notice as provided by the Universal Copyright Convention and to take advantage of a simultaneous publication in a Berne country.

Listed below are the countries with which the United States has international copyright relations.

The first column lists countries that have ratified or acceded to the Universal Copyright Convention of 1952, or the Universal Copyright Convention as revised at Paris in 1971 (the UCC). The countries in the second column are parties to the Buenos Aires Convention of 1910, which is one of the Pan American Copyright Conventions. In the third column are the countries with which the United States has bilateral copyright relations by virtue of a proclamation or treaty.

1. UCC	2. Buenos Aires Convention	3. Bilateral Relations
Algeria		
Andorra		
Argentina	Argentina	Argentina
Australia		Australia
Austria		Austria
The Bahamas		
Bangladesh		
Belgium		Belgium
	Bolivia	
Brazil	Brazil	Brazil
Bulgaria		
Cambodia		
Cameroon		
Canada		Canada
Chile	Chile	Chile
		China
Colombia	Colombia	
Costa Rica	Costa Rica	Costa Rica
Cuba		Cuba
Czechoslovakia		Czechoslovakia
Denmark		Denmark
	Dominican Republic	
Ecuador	Ecuador	
		El Salvador
Fiji		
Finland		Finland
France		France
German Federal Republic		German Federal Republic
German Democratic Republic		
Ghana		
Greece		Greece
Guatemala	Guatemala	
Haiti	Haiti	
Holy See		
	Honduras	
Hungary		Hungary
Iceland		
India		India
Ireland		Ireland
Israel		Israel

Italy		Italy
Japan		
Kenya		
Laos		
Lebanon		
Liberia		
Liechtenstein		
Luxembourg		Luxembourg
Malawi		
Malta		
Mauritius		
Mexico	Mexico	Mexico
Monaco		Monaco
Morocco		
Netherlands		Netherlands
New Zealand		New Zealand
Nicaragua	Nicaragua	
Nigeria		
Norway		Norway
Pakistan		
Panama	Panama	
Peru	Peru	
		Philippines
Poland		Poland
Portugal		Portugal
		Rumania
Senegal		
		South Africa
Soviet Union		
Spain		Spain
Sweden		Sweden
Switzerland		Switzerland
		Thailand
Tunisia		
United Kingdom		United Kingdom
United States	United States	
	Uruguay	
Venezuela		
Yugoslavia		
Zambia		

Chapter 5

PLAGIARISM, PIRACY, AND
INFRINGEMENT

Literary property, like all other goods, wares, and merchandise, attracts the thief. It is as susceptible to larceny as any
other forms of property. It is stolen for any of a wide variety
of reasons, including vanity, but it is usually where the profit
motive appears that steps toward protection are taken. The
poet from whom a line has been plagiarized may complain,
but he rarely sues. If anything can prove to the writer that
what he writes is property, it is the theft thereof.

Plagiarism, piracy, and infringement are often loosely used
as interchangeable terms. There is, however, a distinction. All
of them involve the invasion of another person's literary prop-
perty and imply the copying or taking of it. Plagiarism may
be either infringement of a copyright or noninfringement, in
either case a taking and passing off of an original by ascribing
authorship to the plagiarist.

Infringement is a more technical term which describes the
taking of copyrighted material. Sometimes whole poems and
short stories may be taken and published under the name of
the plagiarist as author. This even happens to larger forms of
writing, as when a complete novel which had been published
seven years before was sold to Little, Brown and Co. as new.
More frequently infringement occurs when a partial use of a
copyrighted work is made.

There can be plagiarism without infringement, as, for instance, where material in the public domain, or works without copyright, or works in which copyright has expired, are reprinted under claimed authorship of the plagiarist.

In some cases there may even be a question of whether there was infringement, as occurred in the case of *Cyrano de Bergerac*. A Mr. Gross wrote and copyrighted a play which he called the *Merchant Prince of Cornville*. In the year 1900 Richard Mansfield produced, in Chicago, Edmond Rostand's *Cyrano de Bergerac*. Thereupon Gross sued, seeking an injunction to prevent the production of *Cyrano* upon the ground that it constituted an infringement of the *Merchant Prince of Cornville*. A consent decree was entered in favor of Gross. Thereafter Edward Vroom contemplated a production of *Cyrano* in New York. Again an action was brought by the owner of the copyright of the *Merchant Prince of Cornville*, but in New York the courts refused to enjoin Rostand's play. George Jean Nathan, who was a friend of Gross, said:

> Plagiarism? the hell with it! I thoroughly believe Rostand swiped my friend's play. But Rostand made it into a beautiful thing, didn't he, so what's the odds?

Piracy is just plain theft. Sometimes it is legally culpable as infringement, sometimes not. Mary Heaton Vorse wrote a story which was published in a magazine, part of a large chain. Some thirty years later the copyright had expired and the magazine was out of business. Thereupon another magazine in the same chain reprinted the story under the name of one of its house authors. Recovery was possible here because after extensive litigation it could be proved that the magazine chain had held the copyright in trust for the author, and that by allowing it to lapse and then using the story wrongfully the chain had invaded her rights. She was paid for the republication.

A collector specialized in examining copyrights, and wherever he found an invalid copyright or an expired copyright, collected the item. Frequently an author's work which appears in a magazine is copyrighted in the name of the magazine. Very few authors go to the trouble of stipulating that a contribution to a periodical should be copyrighted in their names. When, under the old law, the copyright first expired at the end of twenty-eight years, and the magazine, either in or by then out of business, did not seek a renewal, the work of many authors fell into the public domain. The collector in this case made it a business to collect such items and sell them with the rare warranty of no copyright, and in at least one instance was able to collect royalties upon an edition of 500,000 copies of a juvenile anthology. The authors had no recourse. This was piracy.

Under the new law, this sort of "enterprise" is not rewarded until fifty years after the author's death, since the renewal term has been abolished. In the case of authors who have already been dead for some time, this may actually shorten the period of time for which the pirate need wait, but on the other hand, the author himself will not suffer financially and has protection, good for his lifetime plus fifty years, against this sort of piracy.

With the abolition of common-law copyright in virtually all cases, infringement arises solely under the copyright statutes.

In order to recover in an infringement case, the author or proprietor must first prove that he has statutory copyright. For authors or proprietors of works copyrighted prior to January 1, 1978 and therefore falling under the terms of the old statute this means:

a. The work, if published, must have been published with notice of a claim of copyright; and

b. The work must have been deposited and registration claimed; or

c. The work, if unpublished, and copyrightable under the old statute, must have been recorded for copyright.

For works copyrighted after January 1, 1978, this means:

a. The work, if published, must have been published with notice of a claim of copyright, or if not so published, notice must have been omitted either from only a relatively small number of copies, or in violation of an express agreement, or the work must have been registered within five years after publication without notice and a reasonable effort have been made to add notice to the copies already distributed publicly; and

b. The work must have been deposited and registration claimed; or

c. The work, if unpublished, must have been deposited and registration claimed.

Such registration is a prerequisite to suit, although a delay in registration will not defeat the author or proprietor if such registration has been made before the commencement of the suit.

As mentioned earlier, in 1931, *The Washingtonian* Magazine printed material written by Drew Pearson and Robert S. Allen. Shortly thereafter the magazine went out of business, and in 1932 Liveright, Inc., published a book entitled *More Merry-Go-Round*, written by Pearson and Allen, one chapter of which included material which was concededly identical with one of the articles published in *The Washingtonian*. The magazine did not deposit copies until February, 1933, fourteen months after its own publication and six months after the publication of *More Merry-Go-Round*. The Supreme Court held that copyright had been obtained by *The Washingtonian* on publication with notice and that mere delay in registration and deposit did not destroy the right to sue.

d. The action must be brought during a subsisting term of the copyright. For works in statutory copyright prior to January 1, 1978, and thus governed by the old law and the provisions of the new law dealing with the extension of renewal, such action would have to be commenced within twenty-eight years from the date of publication, or if copyright is properly renewed, within seventy-five years of the original date of publication. For works in their renewal period, or for which renewal registration was obtained between December 31, 1976 and December 31, 1977, the action would have to be commenced within seventy-five years of the original date of publication. For works either created or published after January 1, 1978, and thus falling under the provisions of the new law, such action would have to be brought within fifty years of the author's death, or within seventy-five years from publication, or one hundred years from creation, whichever expires first, in the case of anonymous or pseudonymous works, or works for hire. After the expiration of copyright, no action for infringement will lie.

e. The action must be brought by the proper party, i.e., either the author or proprietor of the work. Under the old law, copyright was indivisible and such action could not be maintained by a licensee. Under the new law copyright is divisible, and any owner of any of the exclusive rights may bring a suit for infringement of that right.

f. The work must not be an illegal or immoral one.

On production of the play *White Cargo* by Leon Gordon, a claim was made that it was an infringement of a novel entitled *Hell's Playground*, written by Ida Vera Simonton. The defense was set up that the novel was immoral. The court said:

> . . . neither the book nor the play is elevating. Both are unnecessarily coarse and highly sensual. They nevertheless purport to deal with actual conditions as they are known to exist in tropical countries, and, if such conditions be dealt with in a manner that is not calculated to arouse lust in those who read the book or see the play, it is doubtful if a charge of immorality may be successfully maintained. If the copyright of *Hell's Playground* is invalid upon the ground of immorality, it augurs ill for many present-day novels and magazines, to say nothing of numerous dramas which now meet with public approval.

The plaintiff was successful.

James M. Cain sued for infringement, claiming that one of his novels, *Serenade*, had been used by Universal Pictures Corporation under the title, *When Tomorrow Comes*. The defense was set up that *Serenade* was indecent and immoral and that therefore Cain was not entitled to copyright. The court, while agreeing that there were authorities which deny copyright to works of similar character, said:

> A narrative can have no immoral tendency when derelictions end in punishment or suffering and contrition, followed by merciful forgiveness which brings, as Sharp puts it, "some kind of gray peace." The author did not seem to be conscious of the effect of the final scene. And when the meaning just expressed was called to his attention, he stated that he had not had it in mind when writing. But, whether so intended or not, this scene, which makes one character expiate by death and the other one by penance their guilt and sacrilege, destroys all implications of immorality or impiety in the earlier scenes of *Serenade*.

Not so fortunate in its treatment by the court was the movie *Behind the Green Door*, which was registered for copyright in 1973. When the exclusive distributor of *Behind the Green Door* sued a Texas adult movie theatre for infringement, the owner of the theatre defended on the grounds that the movie was obscene and therefore not deserving of copyright protection. The District Court found that the copyright had indeed been infringed, but said it would not enforce the statutory provisions if the movie were, in fact, obscene. As the court explained:

> Literary and other works that contain references to and explicitly exhibit sexual activities have inundated society in the past few years. . . . Most states have laws making it a crime to display or exhibit obscene materials. The federal government has also condemned the interstate transportation, mailing, and importation of obscene works. Thus the general feeling as reflected in statutory enactments is that obscene matters do not further public welfare or public interest or promote the progress of science or useful arts as called for in the empowering clause of the Constitution. Therefore "Sacrificial days" devoted to the productions of works

which do not advance the public interest or welfare are not entitled to the rewards provided for in the Copyright Act and to judicial protection.

The court then went on to find that under standards developed by the Supreme Court, the movie was obscene and thus not entitled to protection against infringement.

Infringement always involves copying, and whether or not a work has been copied is a question of fact. The essential fact to be determined is whether or not the material copied has originality rather than novelty of invention. Infringement has been defined by the courts:

> A literal reproduction of the whole, or of substantially the whole, of a copyrighted work, if unauthorized, constitutes an infringement, but an infringement is not confined to literal and exact repetition or reproduction; it includes also the various modes in which the matter of any work may be adopted, imitated, transferred, or reproduced, with more or less colorable alterations to disguise the piracy. Paraphrasing is copying and an infringement, if carried to a sufficient extent. Complete or substantial identity between the original and the copy is not required. Copying and infringement may exist, although the work of the pirate is so cleverly done that no identity of language can be found in the two works. In such cases the question of infringement resolves itself into a question of fact on the evidence as to whether or not the copyrighted work was used and paraphrased in the production of the later work . . . To constitute an invasion of copyright it is not necessary that the whole of a work should be copied, nor even a large portion of it in form or substance, but that, if so much is taken that the value of the original is sensibly diminished, or the labors of the original author are substantially, to an injurious extent, appropriated by another, that is sufficient to constitute an infringement.

Ossip Dymow had collaborated with Guy Bolton in the production of a play, *Bronx Express*. Subsequently Dymow wrote a play, *Personality*, with a background of Jewish society engaged in the garment industry, and asked Bolton's aid in the production and adaptation of it. Bolton had the physical possession of Dymow's work. Sometime later Bolton wrote a play called *Polly Preferred*, which was set against a background of theatrical and movie life but which had the same theme, for the court to which Dymow came held that "perhaps unconsciously Bolton took the theme for his play after he had read *Personality* [Dymow] and received the suggestion therefrom." On appeal the court agreed that in each of the plays an ambitious girl is presented, having at least potential charm and willing to have her ambition served by an ingenious young man in financial straits. In each case, though by wholly different means, the man sails very close to the winds of finance and veracity in exploiting the girl as a model of fashion (Dymow) or a movie star (Bolton). Result—gratification of ambition for the girl, and requited affection for the man. Though the higher court found that both plays had this incomplete skeleton in common, it stated that the copying which is infringement must be something "which ordinary observation would cause to be recognized as having been taken from" the work of another. If it requires dissection rather than observation to discern resemblance there is no infringement, on the theory that the subsection of the plot is not susceptible of copyright.

Edna Ferber wrote the novel *Cimarron*, which was subsequently made into a motion picture. One Allen Caruthers brought action against R.K.O. Radio Pictures, Inc., on a common-law copyright of an unpublished manuscript called *The Sooners*. Both dealt with the opening up to settlement of, and the early days in, the territory now the State of Oklahoma. Most of the incidents were common to the Western Frontier and the rough life led by its early settlers. There was an exception; in each there is a faux pas involving a black child. In *The Sooners* a boy Percy, while fanning the dinner table to keep away flies, becomes so absorbed in the talk of the diners that by mistake he strikes one of the guests on the head with a fan. In *Cimarron*, Isaiah, a black child, while fanning flies from his perch in a sort of cradle suspended above the dinner table, becomes interested in the conversation, loses his balance, and falls into a frosted cake. The court said that even if the episode of Isaiah had been suggested by the episode of Percy, it would be insufficient basis for a finding against Miss Ferber, for the episode of Percy is merely glanced at as a supposedly comic accretion to the story, not intrinsic to the development thereof.

A booklet entitled *Opera Stories*, which contained a fragmentary description of the plot and characters of the operas, was held not a copying of the operas.

Copying must be substantial. The taking must either be of a substantial portion of the work which is copied, or be a substantial portion of the work into which the copied matter is incorporated, or both. Of course, the portion taken must be such that the author may claim exclusive ownership. Where a book is copyrighted, its material will be protected, except those portions of it which may be in the public domain, as, for instance, locale, historical data, and other material in which exclusive property may not be claimed.

Basic plots, themes or ideas are generally not copyrightable. Only the originality of expression and writing are protected. Thus, when the author who had submitted a script for a show, *Birdman and Sparrow*, to the NBC television network sued the network over its subsequent production of a juvenile cartoon show entitled *Birdman*, the court held that there had been no plagiarism, despite NBC's access to the original script. The author's script had itself been a parody of "Batman and Robin," the popular cartoon story of a wealthy crime fighter and his young companion, who employ all sorts of elaborate technologies in their fight against crime. The NBC show, however, involved a semi-mythical figure patterned after the Egyptian sun god Ra. As the court explained:

> The idea of larger than life heroes, with juvenile helpers fighting evil doers and embarking on all sorts of fantastic adventures

probably goes back beyond Jack and the Beanstalk and even farther back than Hercules. Such characters have been the staple of comic strip adventures, books, and radio and television juvenile dramas for almost all children who came of age in the twentieth century. Ideas such as these presented by the plaintiff here are in the public domain and may freely be used by anyone with impunity.

Anne Nichols, author of *Abie's Irish Rose*, sued when a motion picture entitled *The Cohens and the Kellys* was produced. Each of these two works was based upon a comic conflict between Jewish and Irish families, a plot that had gone far back in vaudeville history. In each play the grandfather becomes reconciled when he learns that the grandson is to bear his name, and the curtain falls in each with the fathers exchanging amenities. The court said:

Upon any work, and especially upon a play, a great number of patterns of increasing generality will fit equally well, as more and more of the incident is left out. The last may perhaps be no more than the most general statement of what the play is about, and at times might consist only of its title; but there is a point in this series of abstractions where they are no longer protected, since otherwise the playwright could prevent the use of his "ideas," to which, apart from their expression, his property is never extended. *Holmes* v. *Hurst*, 174 U.S. 82, 86, 19 S. Ct. 606, 43 L. Ed. 904; *Guthrie* v. *Curlett*, 36 F. (2d) 694 (C.C.A. 2). Nobody has ever been able to fix that boundary, and nobody ever can. In some cases the question has been treated as though it were analogous to lifting a portion out of the copyrighted work (*Rees* v. *Melville, MacGillivray's Copyright Cases* [1911–1916], 168); but the analogy is not a good one, because, though the skeleton is a part of the body, it pervades and supports the whole. In such cases we are rather concerned with the line between expression and what is expressed. As respects plays, the controversy chiefly centers upon the characters and sequence of incident, these being the substance. . . . If *Twelfth Night* were copyrighted, it is quite possible that a second comer might so closely imitate Sir Toby Belch or Malvolio as to infringe, but it would not be enough that for one of his characters he cast a riotous knight who kept wassail to the discomfort of the household, or a vain and foppish steward who became amorous of his mistress. These would be no more than Shakespeare's "ideas" in the play, as little capable of monopoly as Einstein's Doctrine of Relativity, or Darwin's theory of the Origin of Species. It follows that the less developed the characters the less they can be copyrighted; that is the penalty an author must bear for marking them too indistinctly.

The Sam Spade case raised an interesting question with regard to the copyright of characters and character names. Dashiell Hammett wrote the mystery-detective story entitled *The Maltese Falcon*, including a character named Sam Spade. Hammett sold *The Maltese Falcon* to Warner Brothers. Later he sold certain other stories, in which Sam Spade was a character, to the Columbia Broadcasting System. Warner sought to enjoin Columbia. The court said:

> The practice of writers to compose sequels to stories is old, and the copyright statute, though amended several times, has never specifically mentioned the point. It does not appear that it has ever been adjudicated, although it is mentioned in *Nichols* v. *Universal Pictures Corp.*, 2 Cir., 1930, 45 F. 2d 119. If Congress had intended that the sale of the right to publish a copyrighted story would foreclose the author's use of its characters in subsequent works for the life of the copyright, it would seem Congress would have made specific provision therefor. Authors work for the love of their art no more than other professional people work in other lines of work for the love of it. There is the financial motive as well. The characters of an author's imagination and the art of his descriptive talent, like a painter's or like a person with his penmanship, are always limited and always fall into limited patterns. The restriction argued for is unreasonable, and would effect the very opposite of the statute's purpose which is to encourage the production of the arts.

After a protracted series of lawsuits, Hammett was successful in his contention that Sam Spade was his property and could be used without a charge of plagiarism by a first purchaser. It was during the course of this, and subsequent litigation, that a test for the copyrightability of a character emerged. For plagiarism to occur, the courts have decided, the character must constitute the essence of the story being told.

This test was applied in the case of *Warner Brothers* v. *Film Ventures International*, decided in 1974. Warner Brothers had produced the highly successful film, *The Exorcist*, about the demonic possession of a child, Regan, while Film Ventures had subsequently produced *Beyond the Door*, which told the story of the possession of a pregnant woman named Jessica. Warner Brothers advanced the contention that in the character of Regan they had a property subject to the protection of the copyright laws. The court brought the litigation involving Sam Spade to bear on the issue and held it to mean that a character is copyrightable only if the character "really constitutes the story being told," and is not merely a "chessman in the game of telling the story." Noting that Walt Disney's Mickey Mouse had been protected under this test because "the plot of the piece is quite subordinated to the character's role," the court concluded that even if the story of *The Exorcist* were subordinated to the character of Regan, there was a substantial difference between the character of a demure child who turns into a profane monster and whose possession is driven from her by religious means, and Jessica, a mature woman in the early stages of pregnancy, whose possession exemplifies itself by a more than rapid development of her fetus and whose possession is not expelled by religious faith.

Biography, works which have a historic background, or which lie otherwise in the facts of a given society or locale, must draw upon common source material. No one can claim that source material to the exclusion of others. Everyone has a right to use facts and published records. While this would seem to be almost self-evident, the extent of litigation in which questions have arisen would seem to point to its not being so plain. This applies as well to works which, through the lapse of copyright, have fallen into the public domain.

Hawthorne's *The Scarlet Letter* was used as the basis of a play by Louis J. McCaleb. Thereafter, the Fox Film Corporation produced a photoplay of the same name. Both the play and the photoplay were based on Hawthorne's book and consisted, in large part, of matter copied from that book. McCaleb's claim, in fact, would have given him an exclusive property in material appropriated from Hawthorne. Such material, however, had ceased to be an object of private ownership. Anyone might use it who would, and such similarity and coincidence as might arise from the use of it by several people would not prove infringement by any against the other.

Just as occurrences of a historic or social nature lie within the public domain, so also does locale. Frequently an author seizes upon a part of the world's terrain in which to set his stories. Usually the exotic is sought.

A long-fought litigation, which was in the courts for more than twenty years, arose out of the locale of *The Bird of Paradise*. Richard Walton Tully copyrighted a play under that name in April, 1911. It was produced by Oliver Morosco in September of that year. In February, 1912, Grace A. Fendler brought action to enjoin Morosco and Tully from producing their play on the grounds that it was substantially a copy of her work called *In Hawaii*. The scene of both plays was laid in the Hawaiian Islands, and both told the story of a young American who came to the Islands to work and succumbed to the charms of a native maiden. In both, native costumes, religious rites, songs, dances, and folklore were introduced as a background for the story and formed a significant part of each dramatic composition. There were many points of resemblance and similarities in detail in the two plays. As the court said: "Probably this is inevitable in two plays about Hawaii. The very name Hawaii seems to suggest to Americans the hula dance and the sport of swimming; flowers, sunshine, and music. It suggests, too, the dread disease of leprosy. All these things are introduced, though with varying emphasis, in both plays." Miss Fendler, who had at one time lived in Hawaii, took the historic facts and common stories and embodied them in her play. The court said: "She acquired no exclusive property in them. Others might use them at their will in different combinations and forms."

A parallel example to the failure of Miss Fendler to obtain Hawaii for her own is found in the case involving Zane Grey and his book *The Thundering Herd*. It was one of his typical love stories laid in the Southwest amid the perils of stampeding buffalo and pursuing Indians. Buffalo-hide hunting and Indian fights are vigorously described. It appeared that one John R. Cook had written an autobiography entitled *The Border and the Buffalo*. Its narrative described the situation on the Southwest border shortly after the Civil War, with respect to immigrants, Indians, and buffalo of the period. He described in great detail the numbers and habits of the buffalo, the magnitude of hunting operations, and the strife between the hunters and the Indians. One of the Indian fights described by Mr. Grey in his novel was a fight participated in and described by Mr. Cook. A number of similar incidents were described in both works. The court found, however, that the similar facts described by both were historic facts. They were, therefore, in the public domain. Noting that a large number of other writers of fact and fiction have found in the buffalo a fascinating subject, the court held Zane Grey blameless.

An interesting case involved Robert E. Sherwood and his drama *Abe Lincoln in Illinois*. Shortly after the play was produced Twentieth Century-Fox Film Corp. produced a motion picture entitled *Young Mr. Lincoln*, depicting the same period and events of the life of Lincoln. Sherwood and the Playwrights Producing Company sought an injunction against the film company, claiming that since they had reawakened interest in this period of American history by a dramatization of the formative period of the life of Lincoln, the defendant was guilty of unfair competition in producing and displaying a motion picture depicting the same period and events. The court said with regard thereto:

> Since the source of their material belongs to the public domain, no exclusive right to the use thereof can be acquired even though they were the first to discover its value as a medium to awaken public interest. The use of such material is absolute in the public and no one can be excluded even though by use thereof actual competition is incurred with the pioneer in the particular realm of history or literature. . . . An endless stream of authorities can be cited leading to the conclusion that history and its dominant personalities are public and not private property.

Natural phenomena, historic events, social occurrences are more easily bounded in the public domain than are ideas, plots, and themes. There are what are known as "old" plots and "old" stories. There are many well-known themes for writers. And yet there may be infringement as between the users of the same plot or theme. It is not the plot which is protected, it is the telling. "Plot" is itself a collective word when applied to works of fiction. It implies not only an idea, but a sequence of scenes and situations inhabited by people acting under emotions evoked by the situations, using language to describe their emotions. The same idea or the same plot can be told in innumerable arrangements of incident and scene. Character may be delineated by the choice of emotions running the gamut from A to Z. When the author has impressed an "old" plot with his original arrangements of scenes and incidents, he has created something new, and a new arrangement of scene and incident is, itself, a creation capable of establishing individual ownership. In a suit involving LeRoy Scott's play, *Number Thirteen Washington Square*, the precise question of plagiarism of incident arose, concerning which the court said:

> Plagiarism of incident is less well known, and more difficult of detection—yet in my generation O. Henry's unexpected climaxes have been boldly copied, and in the preceding one, Dickens's

Sketches by Boz had a host of imitators. It is doubtful whether incidents *per se* can become copyrightable literary property, but it does not take many of them nor much casual connection thereof to make what will pass for a plot, or scene, and constitute the action of a play; and that a scene has literary quality and can be copyrighted, and piracy may consist in appropriating the action of a play without any of the words is well settled.

In addition, the choice of language may give to the "old" plot a new and original wealth—not that it is necessary that there should be richness in creation, for the laws which establish ownership of literary property do not have recourse to moral or artistic values for their sanction. And of course similarity of words is the easiest net in which to catch the plagiarist. For the deadly parallel which discloses use of precisely the same words is usually inescapable.

These embellishments of the plot are the creation of the author. Insofar as they are original, they afford protection even though the plot be "old." It is the author's treatment which can be, and is, protected.

Leon Gordon's play *White Cargo* met with phenomenal success. More than five hundred performances were given in New York City, and six or seven companies were on the road producing the play in the United States and England. Ida Vera Simonton brought suit, claiming that Gordon's play infringed her novel, *Hell's Playground*. The action of both the novel and the play took place in the African tropics, in which the central male character, under the pressure of demoralizing influences, lives with a native woman and undergoes dramatic ruin. The difficulties of decision may be seen from the fact that the judge took some fifteen printed pages, discussing similarity, before he came to a conclusion that the facts were such as to warrant the charge of piracy. The plots of both were discussed at length. The judge said: "But, as I understand the law, a play may fairly be subject to charge of piracy, if a substantial number of its incidents, scenes, and episodes are, in detail, arrangement, and combination so nearly identical with those to be found in a book to which the author had access as to exclude all reasonable possibility of chance coincidence, and lead inevitably to the conclusion that they were taken from the book." The court then made a list of the similarities and concluded: "Without access to the book, I think it inexplicable that he should have incorporated into his play such a list of similar and parallel incidents, episodes, and scenes. In addition, many of them are presented in language that is hardly more than a paraphrase of the text of *Hell's Playground*. The difference existing between the novel and the play seems to be no more than Gordon believed necessary in order to adapt complainant's story to the limitations of the stage."

As defined by the court, the paramount question is whether the similarities existing between two plays are mere concidences arising because of the development by two playwrights of a central idea taken from a common source, or whether the similarities are such as reveal plagiarism. The court found for Miss Simonton and awarded her both an injunction and damages.

A similar question of the balance between the development of a central idea taken from a common source and plagiarism was at the heart of a suit brought by the authors of the play *Stalag 17*, Donald Bevan and Edmund Trzcinski, against the CBS television network for its television series *Hogan's Heroes*. Both the play and the series were set in a prisoner-of-war camp in Hitler's Germany. The name of one of the leading protagonists, Sergeant Schultz, was common to both productions, and there were additional similarities between many minor characters as well. In addition, episodes including the baiting, taunting, and outwitting of camp officials occurred in both works, which also shared common themes of the impossibility of escape, the heroism of the prisoners and treachery of informers, and a dramatic mood mixing the grim with the comic. Despite this impressive array of apparent similarities, however, the court found that there had been no plagiarism. The balance of mood in the two works, the court found, was completely different. *Hogan's Heroes* was almost of a slapstick nature, virtually empty of the grim heroism of the play. As the court said, in summing up the difference in the overall tenor of the two works, "These are not just the deliberate changes of a plagiarist, but flow from and result in an entirely different artistic conceptualization and portrayal of the POW situation." What resemblance there was between the works, the court noted, arose "from the nature of the subject matter, a POW camp in Hitler's Germany. The physical and dramatic accoutrements they share are stock items characteristic of the POW camp genre of literature."

A case involving Fulton Oursler and Lowell Brentano is rich with suggestion. They wrote a mystery melodrama, which was very successfully produced, under the title *The Spider*. Thereupon they were sued separately by Margaret Denney Rush, who claimed that their play infringed a play written by her and entitled *Murder in the Astor Theatre*, and by Samuel Fayder and one Kane, who claimed infringement of another play entitled *Eye-Witness*. The two actions were consolidated and tried together. All three of the plays utilized in common the interruption of a stage performance by a murder in a crowded theatre of a person seated in the audience. The court held that this essential similarity was one of idea, and that the dramatic incidents described were not copyrightable, as they lay in the public domain. All of the parties to the action, regardless of priority in copyright, were free to write and produce plays in which one of the incidents was the occurrence of such a murder, whether they obtained the idea from one of the other plays or not. The court said: "When two authors portray the same occurrence in the same setting, presupposing the presence of the same people in the same environment, acting under the same emotions, similarities of incident, unaccompanied by similarities in plot, are not persuasive evidence of copying. The authors having worked with the same material to construct the environment or setting in which the action is laid, such similarities are inevitable, and the products of such labor are comparable to paintings of the same scene made by different artists."

Plagiarism need not be a conscious act of copying. It may also be unconscious. This was held in a case involving George Harrison, formerly a member of the Beatles. Harrison had conceived of the essential motifs of the song, "My Sweet Lord," during an engagement in Copenhagen and had finalized it during a recording session some time later. The song, which was recorded in 1970, used two motifs which were identical, with the exception of a single added grace-note, to the two motifs in another song, "He's So Fine," which had been one of the top hits in England and America in 1963. Although Harrison had no recollection of consciously copying the two motifs of "He's So Fine," the court held that there had indeed been a plagiarism, even though it occurred subconsciously. As the District Court judge stated:

> I conclude that the composer, in seeking his musical materials to clothe his thoughts, was working with various possibilities. As he tried this possibility and that there came to the surface of his mind a particular combination that pleased him as being one that he felt would be pleasing to the prospective listener; in other words, that this combination of sounds would work. Why? Because his subconscious knew it already had worked in a song his conscious mind did not remember. Having arrived at this pleasing combination of sounds, the recording was made. . . . Did Harrison deliberately use the music of "He's So Fine"? I do not believe that he did so deliberately. Nevertheless, it is clear that "My Sweet Lord" is the very same song as "He's So Fine" with different words and Harrison had access to "He's So Fine." This is, under the law, infringement of copyright, and is no less so even though subconsciously accomplished.

Thus, the plaintiff was able to recover.

COMMON ERROR

Frequently, when plagiarism or infringement is alleged, common error or mistake will be established in order to show the taking. So, for instance, in work having a historical or real background there may be errors in dates, or in names, or in the misspelling of names and places, or there may be the taking of an invented character. So when Matthew Josephson wrote his *Zola* he invented characters, including a butler, for Captain Dreyfus. When Warner Bros. produced their motion picture *Zola*, they used the same characters as had been invented by Josephson. Since they were characters that had been added to history as originals, their presence in the Warner Bros. picture was an indication of the use of Josephson's material and indicated plagiarism.

Well illustrative of the idea that copying can be proven by the taking of invented characters and incidents was a suit involving the life of Clara Barton, founder of the American Red Cross. Mercedes De Acosta was the author of an unpublished screenplay entitled *Angels in Service*. The same life story was the subject of an unpublished book entitled *Dedicated to Life*, written by Beth Brown and published in "digest" form in *Cosmopolitan*, entitled *War Nurse—The Biography of Clara Barton*. The court noted that both screenplay and book contained the following characters: Tom Maxwell, Elisha Richards, Mather Richards, Eddie Johnson, Henry Adams, Arthur Holt, and Eyra Jenks. All are fictional characters and names, the invention of the plaintiff. "Eyra" is the product of a mistyping by plaintiff of the name "Ezra." In both screenplay and book the Kelly steel patent is identified as the clue through which Miss Barton discovers misconduct in the Patent Office; in both February 3 is the date assigned to Maxwell's death. The court said:

It is utterly incredible that coincidence can explain defendant Brown's use of these fictional names and incidents invented by plaintiff.

It may well be that defendant Brown mistook plaintiff's fiction for fact; and when she copied she took what she believed to be in the public domain. Her research was chiefly concerned with the hunt for dramatic situations rather than for historical accuracy. There is no doubt, however, that she copied, and since we must ascribe to her the intentions of her assistants, that she intended to copy. The selections she made were made *animo furandi*, with intent to make use of them for the same purpose for which the original author used them.

Identical errors are not to be taken merely as happenstance or coincidence. Sometimes a common error may arise from misstatement of a source available to all. For instance, historical works, biographies, etc., which are in the public domain, or which may be properly used as source material, may contain error. The fact that that error subsequently appears in two works, each author relying upon the same source, will not be available to prove that the other copied. Sometimes in works such as directories and compilations, word lists and dictionaries, errors will be deliberately made for the purposes of proving and entrapping subsequent plagiarists. But it has been held that the copying of a few trap listings, which do not justify an inference of substantial copying throughout the work, will not be sufficient to prove culpable taking.

ACCESS

Obviously there can be no copying unless the copyist has had access to the prior work; therefore in every copyright suit access must be proven. In some way or another there must be proof of possession of the work taken and similarity. That possession need not necessarily be proven by direct evidence.

Where there was a question as to whether a sculptured dog had been copied, the fact that hair conformations and arrangements appeared in substantial identity was taken to show that there must have been access, particularly when measurement with calipers demonstrated identity in measurement, shape, and hair conformations to the minutest detail. The similarities being so striking, access was inferred.

After a plaintiff has established a protectable property right, the further issue, common to all copyright cases, statutory or common law, is: Was the plaintiff's material copied by the defendant? There will seldom be direct evidence of plagiarism, and necessarily the trier of fact must rely upon circumstantial evidence and the reasonable inferences which may be drawn from it to determine the issue. An inference of copying may arise when there is proof of access coupled with a showing of similarity. Where there is strong evidence of access, less proof of similarity may suffice. Conversely, if the evidence of access is uncertain, strong proof of similarity should be shown before the inference of copying may be indulged.

On the other hand, where two writers used the same idea or theme, in fact where both consciously or unconsciously made use of a common fundamental plot involving the usual gangster type of story but told different stories, the mere fact that one had access to the work of the other and made a synopsis thereof for his files does not establish a cause of action for plagiarism.

It is true that where access is admitted, "the probability that the similarities are the result of copying, intentional or unintentional," is high. Access being admitted, there might be, despite the best of intentions, unconscious and unintentional copying, which may amount to infringement. But there must still be similarity. Where there is no access there can be no copying and therefore no infringement. As has been frequently said, if two men independently wrote the "Ode on a Grecian Urn" each could have copyright therein, for similarity without copying is not infringement.

Whether or not there was intention to copy is irrelevant. It has been said:

> If, however, they had read the story or knew of its contents, and if there was a subconscious memory of the story derived from such knowledge, and if the evidence was such that some unconscious and unintentional copying was disclosed by the play when produced, there might be an infringement, notwithstanding the intentions of the parties to avoid infringement.

Signe Toksvig had worked for three years on *The Life of Hans Christian Andersen*. Her work was done exclusively from Danish sources, including the original works and letters of Andersen, and conversations with persons having knowledge of matters and incidents pertaining to the life of Andersen. Margaret Ann Hubbard wrote a novel based on the life of Hans Christian Andersen entitled *Flight of the Swan*. Her work and research were confined to English sources, in the course of which she read and made use of plaintiff's book and included copying from twenty-four specific passages. She acknowledged her indebtedness to Miss Toksvig. The defense was made that Hubbard took from Toksvig's book only that which appeared in quotations which she believed were in the public domain and that she assumed the quotations were taken from Andersen. The court said:

> Even if defendants assumed that the passages appearing between quotation marks were not original translations from Danish sources, that fact would not aid defendants to avoid liability. Intention is immaterial if infringement appears.

Where a property right is proven in material and it is established that one who had access to that property copied it substantially, then whether the copying was conscious or unconscious the property will be protected and infringement will be found.

Assuming a valid copyright:

a. There can be no infringement of copyright unless there

has been a taking of a substantial portion of the copyright owner's protectible material.

b. Some of the material ordinarily appearing in a copyrighted literary or dramatic work is not capable of ownership, is not protectible, and may freely be taken by others, without infringing the copyright. Such material includes:

1. The title, which may, however, be protected under doctrines of unfair competition.
2. The theme.
3. Locale and settings.
4. The "situations."
5. Ordinarily the characters, particularly where such characters are common to the situations of life in which they are depicted, are historical characters, or otherwise well-known types of individuals.
6. Ideas.
7. Bare basic plots.

In general the copyright owner's protectible property consists in the development, treatment, and expression given in the copyrighted work to the elements as hereinabove set forth. The test as to whether a taking of protectible property is a substantial taking is not primarily a quantitative one. The question is one of quality rather than quantity, and is to be determined by the character of the work and the relative value of the material taken, and the test of such taking is one which applies the standards of the ordinary observer.

Chapter 6

FAIR USE, QUOTATION,
BURLESQUE,
AND PERMISSIONS

The constitutional provision which granted exclusive copyright provided that it was for the purpose of promoting the progress of science, and useful arts. The use of copyright material, even to the extent of some copying, may, therefore, under certain circumstances, not be an unlawful use. It may equally as well be lawful. The notion of such lawful use comes under the general description of the term "fair use." The English Copyright Act of 1911 and the Canadian Act of 1921 provide statutory defenses to claims of infringement, including a specific provision that any fair dealing with any work for the purposes of private study, research, criticism, review, or newspaper summary shall not constitute an infringement. Although prior to the signing into law of the 1976 Act, American copyright law had no such statutory provision, substantially the same doctrine had evolved from decisions in the courts.

The 1976 Act has codified this judge-made law along lines similar to the provisions in the English and Canadian acts, and now for the first time, American law has a statutory provision on fair use.

§ 107. Limitations on exclusive rights: Fair use

Notwithstanding the provisions of section 106, the fair use of a copyrighted work, including such use by reproduction in copies or phonorecords or by any other means specified by that section, for purposes such as criticism, comment, news reporting, teaching (including multiple copies for classroom use), scholarship, or research, is not an infringement of copyright. In determining whether the use made of a work in any particular case is a fair use the factors to be considered shall include—

(1) the purpose and character of the use, including whether such use is of a commercial nature or is for nonprofit educational purposes;

(2) the nature of the copyrighted work;

(3) the amount and substantiality of the portion used in relation to the copyrighted work as a whole; and

(4) the effect of the use upon the potential market for or value of the copyrighted work.

Under the judge-made law, there could be no fair use of works protected under common-law copyright. As long as an author kept his work confidential and uncommunicated, no one had the right to use it.

After the work had been published, there might be fair use as well as unfair use. Although codification of the fair-use doctrine by the Copyright Act of 1976 provides the courts with firmer guidance, it does not appreciably alter the line of inquiry through which the courts have approached the question of whether there has been fair use. Prior to the effective date of the new law, courts under the old law would, as they shall continue to do under the new, first find whether there had been any substantial taking, whether there had been any use which might amount to plagiarism. If there had been no plagiaristic use, then, of course, no question of fair or unfair use arose. After the determination of the first question came the question of whether or not that which was taken had been taken fairly. What is or is not a fair use depends upon the circumstances of each particular case. Under the test that gradually evolved, the court would look to "the nature and objects of the selections made, the quantity and value of the materials used, and the degree in which the use may prejudice the sale, diminish the profits, or supersede the objects of the original work." This test is virtually identical to that set forth by the statute, and the examples discussed below will no doubt hold for the decisions reached under the statute as well.

It was never intended that the copyright laws should deprive workers in a given field, such as science or the arts, of all previous works, as otherwise the progress of these arts would be hindered. So when Einstein developed the theory of relativity and published it, an immediate interest was aroused and many persons wrote secondary works in the field. Necessarily, they discussed the previous work and Einstein's revelations, but in each case the question was, did they merely publish Einstein, thus depriving him of his work, or did they utilize him as a jumping-off place?

It has been said that ". . . the law permits those working in a field of science or art to make use of ideas, opinions, or theories, and in certain cases even the exact words contained in a copyrighted book in that field."

The law permits writers of scientific, medical, technical, and similar books or articles of learning to make use of ideas, opinions, or theories and even the exact words contained in copyrighted works in the field. This is done, in the words of Lord Mansfield, so that "the world may not be deprived of improvements, nor the progress of the arts be retarded."

It will be recalled that the constitutional grant of the right to legislate in the field of copyright was for the purpose of promoting "the Progress of Science and useful Arts." In such cases the law implies the consent of the copyright owner to a fair use of his publication for the advancement of science or art.

The proposition is clear that when an author does his own independent research and bases his work on that research there can be no infringement on the other's work regardless of the similarity of the two publications.

The test has been, and will continue to be, whether one has

made an independent production or made a substantial and fair use of the said work. The fact that two works relate to the same subject matter, or are similar to one another, does not make the one an infringement of the other if each is the fruit of independent intellectual effort, nor does the fact of copying an insignificant portion of the copyrighted material make such use other than a fair use. To constitute unfair use there must be a substantial or material taking, but where subsequent work is based in a large part on copyrighted material and mirrors the manner and style used in the prior work, then such use may be unfair. It is a question of fact in each case.

This is particularly so with reference works in regard to the arts and sciences because it has been said any publication in those fields is made as a development toward progress and to a certain extent by common consent and even to the constitutional limitation. Others interested in advancing the same art or science may commence where prior authors stopped. As to such works it sometimes becomes essential to subsequent authors to make use of what precedes them in the precise form in which last exhibited.

Moreover, courts have been willing to interpret the arts and sciences clause of the Constitution liberally in litigation involving fair use. Such was the case in a suit brought by Howard Hughes, the reclusive and wealthy industrialist, to prevent Random House's publication of a biography of him. In 1954 *Look* Magazine had published and copyrighted a series of articles about Hughes's life. In the early 1960s Random House commissioned a biography of Hughes and by 1964 had obtained the services of a writer, John Keats, to finalize the manuscript begun by Thomas Thompson. Upon learning of the proposed biography, Hughes, acting through a corporation created especially for that purpose, bought up the copyright to the 1954 *Look* Magazine articles and five days later sued Random House to enjoin publication of the biography, charging infringement on the magazine articles to which he now held the copyright. The District Court granted Hughes his injunction, but the Circuit Court reversed.

Although it was admitted that small portions of the *Look* articles had been copied, the court found that these constituted an insignificant part of the total biography, as well as of the original articles, and that there had been no commercial injury to Hughes's copyright since the articles had long been out of print. The court also found that there was sufficient public interest in Hughes to warrant publication of the biography. In finding that Random House's use of the *Look* articles fell within the permissible scope of fair use, the court stated the need for defining the arts and sciences broadly.

> Biographies, of course, are fundamentally personal histories and it is both reasonable and customary for biographers to refer to and utilize earlier works dealing with the subject of the work and occasionally to quote directly from such works. This practice is permitted because of the public benefit in encouraging the development of historical and biographical works and their public distribution, so that "the world may not be deprived of improvements, or the progress of the arts be retarded." Indeed, while the Hughes biography may not be a profound work, it may well provide valuable source material for historians and social scientists. Contrary to the district court's view, the arts and sciences should be defined in their broadest terms. . . . particularly in view of the development of the field of social sciences.

The true test of fair use is whether the author's work is the result of his own labor, skill and use of common materials and common sources of knowledge open to all men and whether resulting resemblances are either accidental or arising from the nature of the subject.

A second author may use a previous copyrighted work as a means of reference to the orginal sources. For example, two men writing about Abraham Lincoln would have to draw upon the same historic events and facts and personages, and to some extent there would result some similarity of treatment. Such similarity is sometimes unavoidable and would constitute fair use in the absence of proof of slavish copying or of inadequate research on the part of the subsequent author who relied too much upon the work of the prior author and too little on independent labor.

If one rediscovers a period of history or forgotten worlds, the fact that one has re-established an interest in the subject does not give an exclusive right to the field, and others may enter and write in it. An author may even fairly borrow from his own previous works if they are in a field in which he specializes and in which subsequent works will necessarily bear on the same subject or period.

Use of basic theme, plot, or ideas is fair use up to the point where the particular work alleged to have been taken shows invention, novelty, and originality in the arrangement of incident, character, and writing.

Madeleine Smith, a Scottish girl, was indicted for poisoning her lover. Following the trial a number of persons wrote plays, novels, and stories based on the case. The last one in the field was held entitled to use, not only all that had gone before, but even the contribution of the particular plaintiff, if they drew from it only the more general patterns, that is, "if they kept clear from its expression."

Nor is direct quotation always an unfair use. Such quotation may be made in connection with both fiction and nonfiction. In an article published in the *Saturday Evening Post* on the Green Bay Packers football team, the author incorporated the words of a song "Go! You Packers, Go!" The use of the eight lines of the song was urged as a fair use, on the ground that the song was used in connection with nonfiction. The use of the chorus was held incidental and fair.

J. P. McEvoy wrote a serial story which appeared in *Collier's* entitled "Are You Listening?", and in the course of it used some ten lines out of eighteen of the first chorus of the song "You Can't Stop Me from Lovin' You." The court approved the notion that the author of the original song must have reasonably contemplated such use of words when he created his work, notwithstanding the monopoly conferred upon him by copyright.

When Pearl White died, *The New Yorker* carried an article on her death. She had been famous during her lifetime when the *Perils of Pauline* was being shown every week in the days of the serial movie. In 1914 the plaintiff had published a song called "Poor Pauline," contemporary with the motion-picture serial. When in 1938 *The New Yorker* used the chorus of the song in its article, it was held that publication of a portion of the song was no infringement and that the publication was a fair use.

A more difficult question concerning quotation and fair use arose in the litigation over the publication by Louis Nizer in his *The Implosion Conspiracy* of all, or portions, of some twenty-nine letters written by Ethel and Julius Rosenberg while they were awaiting execution for espionage in 1953. The Rosenbergs' letters had originally appeared in a book entitled *The Death House Letters of Julius and Ethel Rosenberg*, copyrighted in 1953. Suit was brought by the Rosenbergs' sons, Michael and Robert Meeropol, alleging infringement of the copyright. Mr. Nizer, a prominent New York trial lawyer, conceded copying portions of the letters, but asserted the privilege of doing so under the doctrine of fair use.

The question presented by the case, which was decided by the District Court in 1976, was whether limited parts of the letters written by historical figures about public events could be copied verbatim in an historical work dealing with an event in which the writer had been a major participant. In noting the rarity of this question, the court observed that in the only American case discussing the issue directly, Justice Story had held that the copyrighted letters of George Washington could not be republished in their entirety in a work on Washington's life where two hundred and fifty-five of the eight hundred and sixty-six pages consisted of the copyrighted material. In Nizer's case, however, the letters represented less than .85 percent of the material in his book.

As its test for fair use, the court adopted two standards:

(1) whether the taking was limited in scope; and

(2) whether in the context of the entire work, the purpose of using the letters was to illustrate historical facts or to capitalize on the unique intellectual product of the author of the letters.

Applying this test, the court found that Nizer's use of the copyrighted letters was within the scope of fair use. Said the court:

> Whatever their literary quality, the letters are clearly used by defendant to describe the feelings and thoughts of two of the major participants in the Rosenberg trial . . . . it cannot be said that defendant's work derives a significant part of its value from the use of the copyrighted letters . . . . Rather than being used to exploit the individual feelings or expressions of plaintiffs' parents, the excerpts from the letters, like the trial transcript and other source materials, are used to relate certain facts relative to the whole event. These letters in themselves are part of the historical record . . . . Given the public interest in the trial, and the events surrounding it, plaintiffs' copyright should not give them a monopoly on the use and dissemination of facts relating to this historical event.

In reaching its decision, the court balanced the literary value of the Rosenbergs' letters, as well as their commercial value, against the interest of the public in an historical event and decided that because the latter outweighed the former, there had been fair use.

Criticism is an important and proper exercise of fair use. Reviews may quote exclusively for the purpose of illustration and comment. A book, when published, is a fact concerning which anyone is free to avail himself as of any other fact made public. It may be commented upon and discussed, and the author's work reproduced insofar as it may be necessary to make the comment intelligible. And such comment may be serious or humorous. It may even be harsh. The use made is fair if the purpose is criticism. An author who submits his work to the public must expect that kind of use.

Business forms and contract forms, even though embodied in a book, may be used and may be copied for use. The American Institute of Architects published a book of forms called the *Standard Documents of the American Institute of Architects*. They were forms for agreements setting forth the understandings and obligations of owners, contractors, architects, etc., in prospective operations. The use and delivery of six copies of one form by an architect to the owner and contractors with whom he was dealing were held to be a fair use under a well-established doctrine that one who publishes a book explaining a system or publishes a book of business forms contemplates and invites their use as such. The court said: "And where the art it teaches cannot be used without employing the methods and diagrams used to illustrate the book, or such as are similar to them, such methods and diagrams are to be considered as necessary incidents to the art, and given therewith to the public; not given for the purpose of publication in other works explanatory of the art, but for the purpose of practical application."

Publications of the United States Government may be used freely, for the copyright law specifically provides that no copyright shall subsist in any publication of the United States Government. But this does not extend to copyrighted material which may be used in such government publications. It exists only as to the government material.

Utilizing a work for the purpose of checking on one's own work is permissible. So it has been said that it is fair if a competing work is consulted, after an author has himself examined the original sources, for the sole purpose of discovering possible discrepancies or omissions, which, when found, will be investigated and corrected by further independent work. Of course this does not mean that one may check on an obviously incomplete work and take a large amount of matter from prior protected material.

The necessity for comic material raised by the successors to vaudeville in television has brought an increased use of parody and burlesque and with it concomitant litigation. Necessarily, either parody or burlesque involves the use of and reference to the original.

The following principles have been suggested by Judge James M. Carter, who sat in the United States District Court for the Southern District of California:

a. When the alleged infringing work is of the same character as the copyrighted work, viz., a serious work with a taking from another serious copyrighted work, then the line is drawn more strictly than when a farce or comedy or burlesque takes from a serious copyrighted work or vice versa.

b. In historical burlesque a part of the content is used to conjure up at least the general image of the original. Some limited taking should be permitted under the doctrine of fair use, in the case of burlesque, to bring about this recalling or conjuring up of the original.

c. Burlesque may ordinarily take the locale, the theme, the setting, situation, and even bare basic plots without infringement, since such matters are ordinarily not protectible.

d. The doctrine of fair use permits burlesque to go somewhat further so long as the taking is not substantial. It may take an incident of the copyrighted story, a developed character, some small part of the development of the story, possibly some small amount of the dialogue.

In a case involving the dramatization of the copyrighted cartoon strip *Mutt and Jeff*, the defense was made that the infringing production was a mere parody or burlesque of the original. The court's opinion showed that a substantial taking occurred and therefore, the defense of fair use was rejected.

The dividing line between permissible and non-permissible parody is illustrated by four cases, two of which occurred in

1909 in the days of vaudeville, and two in 1955, when television and motion pictures came into conflict. In the first series a parodied imitation of an actress's manner of singing a song, in which no copyrighted material was used, was held nonactionable. On the other hand, where in addition to mimicry or parody of the mannerisms of an actress a copyrighted song was sung, infringement was found. In both cases the actress was the vaudeville star Irene Green. The court said the mannerisms of the artist may be shown without words, and if some words are absolutely necessary, still a whole song is hardly required, and if a whole song was required, it was not too much to say that the imitator should select for impersonation a singer singing something else than a copyrighted song.

In the two more recent cases, one involved the performance by Jack Benny of a humorous sketch, *Autolight*, burlesquing the motion picture *Gaslight*. Benny defended the use on the grounds that his performance was a burlesque. The court held that *Autolight*, which starred Jack Benny and Barbara Stanwyck, took a substantial portion of the film. The court gave considerable weight to the commercial gain involved and distinguished this use from the use in science, technical fields, and criticism, and pointed out that while the line between the permissible and forbidden may be hard to draw, that did not prevent the application of the rule.

In a subsequent case the same court held that a burlesque playlet entitled *From Here to Obscurity*, presented on television, did not infringe on the motion picture *From Here to Eternity*, saying that the burlesque was a new, original, and different literary work. There was some similarity between the burlesque and the motion picture in incident, and in some of the details of the development, treatment, and expression. All such similarities were the result of the intentional use of the motion picture by the writers of the burlesque in order to accomplish the purposes of a burlesque. The use in the burlesque of material appearing in the motion picture was of only such material as to cause the viewer of the burlesque to recall and conjure up the motion picture, or the novel *From Here to Eternity* upon which the motion picture was based, and thus provide the necessary element of burlesque. Since no substantial taking occurred, the court held that the telecast did not disparage or detract from the motion picture.

Dr. Frank C. Baxter, a professor of English Literature at the University of Southern California, who testified in the *Gaslight* case as an expert witness, reviewed the use of burlesque throughout the history of literature, and summarized it as follows:

1. Burlesque as a form of comic art is as old as literature.
2. Burlesque "could not use bitterness or rancor. Burlesque is a happy thing."
3. Burlesque is rarely personal.
4. Burlesque is rarely of a whole work of art.
5. Burlesque changes the tone of the original.
6. It rarely bothers itself with the evil or the sham, the ignominious and the failure.
7. Burlesque is a sort of compliment.
8. It is a manifestation of the comic spirit.
9. Burlesque historically has flourished in those societies where there has been most democratic liberty.
10. Burlesque is a happy toying with serious things.
11. The stage has always laughed at itself.
12. There have been few important novels, verses, or plays that have not been burlesqued.

An acknowledgment by name of the author and work from which material is taken does not establish fair use. It might even establish unfair use, since it might imply that the prior author had given his consent and authorized the use. The mere fact that one acknowledges the name of the person from whom one has stolen does not make the act legal. The question always is was the taking fair, not was an acknowledgment given. Acknowledgment may, however, bear on intention, and while intention plays no part where legal plagiarism is found, intention may play a part in the determination of fair use. Since there are legal uses to which material may be put, whether or not there was such an intention is, like everything else, a question of fact in determining the total issue.

Generally the tests applied by the courts in determining fair use have been similar to that used by the court in the Hughes case discussed above: (1) Was there a substantial taking quantitatively and qualitatively? (2) Did the taking materially reduce the demand for the original copyrighted material? (3) Does the distribution of the material serve the public interest in the free dissemination of information? and (4) Did the preparation of the material require the use of prior materials dealing with the same subject? This test is virtually identical to the statutory criteria set forth in the 1976 Copyright Act.

If too much is taken, if what is taken would serve as a substitute for the original work and impair its distribution, then the use is unfair. Where fair use is made, there is no need to ask for permission, since what is taken is used as a matter of right; to ask for permission is to yield that right. This may give a nuisance value to those who may demand payment for fair use. Permission should be asked only where the use would be unfair without permission. In obvious situations, such as anthologies and compilations, permission should be asked. But for incidental uses, permission should not be asked, otherwise the doctrine of fair use might find itself weakened by custom.

Chapter 7

～ THE EXCLUSIVE RIGHT
TO NAMES AND TITLES

The title or name of a literary work is not protected by statutory copyright. Copyright does not protect the name or title of the work, but it does not follow that the owner of the name or title cannot have a property interest in the title and in its use as against a competitor. A name or title is protected only when its invasion occurs under such circumstances as to establish in a court of equity that there has been unfair competition. Unfair competition means that there has not only been a competitive use of the title, but that competitive use occurred under circumstances which the court can find to be unfair. Necessarily this definition turns on itself, but there is no hard and fast rule for determining the elements of unfair competition, since each name or title stands on its own, and each alleged unfair use requires the separate proof of its unfairness. Each case therefore is, for all practical purposes, a small law unto itself. Among the titles which have been protected are:

"March of Time" vs. "Voice of Time"
"Information, Please"
"The Fifth Column" vs. "Fifth Column Squad"
"The Gold Diggers" vs. "Gold Diggers of Paris"
"Esquire" (Magazine) vs. "Esquire" (Bar)
"Shadow of Chinatown"

"Queen of Flat Tops"
"Blind Youth" vs. "The Blindness of Youth"
"Playboy" vs. "Playgirl"
"Sex and the Single Girl" vs. "Sex and the Single Man"

Generalizations are never more dangerous than in the field of unfair competition, for a writer has "no inherent right in the title to his production." Generally, however, in order to protect a title:

a. The name or title must be arbitrary and fanciful and not be a word or words of common significance, or so-called household words, or words that are merely descriptive.

b. Geographical or historical names cannot be exclusively appropriated. However, recovery has been had under the exceptional circumstances of great public identification with a particular writing, as, for instance, the name of Abraham Lincoln, Oklahoma, South Pacific, etc.

c. The title must have acquired a secondary significance, i.e., it must have become identified in the public mind as the title which is sought to be protected.

d. The title must have been continuously used, i.e., the identification of the title with the work must continue in the public mind.

e. The use of the title must not have been abandoned.

f. The title of a work in the public domain may be used in connection with that work by competing publishers or producers.

g. It is not essential that the works be of the same character or used in the same form.

So, for instance, the obvious competition of book with book, song with song, motion picture with motion picture, does not alone determine, for books, poems, or plays may be in competition with motion pictures, or with each other, and a magazine may be in competition in terms of title with a radio program. The title of a story may not be competitively used. A song title may not be used for motion pictures, radio, or television. In the light of these generalizations each case, nevertheless, stand on its facts.

Where the issue involves the title of a book as distinguished from plays or motion pictures, there may be cases where the reputation of the author rather than the title of the book is important to the sale.

The necessity for both competition and unfairness in the competition was illustrated in a case in which the plaintiff produced a one-reel picture entitled *Inflation*. Plaintiff showed the picture to MGM for purposes of procuring distribution of that picture. MGM produced its own one-reel picture entitled *Inflation*. The court said:

> It is not at all inconceivable that the defendants, after learning that the plaintiffs had produced a picture on inflation, decided to do likewise. They had a perfect right to do so, just as a writer who, after seeing an article or a book on a good timely subject, is licensed to write on the identical topic. Races and imitations of this character are not at all uncommon. . . . Competition alone is not enough; unfairness must attend the rivalry.

To protect the author or proprietor in his property right to a title and its use, there has been developed the doctrine of secondary meaning, which creates a right akin to a property right. It is a term which indicates that a name or title has acquired a new significance as an attribute of the work with which it is coupled, and as indicating that work to the exclusion of others. It implies that the proprietor of the title has, by extensive distribution of the work, by advertising, by promotion and publicity, created in the public mind an identity so that the title comes primarily to mean the work with which it is associated. Once such secondary meaning has been acquired, the title is a form of property in the same general class as other personal property, and if the rights of the owner are violated he is entitled to the same remedies to which the owners of other personal property may resort for redress.

The elements of secondary meaning are, essentially, the following:

1. There must be use, not mere adoption, and the mere deposit of a work in the Copyright Office is not use.

2. There must be a length of use sufficient so that the title will have become identified in the public mind with the work.

3. There must be an extent of popularization, promotion, advertising.

4. There must have been some effort toward promoting conscious connection in the mind of the public between the title and the work.

The question of whether or not a name has attained such public recognition as to give to one person the exclusive right thereafter to use it is a difficult question of fact. If one examines the records of the Copyright Office, one will find many duplications, single titles which have been used fifteen and twenty times. Deciding which person who used a title prior to its next use obtained the right to its exclusive use, must, necessarily, require proof of more than merely the application of the name to a work. The facts which enter into it are, first, of course, what the circulation was; second, when the work was circulated, for it is almost self-evident that a work which has been out of print for twenty-five or thirty years, even though it had had a great sale in its day, is no longer on the market. Where there is no competition there can be no unfair competition. Another of the factors is the amount of money spent in advertising, and general evidence, through reviews and publicity, of the fame attained by the work.

So in the case of *Sex and the Single Girl*, Warner Bros. had spent millions of dollars in the production of the picture and a considerable sum for promotion and advertising, approximately half a million dollars. An injunction was granted to Warner Bros. against Albert Ellis and Lyle Stuart, Inc., restraining them from producing a motion picture entitled *Sex and the Single Man*.

On the other hand, Lyle Stuart was itself successful in a similar suit brought against Pinnacle Books. In this case, Lyle Stuart had published a book entitled *The Sensuous Man*, a sexual "how-to" book which sold 330,000 copies in the hardbound edition, and 6,000,000 copies in a paperbound edition brought out by Dell to which Stuart had sold the paperback rights. To capitalize on what appeared to be a very lucrative market, Pinnacle sought to bring out a similar "how-to" book entitled *The Sensual Male*, which it advertised as a companion book to *The Sensuous Woman* which had also been published by Stuart. In granting Lyle Stuart's request for an injunction, the court not surprisingly held the title, *The Sensuous Man* to be protected under the secondary meaning rule, since Pinnacle's title would be likely to cause confusion among those seeking to purchase *The Sensuous Man*.

Bruno Schelling wrote and published in *Cosmopolitan* Magazine in 1906 a story under the title "Broken Doll." Thereafter, in 1910, and again in 1914, two photoplays appeared under the name *Broken Doll*, but the scenario of neither was based upon the story by Bruno Schelling. In 1921, the *Saturday Evening Post* published a story with the same title not in any way related to Schelling's story.

The Associated Producers, Inc., a motion-picture company, utilized the *Saturday Evening Post* story for a scenario upon which it based a motion picture under the name *Broken Doll* without permission from prior users. During the same year the International Film Service obtained the right to Schelling's story. It brought an action to restrain Associated Producers from utilizing the title *Broken Doll*. The case is interesting because it contains a significant description of the amount of use which would establish an author's rights to the title selected by him. Judge Learned Hand, in the course of his opinion, said: "Ordinarily, I should indeed think that a single publication in a magazine so broadly circulated as *Cosmopolitan* would be prima facie enough. The story presumably has many readers, of whom a substantial number remember the title. That title, billed or advertised as the title of a photoplay, leads them to expect a play based on this story." Nevertheless, the court held that the question was one of fact. The fact that the story had come out only once—and that years ago—that it was never reprinted, and had had nothing but the fugitive publicity of a magazine, was not enough. The court held that, in the face of the subsequent use of the same name in two films, it would be a disingenuous assumption to suppose that there were any substantial number of people who would attribute any secondary meaning to the title at all, and for that, among other reasons, denied the injunction sought.

The titles of plays, of course, provide a fruitful field for theft, in that their titles may be used for both other plays and also for motion pictures. In not every case is the first user entitled to restrain others. Here, too, one who seeks a monopoly must establish his right thereto by proving, on the facts, that his play has attained such public notoriety as to have acquired identification of title and play in the public mind.

Avery Hopwood's play, *The Gold Diggers*, was produced by David Belasco at the Lyceum Theatre and ran for ninety weeks in New York. Subsequently, on tour, five hundred twenty-eight performances were given between September 13, 1921, and April 21, 1923. Gross receipts from the play were more than $1,900,000. In 1923 Mr. Hopwood sold the rights to Warner Brothers to produce the play in motion-picture form. Warner Brothers produced it first as a silent picture in 1923. Its gross receipts were $470,000. Thereafter, they produced it as a talking motion picture, and its receipts were more than $2,500,-000. Such was its success that Warner Brothers tried again, with a new talking motion picture under the title *Gold Diggers of 1933*. Such also was its success that Majestic Pictures Corporation thought to appropriate the title for a picture, under the title *Gold Diggers of Paris*. When Warner Brothers sued, alleging that the attempt to use the title under the form *Gold Diggers of Paris* was with the intent to capitalize on the good will and reputation of Avery Hopwood's play and the motion pictures produced by Warner Brothers, the defendants did little to defend—since there was no obvious defense—except to allege that it was unethical to distribute more than one picture based on the same play within five years. The court brushed the defense aside and said that Warner Brothers' pictures, advertised under the titles *Gold Diggers of Broadway* and *Gold Diggers of 1933*, had become associated in the public mind with Hopwood's play of that title, and thus acquired secondary meaning in the motion-picture field as descriptive of film versions of the Hopwood play.

Now the words "gold diggers" are ordinary words of general description and would ordinarily not be subject to pre-emption by anyone, but despite that fact, having been used by Hopwood and the Warners to the extent to which they had been, they could not be used by a competitor to deceive the public. Warner Brothers were given the monopoly which they craved over the words "gold diggers" for motion pictures.

Edmond Rostand gave Charles Frohman the right to produce his play, *Chantecler*, in English in the United States after it had been first produced in Paris. For several years prior to its production, its title and subject matter, particularly the fact that every character was to represent a barnyard fowl or animal, had been published and announced, and the subject of the play and its ideas had been constantly and widely discussed in the French and European press. In August, 1909, a dramatic piece in the nature of a burlesque was produced in Paris under the name *Chanticlair*. It ran for some weeks. It was also produced in Vienna. William Morris acquired the rights to produce *Chanticlair* in the United States. When Frohman sued Morris, the first question that was raised was that the word "chantecler," of which the word "chanticlair" is another form, was not susceptible of exclusive appropriation by any writer to designate a play. The claim was made that it was a descriptive term which must be left open to all. Even descriptive terms, however, may be fanciful as applied to particular things. "Chantecler" is, in this case, not descriptive of a play. It describes a rooster, rather than a play. Applied to a play, it is fanciful. In its consideration, the court took notice of the fact that Rostand was an eminent playwright, and that the success of his former productions and the uncommon character of his latest effort had caused widespread and intense interest. Even though the French production of *Chanticlair* had preceded Rostand's *Chantecler*, the court held that the right belonged to the eminent author whose talent and reputation created the extraordinary interest of which the defendants sought to reap the benefit. Frohman was granted exclusive right to the use, and the defendants were restrained. They were, however, allowed to continue with the performance of their play under the title *The Barnyard Romeo*.

About 1910 Robert Hilliard was a popular stage idol. He produced, with Marc Klaw, an elaborate dramatic production entitled *A Fool There Was* at the Liberty Theatre in New York City. The play was presented for many years in the United States and Canada, with both artistic and financial success. Large sums of money were expended for actors, actresses, theatres, equipment, and advertising. After the stage presentation, *A Fool There Was* acquired a reputation, and the title became so well known that the General Film Company appropriated it in connection with a photodrama, with full knowledge that Klaw and Hilliard were producing the play. No other play had been presented under that title prior to the production of the drama by Robert Hilliard, although the phrase, "a fool there was," had not originated with him, but with Rudyard Kipling. The plays were not in any way similar, therefore there was no question of copyright. The sole question was whether the title, *A Fool There Was*, was the property of Klaw and Hilliard. The court held that it was, and that they had acquired an exclusive proprietary right, as a trade name, in the title, *A Fool There Was*, in connection with their play.

Once the right to exclusion has been acquired, it may be exercised as against the world, but not forever. Thus, even though an author might be deemed to have acquired a secondary significance for a title and had been held entitled to restrain others from using it, that would not grant him a right in perpetuity. For should the title remain disused for such a period of time that it was no longer connected in the public mind with the work of the author, then others might again use it. But certainly the right acquired would last at least for the life of the copyright.

Names of persons, living or dead, selected for biography or plays, cannot, of course, be acquired exclusively by any author. Any number of authors may write about Washington, Jefferson, Lincoln, Disraeli, or any other well-known figure, whether in the political, artistic, or scientific fields. No one can map out a field in biography and claim it for his own. So Anatole France, Mark Twain, and Bernard Shaw, among others, have written of Saint Joan and used her name as a title. None of them could restrain the others. Special circumstances, however, may sometimes afford protection to an author even though he has used such a name.

John Drinkwater's *Abraham Lincoln* affords an instance of this. When the play was produced in London, it achieved international acclaim. Mr. Drinkwater's reputation soared. All over the United States there was a demand for an American production, and the press book, even before the production of the play by William Harris, Jr., was two huge volumes. Public officials throughout the United States wrote congratulatory letters to Mr. Harris, and it became the play to be seen. A Mr. Ralph Kettering, a stock producer in the Middle West, obtained the rights to a play, *A Man of the People*, which dealt with the life of Abraham Lincoln. He first used the subtitle, "Abraham Lincoln," but as the fame of Drinkwater's play rose, he gradually eliminated the main title of his play so that it eventually was entitled *Abraham Lincoln*. Mr. Harris brought suit in the federal courts in Illinois to restrain Mr. Kettering. Under ordinary circumstances such an action would have failed, for Abraham Lincoln belongs to all. Under the particular circumstance of the renown achieved by Drinkwater's *Abraham Lincoln*, the court expressed its opinion informally to the parties that no other play under that title ought to be produced while Drinkwater's play was running; it would have been an imposition on the public. Accordingly, Mr. Kettering consented to a decree restraining him from producing his play under the name *Abraham Lincoln*.

Test Pilot was used as the title of a copyrighted book by James H. Collins, a well-known flier and test pilot, and was also used as the title of a motion picture produced by MGM. The court held that the words "test pilot" were merely descriptive and therefore could not be exclusively appropriated by Collins any more than could other purely descriptive terms in the absence of a showing of the acquisition of secondary significance.

A similar rule has been applied to the words "confessions," "confidential," "high treason," "inflation," "hubba hubba." A typical case is one in which Ziff-Davis Publishing Company, through one of its subsidiaries, published a magazine called *Eerie Mysteries*, a so-called comic magazine. Avon Periodicals, Inc., published a so-called comic book entitled *Eerie* devoted to the field of weird stories. Both were distributed by the American News Company. Avon claimed exclusive right by reason of priority. The court found that the word "eerie" had appeared in the works of Robert Burns, Charlotte Brontë and De Quincey, and that it was evident that the word is generic, of common usage and origin, with a semantic history of at least six centuries, and therefore in the public domain. It held that a name, generic in origin, cannot be ordinarily exclusively appropriated, and said:

> The first use of a title does not ipso facto give to such user an exclusive right to an uncoined or non-fictitious name. Despite a persistent belief that the first use of a specific name or description gives a power to such user to prevent its employment by others, it is important to find that no such doctrine exists. . . .

It is quite common to find magazines using names startlingly similar. There are *Radio Digest, Radio World, Radio Age, Radio Progress, Radio News, Radio Broadcast; Motor, The Motor, Motor Transport, Motor Record, Motor World, Motor Age, Motor Life; Field and Stream, Forest and Stream; Popular Mechanics, Popular Science*; to cite a few. In the field of comics, a cursory examination of newsstand displays discloses magazines with titles such as: *Weird Science, Weird Worlds; Suspense, Suspense Detective; Man, Bat Man; The Thing, The Beyond; Web of Mystery, Journey into Mystery; First Love, Young Love.*

In the absence of proof of the acquisition of secondary meaning the court decided against Avon, since the use of a title which has acquired no secondary meaning and is descriptive of the publication is open to all.

On the other hand, we have the action of the Dell Publishing Company, which publishes magazines designated as "Modern Magazines"—*Modern Screen* and *Modern Romances*. When another corporation published a magazine entitled *Modern Movies*, it was held that although the word "modern" was not an arbitrary or fanciful word, and was a generic term, the effort on the part of the defendant to publish a magazine entitled *Modern Movies* in the face of *Modern Screen* was unfair competition. That each case stands on its own may be seen from the fact that *College Humor* could not obtain an exclusive right as against *College Comics*. The magazine called *G-Man* could not restrain the use of the title *Ace G-Man*; nor could *Life* restrain the use of the title *More Life*.

Condé Nast once decided that *Bon Ton* was a good name for a magazine. It was. It had been used by the S. T. Taylor Company for some sixty years for a periodical bearing the title *Le Bon Ton*, dealing with styles and fashions in women's apparel. When Mr. Nast made his decision, he acquired from the publishers of a periodical published in Paris, and known as the *Gazette du Bon Ton*, the right to issue in the English language a special edition of the said publication. The S. T. Taylor Company felt aggrieved. They sued Mr. Nast, who was the publisher of *Vanity Fair* and *Vogue*, both in the same field as their magazine *Le Bon Ton*. Unfortunately for Mr. Nast, the court held that the words "bon ton" had acquired a special and unusual meaning because of their use for the long period covered by the existence of Taylor's magazine. The arbitrary application to the said purpose was emphasized by the court, which held that they were not words of the English language, and to many persons would convey no meaning except as a designation of Taylor's periodical, at least so far as publications were concerned. To the court it appeared that the Taylor Company, by its conduct for many years, had acquired a valuable trademark, and should not have such value destroyed or impaired by its use by others. The court said that the natural and probable tendency of Mr. Nast's conduct was to deceive the public, so as to pass off the said magazine to be published by him as the publication of Taylor. Mr. Nast was enjoined.

There may also be protection for the names of characters which have become associated in the public mind with a particular work. Some of us remember that hero of our youth called Frank Merriwell, who figured in some twelve hundred and thirty-six stories written by Gilbert Patten under the pen name Burt L. Standish. The stories revolved around a central character called Frank Merriwell and portrayed his adventures during school and college days and after graduation. They were (as the court later found) "clean, wholesome stories of American life," and were so widely read that Frank Merriwell became a real and impressive figure in the imagination of the boys of the time. News of his name and exploits extended to all parts of the country.

The Superior Talking Pictures, Inc., a distributor of motion-picture films, apparently decided that so good a name ought not to be left unused, and advertised a series of twelve three-reel features of the Northwest Mounted Police using the name Frank Merriwell in the title. The court found the Frank Merriwell stories had definitely become fixed in the public mind with the works of Burt L. Standish. The stories had appeared over a period beginning April 18, 1896, to February 6, 1915, in a magazine published by Street and Smith known as the *Tip-Top Weekly*. Average weekly sales were 100,000, and the total distribution for the period exceeded 98,000,000 copies. After 1915 the stories continued in book form and were sold in papercovered books for ten cents each. There were more than 250 of these papercovered novels, and more than 25,000,-000 copies of them were sold. Some of them, bound in cloth, had approximate sales of 50,000 copies. When Patten sued the Superior Talking Pictures, Inc., the court held that, under the facts, while it was true that his copyright had not covered the titles, the name had become descriptive of and closely identified in the public mind with the author's work. Under the ordinary principles of unfair competition the defendants were restrained from using the name Frank Merriwell.

Other friends of an older generation's youth were Buster Brown and his dog, Tige. Buster and Tige were the creations of Richard L. Outcault. Buster will be remembered as a young male child about five years of age, with blond hair, dressed in bloomers and a pink coat extending a little above the knees, a large white collar and bow, and wearing a sailor hat. He was invariably represented by Outcault with his playmate Tige. Outcault, in 1902, in collaboration with George T. Smith, dramatized Buster and his dog in the form of a musical drama *Buster Brown*. In 1906, Al LaMar and some others produced a play or dramatic sketch under the title *Buster Brown*, and announced it in posters, placards, and newspapers which simulated and colorably imitated Outcault's title. It was not contended in the case that the two plays were in any way alike; the sole question was whether the defendants had appropriated the title and names of the plaintiff's principal characters. Outcault prevailed, and it was held that he had established Buster Brown and Tige as the names of his own particular creatures and was entitled to their sole use.

Now Yukon Jake was a mighty man, and his fame came when E. E. Paramour, Jr., wrote his famous *The Ballad of Yukon Jake*. The poem was printed and reprinted. It was published and republished in magazine form. It was published in bound volumes. Because the name had become so widely known, Mack Sennett, Inc., made a motion picture under the title. Mr. Paramour sued, and the case is interesting because it is one of the few cases in all literary history where the name of a poem was involved in such piracy. The court found that Yukon Jake had been implanted firmly in the public mind as Mr. Paramour's creation, and granted him an injunction and damages.

Once secondary significance has been attained, the property in the title will extend throughout the area in which the title has become known, so that a play produced in New York may be protected elsewhere throughout the United States.

On the other hand, secondary usage is not shown merely by evidence of advertising, widely or over a period of time, a title which is a generic term or in the public domain. The criterion is the achievement of a result, not alone the expenditure of effort.

Advertising under certain circumstances may have no value. When Walt Disney produced *Alice in Wonderland* he spent more than three million dollars on the production and vast sums on advertising. Disney said that his *Alice in Wonderland* had acquired a secondary meaning, in that a motion picture having that title had become established in the public mind as being the Disney picture. Almost simultaneously another picture was produced under the same title. There was no question but that the title *Alice in Wonderland* was in the public domain. The mere fact that Disney had spent more money on his picture and had more widely advertised it was held not to give him an exclusive right even for the short period which would be required for the first run of his picture. The court said that this was the sort of competition which should be encouraged rather than suppressed.

Since each case stands on its own, all criteria become relative. Use of a title for a period of weeks, if sufficiently intensive, may be as satisfactory for all lawful purposes as a period of years. There is no definitive rule as to the length of time required to establish secondary meaning. The question is whether widespread identification has been achieved. It is identification by whatever standards have been established that determines secondary meaning. Priority of use does, however, have some bearing.

Of course no matter when acquired, the property right in a name or title can be lost by abandonment, which is, like all other questions, a question of fact. Nonuse of the name or title over an extended period of time may be one of the facts which enter into the question of whether or not the title has retained its identification in the public mind. So where a title had been used for six months and not used for three and one-half years thereafter, it was held to be abandoned.

When a work which has been copyrighted falls into the public domain, or is otherwise in the public domain, that work may be reprinted, using both the name of the work and of the author. The leading case on this is *Clemens* v. *Belford,* in which Samuel L. Clemens sought to obtain exclusive use to his pseudonym Mark Twain, and was denied relief in connection with the use of works which had been produced under that pseudonym after the copyright term expired.

Edward S. Ellis was an outstanding author who had written juvenile and historical works. Among his earlier juvenile works were two, one entitled *In the Apache Country* and the other *The White Mustang.* Neither of the books had been copyrighted, and thereafter some book publishers printed copies of each of Ellis' books under his nom de plume of Lieutenant R. H. Jayne, with the name "Edward S. Ellis" and "Ellis" printed on the covers and wrappers. It was conceded that the publishers had a right to print the books, but it was contended that in the absence of permission, the author's name could not be used. The court held that the publishers had the right to use the name since it was a true statement of fact with regard to authorship of a work in the public domain.

The music of Dmitri Shostakovich, Serge Prokofiev, Aram Khachaturian, and Nicolai Miaskovsky was used in connection with a motion picture known as *The Iron Curtain*. Their names were used in what is known as "credit lines," and one of the composers was shown placing a record of his music on a phonograph. The music was in the public domain and enjoyed no copyright protection. The court held that the use of their names in connection with the publication or use of their works was permissible.

The field of unfair competition in which all of these cases fall establishes only the broadest of principles, but those principles are equitably applied to the facts of every case. As Judge Learned Hand has said:

> There is no part of the law which is more plastic than unfair competition.

Chapter 8

PROTECTION OF IDEAS

The very word "idea" suggests the difficulty which arises in any legal attempt to give it form and definition for purposes of enforcement. It has a philosophical meaning. It may mean thought, conception, or notion. It may mean opinion or belief. It may mean plan or project. When ideas reach the form of being plans or projects, particularly for the exploitation of an idea, then payment may be sought and legal obligation ascertained. Because of the multiplicity of meaning which the word "idea" may have, there was great difficulty in finding methods for the enforcement of the obligation which arose out of the communication of ideas and their use for practical ends.

Originally, as Augustine Birrell, in his charming lecture on "Literary Larceny," said: "Ideas, it has always been admitted, even by the Stationers' Company, are free as air. If you happen to have any, you fling them into the common stock and ought be well content to see your poorer brethren thriving upon them."

The first attempts at enforcement were in the field of copyright, and since copyright implied monopoly there was a strong prejudice against erecting a monopolistic property in ideas.

"Property," said the court, "is a historical concept; one may bestow much labor and ingenuity which inure only to the public benefit; 'ideas,' for instance, though upon them all civilization is built, may never be 'owned.' The law does not protect them at all, but only their expression."

Yet another court referred to ideas as comparable to *ferae naturae*, in which property rights are dependent upon possession, and are lost as if by escape of a wild animal. Abstract ideas cannot be made the subject of a property right.

And so throughout the development of the copyright law, ideas as such could not be protected. In the *Abie's Irish Rose* case the court said: "Though the plaintiff discovered the vein, she could not keep it to herself; so defined, the theme was too generalized an abstraction from what she wrote. It was only a part of her 'ideas.' "

In *The Bird of Paradise* case the court said: "There may be literary property in a particular combination of ideas or in the form in which ideas are embodied. There can be none in the ideas."

Again the thought was expressed: "The object of copyright is to promote science and the useful arts. If an author, by originating a new arrangement and form of expression of certain ideas or conceptions, could withdraw these ideas or conceptions from the stock of materials to be used by other authors, each copyright would narrow the field of thought open for development and exploitation, and science, poetry, narrative, and dramatic fiction and other branches of literature would be hindered by copyright, instead of being promoted."

And so the ideas behind books on science, medicine, art, painting, mathematics, bridge building, etc., can never be claimed under copyright as the exclusive property of any author. For when a work of art or literature has been copyrighted the owner is protected only in the method of expression of the idea contained in the copyrighted work and not in the use of the idea.

Into this stream of cases based on copyright for the protection of ideas there came a modern intruder. This was the notion that where the idea consisted in a plan or project capable of commercial use, there ought to be protection when such idea was conveyed for that purpose. The development of that concept has occurred within the past fifty-odd years, and today, under certain circumstances, ideas may be protected. A first step toward such protection is the requirement of proof that the idea is original. When an inventor patented an idea in which two additional seats were to be inserted in a coupé or roadster model of an automobile behind the front seat or from the side walls of a car, and communicated that idea to General Motors, he sought to recover when they used it, and said that otherwise General Motors would be unjustly enriched by the idea. The court said that the first requirement was a showing of novelty and originality in the idea, and that in the absence of such showing no recovery could be had.

In addition to novelty and originality the idea must be reduced to what is called concrete form. So, when a Mr. Thomas suggested to the Reynolds Tobacco Company that they advertise one of their brands of cigarettes as burning much slower than others, and suggested that they prove this by actual tests, he was unable to recover on his claim that the company had used his idea for advertising, for the court held that there was no property right in the offer of an abstract idea unless such idea had been reduced to concrete form, saying that originators of ideas have ample protection, since they are in control of them until they have produced an express contract providing for compensation. It held that since the letter in which Thomas submitted his idea did not contain concrete suggestions for advertising purposes, he could not recover in the absence of an express agreement to pay.

An author had an idea to build a motion picture around the colorful story of the Palace Theatre in New York City, with the old vaudeville characters, and transmitted that idea to RKO Pictures. The court held that the idea was so abstract that the author had no property right, since it was not embodied in tangible form.

Reggie Bowen had an idea for a radio program involving the use of local orchestras. He planned that broadcasts be given in different large cities each week through the facilities of the network. The artists would include famous names in comedy, song, and drama to be worked into the local musical background. He transmitted the idea to the Wrigley Company, and claimed thereafter that they used the idea. The court said that it was merely an idea or scheme in which there was no property right, and since the idea had not been reduced to concrete form, it was not protected where Mr. Bowen voluntarily communicated the idea to Wrigley without protecting it by contract. The court said that whatever interest he had in the idea became common property on disclosure.

On the other hand, where writers submitted to a radio broadcasting company a fully-developed and recorded program, entitled *Hollywood Preview*, which consisted of the production of a play for the purpose of obtaining the public's opinion as to the advisability of turning the play into a picture, the submitted program was held to be a "concrete idea" rather than a "submitted idea" and subject to protection in property right.

The third requirement for the protection of an idea is that the idea be submitted under circumstances which imply an obligation.

Lloyd K. Belt had an idea for a type of radio program in which the utilization of student talent selected from different high schools could be made and recorded as a student assembly, retaining the atmosphere of school by referring to the show as a "class," to the acts as "assignments," and to the action as "recitations." There was to be a rendition of several pieces by the school glee club. A bank entered into an agreement at first with Mr. Belt to utilize the idea, but later on carried the plan forward without his assistance. He sued the bank, and the court said that, even though the contract between Belt and the bank had been terminated, that did not erase the facts of disclosure under circumstances whereby he was to get a contract, and since a contract was implied from the conduct of the parties, it held that he was entitled to compensation.

John W. Shaw had an idea for an advertising campaign for the Ford Motor Company. It was contained in a slogan "Get the Feel of the Wheel." Mr. Shaw contended that the negotiations between him and the Ford Company had resulted in an implied contract to pay him. He asserted that the ideas and material submitted by him to Ford had been used without authorization in a subsequent campaign. The court said that such property interest is recognized and protected and set the case for trial.

A Mr. Healy had submitted to R. H. Macy & Company a Christmas advertising campaign involving three slogans, one of which Macy's used, "A Macy Christmas Means A Happy New Year." Healy had submitted not only the slogans but a complete advertising plan with words and sketches and carefully worded advertising material. He testified that when he went to Macy's he had said to the gentleman in charge that his object was to sell it, and was told that in the event Macy's used the idea, they would purchase it. There was no express contract determining the amount he was to be paid, but it was held that he was entitled to recover the reasonable value in view of the fact that the conversation had taken place.

The case involving *Mr. District Attorney* is of particular interest. Alonzo Deen Cole had produced a combination of ideas for a radio series in concrete form, which bore the title *Racketeer & Company,* and he had submitted it to Phillips H. Lord, Inc., for sale. He asserted that the Lord, Inc., production, *Mr. District Attorney,* was similar to his program, and testified as to certain amounts paid in commercial radio as being a fair yardstick. He also testified as to certain conversations had with Mr. Lord, from which a contract might be inferred. The court said that an express contract would afford him protection even as to his mere idea, but, the court said, since they were dealing with a specialized field, having customs and usages of its own, he was also allowed to have the jury consider an implied contract and to recover on the basis of the value, utilizing the sum of $500 for a half-hour broadcast as a yardstick.

On the other hand, unsolicited disclosures of an idea do not create any enforceable contract implied in law. Contract protection is necessary upon disclosure to prevent a public dedication.

The law ordinarily will not imply a promise to pay one who voluntarily confers a benefit upon another. However, where the benefit consists of a voluntary disclosure made in confidence with expectation of payment therefor, the law will provide a recompense. The law will imply a contract or promise to pay by the one obtaining the information, providing the information is voluntary, and provided further that there are the elements of a contract or implied contract, including some standard of measurement of damage. It is customary for advertising agencies and television production companies and the like to require persons who submit ideas to them to sign a release which bars any claim for breach of contract in connection with the idea submitted. Any payment made is voluntary. Such was the case involving Lor-Ann Land against Jerry Lewis Productions, Inc. Miss Land, a secretary, spoke to Jerry Lewis, a motion-picture producer, in Blum's soda fountain, and asked him to consider a script she had written with him in mind. Lewis sat down with her, and there ensued a conversation in which she outlined the ideas of her script. Two days later she wrote him she was planning to mail her script the following week. In reply she received a letter from Lewis's manager enclosing a release form for her to sign and return with her script. She did so and returned it to Lewis. The following month the script was returned to her with regrets. When the case came up on a motion for judgment by the defendants, the court said:

> Producers may become obliged to pay for commonplace ideas, no matter how tired, threadbare, faded, and shopworn the ideas, if

they have conducted themselves in such a manner that a promise to pay can be inferred. The inference may easily arise, for example, even from the conduct and telephone calls of the producer's secretary.

Yet, said the court, in spite of ease of inference, there must be some type of agreement, an agreement made in advance. In Miss Land's case the court said that while the release might have barred recovery for the ideas expressed in the script, it would not necessarily provide immunity for ideas disclosed earlier in the soda fountain, saying, "In this State [California] producers who discuss plots with would-be script writers, even at cocktail parties or in soda fountains, do so at their peril." The court set the case for trial as to whether she had disclosed anything new and original under conditions which would give rise to an implied contract.

In all of the cases there has been, as far as we can ascertain, only one verdict at the hands of a jury in a case based upon the disclosure of an idea. In that case David Robbins sued on the theory that he had disclosed an original idea developed and expressed in program format for the program known as "Dotto." The format was tangible enough physical property of value in such concrete form as to give rise to an action for its appropriation for profit upon the theory of an implied contract to pay for such a utilization. The court considering the case said:

> To establish a contract implied in fact plaintiff would have to show that the parties in their dealings with each other in regard to the subject matter understood that if the defendants used the plaintiff's idea and material it would pay what it was reasonably worth; that upon that understanding defendants did so use the material; and that this arrangement was arrived at not by express words but by such conduct, looked at in the context of the trade and their familiarity with it, that makes it clear that such was the understanding they reached.

The court discussed damages and said:

If in support of the theory of contract implied in fact no proof of market value can be made, recourse should be had to the method of proof competent on the quasi-contract theory, the actual profits made by defendant's appellants through the utilization of plaintiff's material.

This would constitute a practical and reasonable alternative in evaluating damage if, as the present record suggests, no independent market value may be established for the material in format. So that this method constitutes not only the basis for establishing damage in quasi-contract but it is also an alternative method in an action on implied contract under the indicated circumstance of the absence of an established market.

The Court of Appeals of the State of New York said with regard to the law:

> In this case the parties negotiated for the conveyance of the plaintiff's property and failed to agree upon the terms. Since the property was thereafter taken and made valueless for its owner, the law imposes an obligation to pay its reasonable value where the parties dealt with each other in the context of an intention of payment for its use. . . .
>
> Opinion evidence of the value of the property was properly admitted. . . .

The verdict of the jury was upheld and a judgment of approximately $188,000 was paid.

It is thus evident when all the elements of novelty, originality, disclosure under promise to pay or implied promise to pay, are present, and opinion evidence is available as to value of the idea which has been submitted in concrete form, then an idea can be protected.

Chapter 9

✎ LIBEL

Libel is one of the most troublesome dangers in the fields of communication. Even writers who might be presumed to be aware of the danger inherent in the publishing of unlawful references to other human beings and institutions suffer inadvertently. Supreme Court justices, cabinet ministers, law school professors, and others have been amerced in damages.

Although the First Amendment to the Constitution provides that Congress shall pass no law limiting the freedom of the press, and although all of the states have such provision in their constitutions, libel is an exception to the limitation. For libel lies in that category of "fighting words" which, from earliest times, have notoriously tended to a breach of the peace, and is therefore excluded from the constitutional protection of free speech.

Since libel is a limitation on free speech the tendency in recent cases has been to permit a wide latitude of discussion and criticism, particularly where public interests and persons in the public eye who are seeking to influence society are concerned. Freedom of expression upon public questions is secured by the First Amendment, and the Supreme Court has expressed its belief in the controlling significance of "public issues" and "public questions" as the keystones of privileged speech.

The dignity of man in terms of reputation and position in the community when attacked by libel is determined by the mores of the society in which such attacks occur and the time when they are made.

Throughout the United States words that in one community might even be considered laudatory are libelous in another. The personality of man is a condition and a function of man considered as a part of the group. So a scale of words may place particular language either high or low, as it affects the values ranging from inane conceit and vapid vanity to a sense of pride and honor which have objective justification. In the relationship of people, whether it involves their home, their business, their health or sex life, libelous words may intrude to do substantial damage. It is for this damage that the law of libel gives recourse.

Libel, like other ills, may be prevented by careful and studied examination before the emission of material. Libel in law is a tort, that is, a civil wrong, which is distinguishable from slander by the permanence of form which it has. It has been said: "What gives the sting to the writing is its permanence of form. The spoken word dissolves, but the written one abides and perpetuates the scandal." That permanent form may be printed or written words, pictures, cartoons, effigies, or any expressive symbol which may be utilized for communication. Slander is of lesser degree because it occurs in the more temporary form of the spoken word. The tort of libel is a creature of the common law whose expressions and definitions are found in the judicial decisions of the courts and in statutes. In addition, libel is a crime in many states of the Union. It is so created by statute which defines the nature of the libel and also defines the privileges and immunities to libel.

Criminal libel, which is far less resorted to than civil libel for redress, is prosecuted by an organized society rather than by the individual who has suffered.

The definitions of libel are many. With the laws of fifty states and the courts of the United States all to be looked to, it is obvious that in almost every case some new distinction will be added. The United States Supreme Court has defined it as follows: "A libel is harmful on its face; if a man sees fit to publish manifestly hurtful statements concerning an individual without other justification . . . the usual principles of tort will make him liable if the statements are false or are true only of someone else. An unprivileged falsehood need not entail universal hatred to constitute a cause of action." (*Peck* v. *Tribune*.) One should note in connection with this definition the statement that it need not cause all of society to hate the person libeled, thus limiting the area within which the libel must circulate to have effect. The Supreme Court of the United States has also defined libel as "an utterance tending to impugn the honesty, virtue, or reputation, or publish the alleged or natural defects of a person and thereby expose him to public hatred, contempt, or ridicule." Observe here the inclusion in the definition of the "alleged or natural defects." (*Dorr* v. *U.S.*) Another of that court's definitions holds: "Every publication, either by writing, printing, or pictures, which charges upon or imputes to any person that which renders him liable to punishment, or which is calculated to make him infamous, odious or ridiculous, is *prima facie* a libel. . . ." (*White* v. *Nicholls*.)

In New York it has been stated: "A malicious publication tending to expose a person to ridicule, contempt, hatred or degradation of character is libelous." (*Byrnes* v. *Mathews*.) "A publication is libelous on its face when the words impute to the plaintiff the commission of a crime or a contagious disorder tending to exclude him from society, or when the injurious words are spoken or published with respect to his profession or trade, or to disparage him in a public office, or tend to bring him into ridicule and contempt." (*McFadden* v. *Morning Journal*.)

Another New York court held that "Words which tend to expose the character of the plaintiff to the ridicule and contempt of the community, whether they impute a punishable offense or not, are actionable when put forth in the shape of written or printed slander. The proposition that the imputation of a previous, vicious and corrupt life tends necessarily and directly to degrade the individual in the estimation of the community at the time of the publication of the libel is too obvious to require argument. Where a libel was published imputing corrupt conduct to the plaintiff in his office of a Senator of the State, his term of office having expired, it is a mistake to suppose that the ground of the action is the libel upon his official character. It is the calumny against his private character, charging him with having been guilty of previous misconduct, seriously impeaching his integrity and honor, and which tends to degrade him in the opinion of the public, of which he complains." (*Cramer* v. *Riggs*.)

So each of the courts in defining libel has added varied words and terms. A general summation of the judicial definitions of libel would probably serve to crystallize its meaning: False written or printed words, symbols, signs, pictures, or other methods of expression which expose or tend to expose a person to contumely, contempt, shame, disrepute, and ridicule, including words which tend to degrade the individual or lessen him in the estimation of an appreciable portion of the community, or that portion of the community which affects or may affect his personality or his business, profession, or calling, and malicious publications tending to blacken reputations or to expose the object of the libel to public hatred, contempt, and ridicule are libelous. A communication is libelous which offers the idea either that the person to whom it refers has been guilty of some penal offense or that he has been guilty of some act or omission which, although not a penal offense, is disgraceful to him as a member of society, and the natural consequence of which is to bring him into contempt among honorable persons. Or if a communication points out that he has some moral vice or physical defect or disease which renders him unfit for intercourse with respectable society and, as such, would cause him to be generally shunned or avoided; or that he is a notorious, bad, or infamous character, it is libelous. Communications are libelous which impair the character by imputing vicious motive or unsocial conduct; which reduce the respectability; which lessen the social position by exposing to shame, to disgrace, and to ridicule; which imply lowered mentality or loathsome physical disease; or which make a criminal charge or charge of other unlawfulness. Generally, communications are libelous which tend to degrade in the estimation of the community, to deprive the individual of public confidence and the temporal advantages which result naturally from a reputation for honesty and sobriety; which would cause him to be shunned or avoided in his business, profession, or occupation.

In addition to the judicial definitions the laws of the several states contain statutory definitions. For instance, California provides:

> Libel is a false and unprivileged publication by writing, printing, effigy, picture, or other fixed representation to the eye, which exposes any person to hatred, contempt, ridicule, or obloquy, or which causes him to be shunned or avoided, or which has a tendency to injure him in his occupation.

Texas provides an unusually detailed description:

> The written, printed or published statement, to come within the definition of libel, must convey the idea either:
> 1. That the person to whom it refers has been guilty of some penal offense; or
> 2. That he has been guilty of some act or omission which, though not a penal offense, is disgraceful to him as a member of society, and the natural consequence of which is to bring him into contempt among honorable persons; or
> 3. That he has some moral vice, or physical or mental defect or disease, which renders him unfit for intercourse with respectable society, and such as should cause him to be generally avoided; or

4. That he is notoriously of bad or infamous character; or

5. That any person in office or a candidate therefor is dishonest and therefore unworthy of such office or that while in office he has been guilty of some malfeasance rendering him unworthy of the place.

From both the common-law definitions and the statutes we may gather the truth of what the Supreme Court of the United States said when it quoted Lord Mansfield with approval: "Whenever a man publishes, he publishes at his peril," paraphrasing Pollock, who in his work on tort said: "A man defames his neighbor at his peril."

The definitions are not enough. They act as a guide for determination. Words have many facets and many interpretations. Their values change with time, with place, and with association. Whether or not a word has a libelous connotation will therefore require analysis and perception in terms of its milieu and period. Words are but symbols and, like all symbols, have a varying impress. The red flag elates the Russian but enrages John Bull. To bear the cross is noble; to double-cross, corrupt. Dealers in the symbols of communication must develop a hypersensitivity so that the buzzer, the gong, or the light, sounds and appears in the mind and warns of the impending danger. As Mr. Justice Holmes has said: "A word is not a crystal, transparent and unchanged; it is the skin of a living thought and may vary greatly in color and content according to the circumstances and the time in which it is used." As the relationships of men and women change, as their forms of organization change, the significance of allegedly libelous words changes. The libel of yesterday may be praise today, or vice versa.

This is particularly true of words with political and social imputation. Currently, the word "Communist" is a word and appellation of frequent use. To call a man a "Communist" in Moscow would certainly not be objectionable to him. It might even be a term of highest praise and social esteem.

To call a man a "Communist" in New York might in some circles be deemed praise. In some it might be harmful, and in some it might even be a word legally libelous. If one were to call a man in the Deep South a "Communist," it might hold him up to scorn in his community and certainly be libelous if he were running for office.

So important is the element of currency that the courts of New York, within a period of two years, wrote conflicting opinions as to whether or not the word "Communist" is libelous within a period of transition. The political animus of the word changed that quickly. So the word "Fascist" could be a word in point of place and time that was either libelous or nonlibelous. When Winston Churchill was praising Mussolini and countenancing colored shirts in England, the word "Fascist" would not be libelous. After the "stab in the back," it could have been libelous. The word "Nazi," at a time when men were praising Hitler for causing smoke to rise from all the stacks in Germany, might not be libelous. After the disclosures of Büchenwald, it might be. Undoubtedly while we were at war it was. Thus the word "atheist" might be a word of disapprobation in a devoutly religious country and a word of praise in other countries.

Many other words have been accepted as having new significances in the light of the day in which they are used, and many slang words and expressions have been accepted as having the meaning which the public ascribes to them, despite their dictionary definition, or sometimes despite the fact that they do not appear in the dictionary at all. The courts, in libel actions, are constantly taking cognizance of the presence of new words and their changing connotations. One of them has said: "Dictionary meanings, however, are not conclusive. English is not a dead but a virile language, flexible, progressive, continually being enriched from all sorts of sources, its common speech made piquant and interesting by slang and jargon, often better understood by the man in the street than the classic diction of its great masters. The noun 'combine' meaning a secret combination for the purpose of committing fraud, a conspiracy, was added to the language by a witness on a famous trial in the City of New York in 1886, and is now a dictionary word. Of course there are innumerable instances of like character."

Similarly, in a case involving the use of the word "racket," it was held: "The meaning for which the plaintiff contends is that it is the engaging in an occupation to make money illegitimately, and implies continuity of behavior. The less recent meaning, for which the defendant contends, is that it is a trick, or a dodge, or a scheme, and that in the context in which it was used it had reference to the single incident which precipitated the publication, and does not necessarily imply continuity of behavior. Which meaning should be accepted is a question of fact for the jury."

In a case in which libel consisted of a statement in which it was said that the plaintiff gave a "rubber check," it was held: "It would appear that a jury will be entitled to say whether the plaintiff, by closing his account while a check was outstanding, was guilty of issuing a 'rubber check.' Such a term is slang, and the precise definition has not been so firmly fixed that this court can take judicial notice or, for that matter, be expected to know its precise meaning as a matter of law."

When libel is considered as having been stated, not through a single word, but rather by a group of words, then the problem of construction becomes more involved. Recognizing this, a court has held: "Perfectly innocent words, standing by themselves, may be thrown into such juxtaposition that together they become libelous."

There are, however, certain general canons of construction adopted by the courts which are helpful if one considers language, even before its use, in the light of what its implications will be when used and, if used, challenged. Words should be construed according to their plain and obvious meaning. They should be understood to mean what they would ordinarily be understood to mean by persons generally of ordinary ability and intelligence. In the case of the printed word, the test of interpretation would be measured by the ordinary intelligence and understanding of persons acquainted with the subject or topic being discussed in the light of the community's general understanding. If the words are capable of a fair and natural construction which is not libelous, then the critical or malignant mind may not torture the expression into a charge of criminal or disgraceful conduct. Merely possible and farfetched constructions will not make inoffensive language offensive. The test is whether, to the mind of an intelligent man, the tenor of the article and the language used naturally imports a criminal or disgraceful charge.

One court said: "It is inconsistent with a due regard for the protection of the public from libelous attacks that obsolete or antiquated and practically unused meanings of words should be searched for and studied out, to show that at some remote period of history they were not opprobrious, in order to shield a party publishing and using them in respect to another in that now only used and universally established sense, that holds him up to public reproach and indignation. . . ." Another court has held that "The libel law is not a system of technicalities, but reasonable regulations whereby the public may be furnished news and information, but not false stories about anyone. When the truth is so near the facts as published that fine and shaded distinctions must be drawn and words pressed out of their ordinary usage to sustain a charge of libel, no legal harm has been done. . . ."

In a recent decision a court wrote that a newspaper publication must be measured by its natural and probable effect on the average lay reader's mind in determining whether it is libelous.

In determining whether words are libelous, they must be given their ordinary popular meaning, and if they are susceptible of two meanings, one of which is libelous and the other innocent, the libelous meaning should not be adopted and the innocent meaning rejected as a matter of course, but the jury should determine in what sense the words are used. In construing words alleged to be libelous, the court cannot invade the realm of conjecture but must confine itself to the natural, ordinary, and commonly accepted meanings of the words themselves, considered with other facts alleged in the complaint.

Nor is a statement of fact in fictional form relieved of liability. Words that depict as imaginary events twisted or distorted from real life are actionable. If a newspaper publishes news as fiction or fiction as news, it does so at its peril, for the courts have said that reputations may not be traduced with impunity, whether in the literary forms of works of fiction or in jest.

Curtis B. Dall, son-in-law of President Franklin D. Roosevelt, sued Time, Inc., for libel. He alleged the following statement was made in *Time* Magazine:

> Son-in-Law. "Yesterday Curtis B. Dall, son-in-law of President Roosevelt, shot himself in the White House in the presence of his estranged wife and Mrs. Roosevelt. He died later in the day."

The above statements were in quotation marks. Immediately thereafter was the following, which was not quoted:

> If such an event were so briefly reported in the U. S. Press, neither readers nor publishers would be satisfied. Yet almost an exact parallel of that tragedy occurred in the Hotel Continental apartment of Premier Gaston Doumergue last week. Mention was limited to a few slender paragraphs in New York newspapers and a close-mouthed silence on the part of French officialdom.

Then followed another paragraph, also not quoted, which gave details of the suicide of one Enzo de Bonze, son-in-law of the French Prime Minister, Gaston Doumergue, in the presence of the Prime Minister's wife. At the trial it was shown that, when the article appeared, Mr. Dall was considerably upset in his business relationships and a great many people called his office to inquire whether he had in fact committed suicide, and thereby both he himself and his partners were caused great embarrassment. *Time* claimed that the use of a hypothetical comparison to make clear the significance of news was a journalistic device very familiar to its readers. The managing editor of *Time* testified that the part of the article in quotation marks was not really a quotation, but what he termed "the imaginary mind of *Time*, but not the serious reporting mind of *Time*." He called the first paragraph a "Dutch lead" and he then defined that to mean "to get the reader's attention with a startling statement which may or may not be true, but to get his attention and then carry him on into the story and tell him what you have to tell him." A verdict for *Time* was set aside by the court on the ground that the article tended to injure Mr. Dall, no matter what the intention of *Time* may have been. The court stated that words need not necessarily impute actual conduct to the plaintiff. It is sufficient that they render him contemptible and ridiculous.

In doing this the court followed one of the leading cases in New York, *Triggs* v. *Sun Printing & Publishing Association,* where the words published were alleged to have been so merely in jest. The court stated: "If, however, they can be regarded as having been published as a jest, then it should be said that however desirable it may be that the readers of and the writers for the public prints shall be amused, it is manifest that neither such readers nor writers should be furnished such amusement at the expense of the reputation or business of another. In the language of Joy, C. B.: 'The principle is clear that a person shall not be allowed to murder another's reputation in jest'; or, in the words of Smith, B., in the same case: 'If a man in jest conveys a serious imputation, he jests at his peril.' We are of the opinion that one assaulting the reputation or business of another in a public newspaper cannot justify it upon the ground that it was a mere jest, unless it is perfectly manifest from the language employed that it could in no respect be regarded as an attack upon the reputation or business of the person to whom it related."

LIBEL IN POLITICS AND PUBLIC AFFAIRS

Prior to 1964, publishers printed materials susceptible of a defamatory meaning at their own peril. However, in 1964, the case of *New York Times* v. *Sullivan* reached the Supreme Court of the United States. In a landmark decision in that case, the Supreme Court of the United States elaborated the First and Fourteenth Amendment guarantees of free speech and press as they bore on the problem of accommodating the law of defamation to our historic policy of fostering free and un-inhibited discussion of matters of public interest.

In *Sullivan*, the court held: "The constitutional guarantees require . . . a federal rule that prohibits a public official from recovering damages for a defamatory falsehood relating to his official conduct unless he proves that the statement was made with 'actual malice'—that is, with knowledge that it was false or with reckless disregard of whether it was false or not."

The court there noted that

The general proposition that freedom of expression upon public questions is secured by the First Amendment has long been set-tled by our decisions. The constitutional safeguard . . . "was fashioned to assure unfettered interchange of ideas for the bringing about of political and social changes desired by the people." . . . We consider this case against the background of a profound na-tional commitment to the principle that debate on public issues should be uninhibited, robust, and wide open. . . .

In subsequent cases, the court expressed its belief in the con-trolling significance in "public issues" and "public questions."

It further held that an erroneous statement is inevitable in free debate and it must be protected if the freedom of expression is to have the "breathing space" that it needs to survive. The court said, "Speech concerning public affairs is more than self-expression; it is the essence of self-government." Where there is tension between the interest in preventing and redressing attacks upon reputation and the interest and the values nurtured by the First and Fourteenth Amendments, the court took the position that the Constitution must limit the rights afforded by the law of defamation. This interest of the people in limiting the right to sue for libel, was formulated in the "public figure" rule developed by the court, and was applied to bar suits of candidates for Congress and even to persons connected with public officials, and was extended to bar suits by persons in the public eye, such as General Edwin Walker, the John Birch Society, and Linus Pauling. When Linus Pauling sued, the court said:

> We also feel that a rational distinction cannot be founded on the assumption that criticism of private citizens who seek to lead in the determination of national policy will be less important to the public interest than will criticism of government officials. A lobbyist, a person dominant in a political party, the head of any pressure group, or any significant leader may possess a capacity for influencing public policy as great or greater than that of a comparatively minor public official, who is clearly subject to *New York Times*. It would seem, therefore, that if such a person seeks to realize upon his capacity to guide public policy and in the process is criticized, he should have no greater remedy than does his counterpart in public office.

For similar reasons, the John Birch Society was also disqualified from suing.

This privilege to criticize public persons, persons in the spotlight, was not, however, an absolute privilege. If it could be proven that the words had been published with actual malice or with reckless disregard for the truth, an action for libel would still lie. Thus Wallace Butts, a well-known figure in the college football coaching ranks, won his action against the publisher of the *Saturday Evening Post* which had published an article charging him with having fixed a football game between the University of Georgia and the University of Alabama. In permitting Butts's suit, the court held that a public figure "may recover damages for defamatory falsehood whose substance makes substantial damage to reputation apparent, on a showing of highly unreasonable conduct constituting an extreme departure from the standards of investigation and reporting ordinarily adhered to by responsible publishers."

Not as successful, however, was General Edwin Walker, a private citizen at the time of instituting the libel action, but one who had attained some political prominence. He sued the Associated Press for distributing a news dispatch which, in giving an eye-witness account of the riots attendant to the integration of the University of Mississippi, stated that General Walker had taken command of the violent crowd, had personally led a charge against federal marshals, and had encouraged and advised the rioters. In upsetting a state court verdict awarding the General $500,000 for compensatory damages, and $300,000 for punitive damages, the Supreme Court held that in contrast to the Butts article, the Associated Press had received the information from a correspondent who was present at two of the events and gave every indication of being trustworthy and competent. His dispatches were internally consistent and would not have seemed unreasonable to one familiar with General Walker's prior publicized statements on the underlying controversy.

At one point it seemed that the constitutional guarantees announced in the *New York Times* case might be extended beyond news reports involving public figures, to include reports involving areas of public concern, regardless of the fame or anonymity of the plaintiff. Thus in *Rosenbloom* v. *Metromedia*, a case involving a private citizen who was arrested for possessing obscene materials and labelled a "peddler of girlie books" in a radio broadcast, it was held by a plurality of the Supreme Court that the social importance of the issue reported on, and not the status of the person as a public figure, protected the radio station against liability for defamation. However, more recent Supreme Court decisions indicate a sharp reversal of this trend and have rejected the *Rosenbloom* criteria, while at the same time substantially narrowing the definition of who is a public figure. As a result, the likelihood of successful suits against publishers who print material susceptible of defamatory meaning even in the absence of malice has been greatly increased.

This reversal of the *New York Times* trend first became apparent in the case of *Gertz* v. *Robert Welch*, involving a suit over an article published by the John Birch Society which portrayed a prominent Chicago lawyer as a communist-fronter, and which accused him of having "framed" a Chicago policeman in a murder case, in addition to implying that he had a criminal record. Although Mr. Gertz was a prominent community figure, had authored four books, and had appeared on radio and television programs, the Supreme Court held that he was not a public figure and did not have to prove actual malice to win his action. The category of "public figure," the court said, should only be applied to those "who have voluntarily thrust themselves to the forefront of particular public controversies in order to influence the resolution of the issues involved."

This narrowing of the public figure exception was given a particularly literal application in the 1976 case of *Firestone* v. *Time Magazine*.

After six years of marriage, Russell A. Firestone, Jr., heir to the tire fortune, won a much-publicized divorce in a suit initiated by his wife, Mary Alice Sullivan Firestone, an active member of the sporting set. In its "Milestones" column, *Time* Magazine had reported that the divorce had been granted on the grounds of mental cruelty and adultery, adding that the trial, which had run, on and off, for seventeen months, had produced enough testimony of extra-marital adventures, as the judge put it, "to make Dr. Freud's hair curl." Although the judge's comment was accurately reported, and although Mr. Firestone had based his counterclaim for divorce on the grounds of adultery and mental cruelty, the court had not, technically, made these the bases for its decree, although the report of its decision was somewhat unclear. Mrs. Firestone sued *Time*.

During the long divorce trial, Mrs. Firestone had held several news conferences. Nevertheless, the Supreme Court held that she was not a public figure because she "did not assume any role of special prominence in the affairs of society other than perhaps Palm Beach society, and she did not thrust herself to the forefront of any particular public controversy in order to influence the resolution of the issues involved in it."

In an opinion authored by Justice Rehnquist, the court went on to say that a divorce trial was not itself a "public controversy," and that private plaintiffs should not lose their right to bring a defamation suit simply because they had been engaged in civil court proceedings.

The court's decision was especially harsh since the official report on which the *Time* article had relied, was itself ambiguous about the grounds for which the divorce had been awarded. Nevertheless, Justice Rehnquist wrote, *Time* might well be liable for its "Milestones" piece, even if the meaning of the trial court's decision was unclear, since ambiguity in an official report "does not license [*Time*] to choose among several conceivable interpretations the one most damaging to [Mrs. Firestone]." In so ruling, the court apparently rejected an earlier case involving *Time* in which it had been held that where an official document is ambiguous, the choice of one of several rational interpretations is insufficient to support a finding of actual malice.

Finally, the *Firestone* case is important because Mrs. Firestone did not claim any damage to her reputation, long the traditional basis for a libel action. Rather, her complaint seemed based on emotional injuries, usually associated with actions for invasion of privacy. In allowing her libel action to proceed, the Supreme Court not only marked a sharp departure from its approach in the *New York Times* case, it also expanded the common-law action of libel to include an award for damages resulting from a publisher's negligence, without proof of actual injury to the plaintiff's reputation.

As a result of both the *Gertz* and *Firestone* cases, it is clear that the Supreme Court is taking a less protective attitude toward First Amendment rights when weighed against the rights of individual plaintiffs bringing defamation suits. Since under current law the several states may determine their own standard for fault in a libel action, so long as they do not impose liability without fault, and since both the *Gertz* and *Firestone* decisions have narrowed the scope of the public figure exception, it is likely that publishers will either have to impose some form of self-censorship on their news reporting, or be forced to contend with an increasing number of libel actions brought against them by individuals who need only prove negligence in order to collect damages.

CRITICISM IS AN EXCEPTION TO THE LAW OF LIBEL

When people submit their work to the public, whether as artists, writers, actors, playwrights, athletes or members of the professions, then that work is subject to criticism, not only fair but unfair. This exception to the law of libel has been summed up in the following language:

> The law does not give reparation for all derogatory or disparaging words. If the articles in question are nothing more than a fair and honest comment on a matter of public interest, they

are not libelous. The rule is well settled that the acts and conduct of one who, by his position or occupation, commands the attention and interest of the public, may lawfully be made the subject of candid and honest comment and criticism, not only by the press, but by the people generally. Everyone has a right to discuss the personal deportment, behavior, and qualifications of one who occupies the public eye much more freely than he has to talk about a private individual in whose affairs the public has little or no interest. Just and reasonable criticism of a public person is not libelous. It would indeed be a sorry day for the country if men in public life were beyond censure. (*Hoeppner* v. *Dunkirk Printing Co.*)

On another phase of fair comment the higher court said:

Everyone has a right to comment on matters of public interest and concern, provided he does so fairly and with an honest purpose. Such comments or criticisms are not libelous, however severe in their terms, unless they are written maliciously. Thus, it has been held that books, prints, pictures, and statuary publicly exhibited, and the architecture of public buildings, and actors and exhibitors are all the legitimate subject of newspaper criticism, and such criticism fairly and honestly made is not libelous, however strong the terms of censure may be.

New Mexico and Texas provide, by statute:

It is no offense to publish any criticism or examination of any work of literary science or art, or any opinion as to the qualifications or merits of the author of such work.

As to authors, Lord Ellenboro has said:

Every man who publishes a book commits himself to the judgment of the public, and anyone may comment on his performance. The critic does a great service to the public who writes down any vapid or useless publication such as ought never to have appeared. Nothing can be conceived more threatening to the liberty of the press than the species of action before the Court.

In one of the opinons in the remarkable series of libel cases which were brought by James Fenimore Cooper, the court said:

To say that he is an author, editor, or reviewer is but saying that he is engaged in a profession which has been and may be made eminently useful to mankind and which would, therefore, seem to call for peculiar protection and encouragement. That the law should allow his production to be criticized with great freedom is not denied.

The court concluded that no action would lie for criticism of the works of an author in the abstract unless

> the criticism be grossly false and work for a special damage to the proprietor of the book at which the strictures are leveled. (*Cooper* v. *Stone*.)

Calling an author a plagiarist is an attack upon him in his professional integrity and ability, and it therefore follows that such a charge is a libel per se; that is, one which requires no further proof of special damage. For instance, Georgette Carneal wrote a book entitled *The Great Day* which was published by Liveright, Inc. Walter Winchell wrote in his column in the *Daily Mirror*: "Helen Woodward rewrote Georgette Carneal's tome *Great Day*." Miss Carneal sued, alleging that by this comment Mr. Winchell had libeled her, since it would tend to show that she had falsified her authorship of the novel and also would make people believe that she had had to have her book rewritten prior to publication, and had not given credit therefor. Miss Carneal alleged that such a charge against an author was serious, and would tend to discredit her in the field of her professional endeavor. Mr. Winchell moved to dismiss her complaint, but it was held good.

Dr. Louis Berg was a physician specializing in neurology and psychiatry, as well as an author. He wrote two articles attacking certain radio programs and their effect upon the audience. The court said: "He could hardly expect a gentle or meek reply. On the contrary, he could expect what he had given and should be willing to take it."

The court further said:

> When the plaintiff thus submitted his professional work to the public and thereby appealed for its support and approval, he was

bound to expect, with equal equanimity, praise or blame directed at the work itself. Fair and legitimate criticism is always permitted upon any work to which the attention of the public has been invited. It would not be a libel upon the plaintiff to say that the product of his pen was not good. Whatever is written cannot be said to be libelous except something which decreases or lowers plaintiff is his professional character. . . . Criticism of so much of another's activities as are matters of public concern is fair, if the criticism, even though defamatory, is based on facts truly stated, free from imputations of corrupt or dishonest motives on the part of the person whose work is criticized, is an honest expression of the writer's real opinion or belief, and is not made solely for the purpose of causing hurt to the other. Mere exaggeration, slight irony or wit, and all those delightful touches of style which go to make an article readable, do not push beyond the limits of fair comment. Facts do not cease to be facts because they are mixed with the fair and expected comment of the storyteller who adds to the recital a little touch of his piquant pen. . . .

The criticism need not express an opinion with which any person of reasonable intelligence and judgment could possibly agree. Unlike a personal attack upon a public man, the fact that the comment or criticism is one which is not reasonably warranted by the facts upon which it is based or is fantastic or extravagant, is immaterial. If the public is to be aided in forming its judgment upon matters of public interest by a free interchange of opinion, it is essential that honest criticism and comment, no matter how foolish or prejudiced, be privileged. It must not constitute an attack upon the author except in respect to the worth of his work. . . .

Judge Learned Hand simply stated the rule:

It is indeed not true that all ridicule . . . or all disagreeable comment . . . is actionable; a man must not be too thin-skinned or a self-important prig. . . .

This rule, which allows for fair and free comment, applies to all professions and all persons who submit their work to the public. This includes teachers, ministers, editors, lawyers, doctors, architects. The privilege, however, may never be used as an occasion for personal attack.

Charles Reade sued the *Round Table Magazine* for an article entitled "Did Charles Reade Write 'Griffith Gaunt'?" which asserted doubt whether he was the real author of the work. The court said in finding judgment for Reade:

> In criticizing the products of an author, the law allows considerable latitude. The interests of literature and science require that the products of authors shall be subject to fair criticism; that even some animadversion may be permitted, unless it appears that the critic, under the pretext of reviewing the book, takes an opportunity of attacking the character of the author, and of holding him up as an object of ridicule, hatred, or contempt. In other words, the critic may say what he pleases of the literary merits or demerits of the published production of an author; but with respect to his personal rights relating to his reputation, the critic has no more privilege than any other person in assuming the business of criticism. For instance, he may say that the matter is crude, forced, and unnatural, that it betrays poverty of thought and abounds with commonplaces and platitudes, being altogether flat, stale and unprofitable, and that its style is affected, obscure, and involved. He may say that it is execrable, but he cannot say that the author himself is execrable, or that he is personally affected or absurd or wayward.

The obverse of the picture is a special sensitivity on the part of the law to see that such professional persons are not unnecessarily attacked so that they will be injured in their profession, business, or calling. The general doctrine has been laid down:

> The law allows this form of action, not only to protect a man's character as such, but to protect him in his occupation also against injurious imputations. It recognizes the right of a man to live, and the necessity of labor, and will not permit one to assail by words the pecuniary credit of another, except at the peril, in case they are untrue, of answering in damages.
>
> The principle is clearly stated by Bayley, J., in *Whittaker* v. *Bradley:* "Whatever words have a tendency to hurt, or are calculated to prejudice a man who seeks his livelihood by any trade or business, are actionable." When proved to have been spoken

in relation thereto, the action is supported, and unless the defendant shows a lawful excuse, the plaintiff is entitled to recover without allegation or proof of special damage, because both the falsity of the words and resulting damage are presumed. . . . "Words," says Starkie, "are libelous if they affect a person in his profession, trade or business, by imputing to him any kind of fraud, dishonesty, misconduct, incapacity, unfitness, or want of any necessary qualification in the exercise thereof." (*Moore* v. *Francis*.)

THE SO-CALLED DOCTRINE OF ANONYMOUS LIBEL

It is not essential to recovery in an action for libel that the complaining party be correctly named in the alleged libelous writing. A different name or no name will not protect if the writing was really intended to be of the complainant. On the other hand, the use of a name unknown to the writer to describe a person will not subject the writer to damages if he did not intend to describe the named person. An important case in point is that which was brought against James T. Farrell in connection with a book written by him entitled *Bernard Clare*. It dealt with an aspiring young writer by the name of Bernard Clare, who went from Chicago to New York City to pursue a writing career, who never actually did any writing for publication. Clare's thoughts, hopes, observations, and sordid experiences were dealt with in considerable detail. The plaintiff was named Bernard Clare, but had never gone from Chicago to New York City, or did any writing in New York City or the eastern United States. Apart from the identity of plaintiff as a writer, the book did not identify him as the person about whom the author was writing except through the coincidence of name. The court said:

It would be an astonishing doctrine if every writer of fiction were required to make a search among all the records available in this nation which might tabulate the names and activities of millions of people in order to determine whether perchance one of the characters in the contemplated book designated as novel may have the same name and occupation as a real person. At least some latitude must be given authors in their selection of names for characters so that the production of fictional literature may continue, and the mean, the base, and the good of the characters therein fearlessly portrayed. In a country of this size, which contains all nationalities, it seems quite obvious that, if an author used a name which was possessed by no one, it would be pure accident. Obviously there are no readily available records which would furnish anyone all the desired information in that regard. Although some type of search, the extent thereof depending upon the type of material contained in the book and other circumstances, might reasonably be required in some cases, it seems absurd to place upon the author of this book the Herculean task and duty to search every directory, gazetteer, or telephone book for that purpose. (*Clare* v. *Farrell.*)

The mere fact that plaintiff might have suffered damages through the ignorance of people in assuming that the novel depicted plaintiff's life was not sufficient to establish a cause of action.

But suppose the character to be real and the name to be fictitious. Here we have a case frequently occurring in fiction, where description and characteristics are drawn from living persons, even though the names of the characters differ from those borne by the person or persons described. The author will be unprotected if such person can prove that reasonable persons believed he was meant to be the individual who was described in the fiction.

One Neil Callahan sued Doubleday, Doran and Co. and the author, Josef Israels II, on the grounds that a character called "Ralph Holloran" in a book published by that firm really represented him. He alleged that the defamation was accomplished in the literary form of a work of fiction, and that the libel consisted of a skillfully painted picture. The background was made up of many allusions not in and of themselves libelous, to incidents, circumstances, and facts in the life and associations of himself and his wife. In the foreground were set forth the alleged libelous statements. The court said with regard thereto: "The background and shadows alone were not harmful. The distorted figures and false lights in the foreground were in and of themselves damaging. The combination and setting, and the ruinous result of the finished picture, however, was the evil accomplished. I think, under the circumstances, that plaintiff was justified in his allegations of fact in exhibiting the entire picture so that the full libel might be exposed, not alone in its central figures and highlights, but also in its minor features, details and shadings." (*Callahan* v. *Israels*.) Since the plantiff alleged the application to him of the defamatory matter, the complaint was held good.

It is not enough, in such a case, for the person complaining merely to state that he was the particular person intended, nor is it enough to state that the character in the book resembles an actual person. The question which such a person must establish to the satisfaction of a jury is whether it can reasonably be believed that the character in the allegedly libelous work is intended to portray the person complaining. If the work is reasonably understood as portraying an actual person, it is not only immaterial that the author or playwright did not so intend, but it is equally immaterial that he had no reason to expect that it would be so understood, as if, for instance, he did not know or had no reason to know of the existence of the actual person.

If we can assume a case in which the author coins a name and creates an entirely imaginary character which, nevertheless, can, under that name and description, reasonably be believed to describe a living person, then the author is liable. Of course, anyone complaining of such libel has the burden of proving the application to himself.

George Bronson Howard wrote a sensational novel called *God's Man*. The novel depicted somewhat realistically the adventures of one Arnold L'Hommedieu in New York's underworld and elsewhere, and contained chapters entitled "Arnold's Adventures in Plunderland," "Sons of Subterranea," among others. A chapter, which in the table of contents bore the caption "Justice—a la Corigan," in the body of the book was headed "Justice—a la Cornigan." The hero was brought into Jefferson Market Court in New York City (a court in which Joseph E. Corrigan frequently sat as magistrate) in a chapter which described the disposition of cases by a Magistrate Cornigan. Another chapter, entitled "The Gay Life," portrayed Cornigan even more offensively as an associate of low and depraved characters. Magistrate Joseph E. Corrigan sued, alleging that the magistrate described in the book as "Cornigan" was intended to mean him. The court said that the inference from the unsavory details, as related to the facts, was unmistakable; that the author Howard deliberately intended to vilify Magistrate Corrigan under the barely fictitious name of Cornigan, and the plaintiff sustained a verdict against Bobbs-Merrill Co., publishers of the book, of $25,000.

The court said that the publishers were as chargeable with publication of libelous matter as if it were spoken of Magistrate Corrigan, even though they were unaware of his existence, or that it was written concerning any existing person. Proof that the chapter actually referred to a living person would sustain his cause of action. Holding to the effect that there was no intention to defame a particular man, or indeed to injure anyone, does not prevent recovery of compensatory damages by one who connects himself with the alleged libel in the publication. At least this may be held in the absence of some special reason for a positive belief that no one existed to whom the description answered. The question is not so much who was aimed at as who was hit. The court continued that works of fiction not infrequently depict as imaginary events in courts of justice or elsewhere which are actually drawn or distorted from real life, saying:

Dickens, in his *Pickwick Papers*, has a well-known court scene of which Mr. Sergeant Ballantine says in his "Experiences" that Mr. Justice Gaselee "has been delivered to posterity as having presided at the famous trial of *Bardel* v. *Pickwick*. I just remember him and he certainly was deaf." Goldwin Smith, the distinguished historian and publicist, said of Disraeli's veiled attack upon him as "The Oxford Professor" in the novel *Lothair* that (*Reminiscences*, p. 171): "He afterwards pursued me across the Atlantic, and tried to brand me, under a perfectly transparent pseudonym,—if 'Oxford Professor' could be called a pseudonym at all,—as a 'social sycophant.' There is surely nothing more dastardly than this mode of stabbing a reputation." The power of Charles Reade's descriptions of prison life in *It's Never Too Late to Mend* and the abuses of private insane asylums in *Hard Cash* are undeniable, although the truth of some of his details was challenged. The novel of purpose, such as *Uncle Tom's Cabin*, often deals with incidents and individuals not wholly imaginary. Reputations may not be traduced with impunity under the literary forms of a work of fiction. (*Corrigan* v. *Bobbs-Merrill Co.*)

An interesting case is the action of *Lew Brown* v. *New York Evening Journal*. Brown was the author of numerous popular songs, including one called "My Song," made popular by Rudy Vallee in the *Scandals*. In one of its columns entitled "The Voice of Broadway," the *New York Evening Journal* printed a note that the song had been written by an eighteen-year-old high-school boy. Brown asserted that "My Song" was an original composition of his and that the imputation of the article was that he was inefficient, dishonest, and lacking in professional ability. The article, as printed, did not contain the names of Brown and his collaborator. The court said, "That the libelous matter did not specifically mention plaintiffs by name is unimportant if the complaint shows that it referred to plaintiffs and would be so understood by the readers." (*Brown* v. *New York Evening Journal.*)

Frequently there is inserted in the beginning of a book the legend: "The characters in this book are fictitious; any resemblance to living persons is purely coincidental." The phrase is probably meaningless in the event of suit based on material contained in the book, if a real person is intended. It is obvious that one cannot delineate a character by a carefully drawn portrait, locate the character in time and place as if it were a real character, and avoid the consequences of such a portrait if it is libelous. If it is nonlibelous, of course, the question does not arise. The only possible use to which this sentence might be put is in the event of action by a person who was not known to the author and where the portrait, if applied to a living person, would be purely accidental. In that event the sentence might have some weight as indicating lack of intention and malice.

ERRORS AND MISTAKES

Although libelous statements may be printed through error or mistake, liability nevertheless follows.

Mr. Justice Oliver Wendell Holmes laid down the law in *Peck* v. *Tribune Company*, saying: "There was some suggestion that the defendant published the portrait by mistake, and without knowledge that it was the plaintiff's portrait, or was not what it purported to be. But the fact, if it was one, was no excuse. If the publication was libelous, the defendant took the risk. As was said of such matters by Lord Mansfield, 'Whenever a man publishes, he publishes at his peril.' . . ."

Everything printed or written which reflects on the character of another and is published without lawful justification or excuse is a libel whatever the intention may have been. The mistake of a reporter may bring about liability. A newspaper cannot avoid responsibility by saying that a reporter, by mistake, used the wrong person's name.

The *Bee-News*, published in Nebraska, published in its home edition a large flashlight picture reaching across four columns, showing a wrestling match in a barn loft. The picture showed some forty people, including some girls. The large-type headline above the picture read: "Battle in Barn. Days of Old Live Again." In the half column right under the picture was this paragraph: "In Tom Walker's barn, west of Florida, two rasslers rassled it out Wednesday night. John Hodges of Tech High took on John Shepard, who takes care of pots and pans in a downtown café." To attract attention to this unimportant event, a semi-ludicrous report describing the meet, at which no admission was charged, was added: "The crowd had a swell time, which it proved by tossing into the ring $18.30 to the men, which was divided between the pot massager and the high-school student."

Inadvertently the reporter had stated that the fight had occurred in Tom Walker's barn, whereas it was actually held in the barn of a D. H. Walker two and a half miles away. Tom Walker sued, his contention being that the publication injured his good name and reputation as a husband and father. The newspaper defended on the ground that its reporter had inadvertently, but in good faith, written the story, placing the event in the barn of the wrong Walker. The court held that the mistake was not a defense to the publication but, fortunately for the newspaper, held that the publication itself was not libelous per se.

HEARSAY OR RUMOR

Still another source of inadvertent error may creep into published matter when the information upon which the story is based comes from third persons, or rumor. When such stories are printed, they are frequently preceded by such words as, "it is alleged," or "it is said." The mere fact that someone else has spread a libelous rumor or gossip is no defense to a subsequent publication of the libel in reliance on the rumor or gossip. If the libelous statements are untrue, then no protection is afforded by the fact that they are based upon hearsay, however reliable that hearsay may be. This is one of the instances where the rule that one publishes libel at his peril is most apparent.

A young man brought an action in libel against two papers, the Boston *Post* and the Boston *Daily Record*. The action was based upon stories in which it was said that "it was alleged" that a young man was a member of a gang of extortioners and that the gang told a garage proprietor they had been hired to kill him, but would spare him if he paid them $25, which he did. It was held that the paper was not excused by the fact that the charge was qualified by the words "it is alleged" or their equivalent, unless the boys were actually guilty of extortion.

Divorcing one's self from a story by attributing it to others is not permissible as a defense in libel. Nor does the plea of typographical error avail. In a New York case, the defendant newspaper published a map purportedly showing the location of disorderly houses in a certain part of New York City. By mistake, the house occupied by the plaintiff was marked on the map as such a house, instead of the house next door, which the map was intended to indicate. The court, holding for the plaintiff, said: "It has nowhere been decided as yet that where either an individual or a published newspaper, intending to refer to 'B,' makes a slanderous attack upon 'A,' it is a privileged communication. The plea of typographical error does not in any respect alter the situation. It may go to the question of exemplary damages, but to the right of the plaintiff of recovery, typographical errors afford no answer."

LIBEL OF THE DEAD

Generally the cases which have been brought arising out of libels of the dead fall into three categories: first, in which the libel is directly of the deceased; second, in which the libel indirectly tends to affect the reputation of the living; and third, in which the libel of the dead contains a direct libel of the living.

As an example of the first classification we have an action in which it was said of a girl who had died in the course of an abortion that she was pregnant and had had a miscarriage. Her mother sued. The court said: "It would seem plain that the imputation on the character of the daughter did not necessarily or naturally affect the reputation or character of the plaintiff, and as it is only injury to reputation which gives a right of action, it is apparent that the present action in this respect cannot be maintained." (*Sorensen* v. *Balaban.*)

In Iowa a newspaper story was published entitled "Hunting a Dead Man." It involved a charge against the deceased of counterfeiting and burglary. In the course of the article it was stated that the dead man was known to have been a leader of a gang of counterfeiters and had been a well-known desperate character. His mother sued for libel. The court said that the only question presented to it was whether the mother could recover damages for a libel published of and concerning an adult son after his decease. The damages which were sought to be recovered were for the humiliation, shame, and mental anguish of the mother caused by the alleged libelous publication concerning her deceased son. In its opinion the court said:

There is no doubt that for the publication set out in plaintiff's petition defendant was subject to a criminal prosecution, provided the article was published without sufficient justification. But is it liable civilly to the mother of the deceased? She does not sue in a representative capacity, and, if she had, she could not recover, for it is manifest no injury was done to the estate of her deceased son. It seems that contemptuous demeanor toward a corpse was, by the Roman law, an insult to the heir of the deceased and that action could lie therefor. The rule that an heir may recover for a libel of one deceased does not seem to have gained a foothold in this country, and we know of no principle that will sustain such an action. There was nothing in the article which tended in any manner to reflect on the plaintiff, and her sufferings were of the same kind as that produced by the publication upon any of the other relatives, or close friends of the deceased. To permit a recovery in this case would allow the mother of any person libeled to bring suit in her own name for the consequential damages done to her feeling, and the death of the person libeled would be a wholly irrelevant matter; for the suffering is in kind the same whether the person libeled be living or dead. We have not been cited to an authority, and, after a diligent search, we have been unable to find one, which authorizes a recovery in such a case.

The second class of cases concerns allegations with regard to the dead in which living persons are named and connected with the dead as relatives. Jack Rose, known as "Baldy Jack Rose," was a well-known criminal who was involved in the famous Lieutenant Becker case in New York, which rose out of the murder of Herman Rosenthal, the gambler. A Jack Rose other than "Baldy Jack" died and the *New York Daily Mirror* printed an article of and concerning Jack Rose, the deceased, wherein he was erroneously identified with "Baldy Jack Rose," a person described in the article as a self-confessed murderer who has "lived in constant fear that emissaries of the underworld . . . would catch up with him and execute gang vengeance." The article named the surviving wife and children of the deceased Jack Rose, the plaintiffs in the action brought against the *Daily Mirror*, but made no other direct reference to them. The Court of Appeals of the State of New York held:

> Defendant does not deny that the publication complained of was a libel on the memory of the deceased Jack Rose. Plaintiffs make no claim of any right to recover for that wrong. They stand upon the position that the publication—while it did not affect their reputation in respect of any matter of morals—tended to subject them in their own persons to contumely and indignity and was, therefore, a libel upon them . . . In this State, however, it has long been accepted law that a libel or slander upon the memory of a deceased person which makes no direct reflection upon his relatives gives them no cause of action for defamation. (*Rose* v. *Daily Mirror*.)

In the third class would fall those cases where, not only were relatives named in connection with the deceased, but the con-

nection was such as to contain invidious implications or statements affecting the named person's reputation and his moral
disposition. Here the relative or descendant might have a cause
of action, but it can readily be seen that this distinction arises
out of the fact that there is a libel of the descendant or relative
which is independent of the libel of the deceased.

As to a mere statement of death, *The New York Times* in its
obituary column carried the notice "Died—Brooklyn: Cohen-
Bealey, 133 St. Marks Avenue, May 6." One Zealey Cohen of
Brooklyn, under the theory that he had thereby been held up
to scorn and ridicule and that his reputation had been injured,
sued for libel, even though the given name was different. The
court held:

> The question then whether this publication could be a libel
> per se involves the inquiry as to whether it could have injured
> the reputation of the plaintiff. Here is a bare item of news in a
> newspaper. The item states that an event has come to pass which
> is looked for in the history of every man, is regarded as beyond
> his control, and, therefore, does not permit the inference that the
> man has done any act or suffered any act which he could not have
> done or which he need not have suffered. Prematurity is the sole
> peculiarity. How can the publication of such an event, merely as
> a matter of news, hold up the subject to scorn, to hatred, to con-
> tempt, or to ridicule so that his reputation is impaired? Such
> publication may be unpleasant, it may annoy or irk the subject
> thereof, it may subject him to joke or to jest or to banter from
> those who knew him or knew of him, even to the extent of affect-
> ing his feelings, but this in itself is not enough.

On the other hand, where a story of the dead also contains a
libel of the living, action may be maintained.

The Rev. Francis J. Quinn, pastor of a church in Syracuse,
New York, for more than twenty years, was erroneously described in the *New York Sun* as a man who had been asphyxi-
ated in a lodging house in New York City under disgraceful
circumstances. The publication was held to be libelous.

In a Massachusetts case a statement that a woman's husband

had committed suicide was held not to cast libelous aspersions upon the widow.

In Missouri, Violette H. Bello sued the publisher and the author for alleged libels of her husband, the stepfather of Jean Harlow, arising out of the publication of the book entitled *Harlow—An Intimate Biography*. The court held that since she was not directly libeled and was not even mentioned in the book, she had no cause of action.

It may be stated as a general proposition that there is no civil libel suit arising out of the libel of the dead and that the relatives of the deceased person have no cause of action unless they are themselves directly libeled thereby.

LIBEL OF WOMEN

Sex and its ramifications have always bothered our lawmakers, and the law has reflected changing attitudes as the relationships between men and women have changed. In this decade there have been many changes in sexual mores and manners and in the relationships of the sexes. Many laws have been passed in many fields, including divorce laws, laws on abortion, and laws prohibiting discriminatory advertising. A vigorous women's liberation movement has been behind much of this legislation. The Kinsey Report and other taxonomical studies have shed new light on the results of these changes in mores. We now know that more than one-third of first-born children are born out of wedlock. Nevertheless, many of our laws make punishable language which would suggest unchastity on the part of women or charge them with what was once sexual misconduct, but is now almost generally accepted. Among those statutes in the field of libel, providing criminal or civil penalties are:

> Alabama: "Any words, written, spoken or printed, of any woman, falsely imputing to her a want of chastity, are actionable without proof of special damages."

Florida: "Whoever speaks of and concerning any woman, married or unmarried, falsely and maliciously imputing to her a want of chastity, shall be punished. . . ."

Georgia: "Any person who shall willfully or falsely utter . . . statements derogatory to the fair name or reputation for virtue of any virtuous female shall be guilty of a misdemeanor."

"It shall be unlawful . . . to print, publish, or cause to be printed and published . . . the name or identity of any female who may have been raped or upon whom an assault with intent to commit rape may have been made."

Indiana: "Every charge of incest, fornication, adultery, or whoredom, falsely made by any person against a female . . . shall be actionable in the same manner as in the case of slanderous words charging a crime the commission of which would subject the offender to death or other degrading penalties."

Kentucky: "Any accusation of incest, fornication or adultery against a female shall be actionable. . . ."

Maryland: "All words spoken falsely and maliciously touching the character or reputation for chastity of any woman, whether single or married, and tending to the injury thereof shall be slander. . . ."

Michigan: "Words imputing a lack of chastity to any female are actionable in themselves. . . ."

Nevada: "Every male person who shall in any language or words whatsoever, either truthfully or falsely, orally declare, in the presence of two or more other persons of good general reputation in the locality in which they reside, that he has had carnal knowledge of any certain female person other than his lawful wife . . . shall be deemed guilty of a misdemeanor. . . ."

New York: "In an action of slander of a woman imputing unchastity to her, it is not necessary to allege or prove special damages."

North Carolina: "Where doubts have arisen whether actions for slander can be maintained against persons who may attempt, in a wanton and malicious manner, to destroy the reputation of innocent and unprotected women whose very existence in society depends upon the unsullied purity of their character, which may amount to a charge of incontinency, shall be actionable."

North Dakota: "A person who, in the presence and hearing of a person other than the female slandered, whether such female is present or not, maliciously speaks of or concerning any female of the age of twelve years or upwards, not a public prostitute, any false and defamatory words or language injuring or impairing the reputation of such female for virtue or chastity, is guilty of a misdemeanor."

Ohio: "No person shall write, print, or publish a false or malicious libel of, or concerning . . . a female of good repute, with intent to cause it to be believed that such female is unchaste."

Oklahoma: "If any person shall orally or otherwise, falsely and maliciously or falsely and wantonly impute to any female, married or unmarried, a want of chastity, he shall be deemed guilty of slander."

Pennsylvania: "Whensoever any husband shall have deserted or separated himself from his wife, or neglected or refused to support her, . . . it shall be lawful for her to protect her reputation by an action for slander or libel."

South Carolina: "Whoever publishes or causes to be published the name of any woman, maid or woman child upon whom the crime of rape or an assault with the intent to ravish has been committed or alleged to have been committed in this State . . . shall be guilty of a misdemeanor."

Tennessee: "Any words, written, spoken, or printed of a person, wrongfully and maliciously imputing to such person the commission of adultery or fornication, are actionable, without special damage."

Texas: "If any person shall, orally or otherwise, falsely and maliciously . . . impute to any female . . . a want of chastity, he shall be deemed guilty of slander."

Utah: "If any person shall orally or otherwise, falsely or maliciously or falsely and wantonly, impute to any female, married or unmarried, a want of chastity, he is guilty of criminal slander."

Virginia: "If any person shall falsely utter and speak, or falsely write and publish, of and concerning any female of chaste character, any words derogatory of such female's character for virtue or chastity, or imputing to such female acts not virtuous and chaste, he shall be punished. . . ."

Washington: "Every person, who, in the presence or hearing of any person other than the female slandered . . . shall speak of . . . any female of the age of twelve years or upwards, not a common prostitute, any false or defamatory words . . . which shall injure or impair the reputation of any such female for virtue or unchastity, or which shall expose her to hatred, contempt or ridicule, shall be guilty of a misdemeanor. . . ."

Wyoming: "That any person who shall falsely and maliciously by word, oral statement, speech, or otherwise accuse or . . . . impute to any female a want of chastity . . . shall be guilty of slander. . . ."

Chapter 10

✦ THE RIGHT OF PRIVACY

The invasion of a person's privacy through media of public communication was not protected at common law. An English court said:

> If my camera, during a choppy Channel crossing, catches the Prime Minister in the throes of sickness, and if the picture is used as an adjunct to the announcement of a sure guard against sea-sickness, what then? Why, the Prime Minister might not grin, but he would have to bear it.

In the United States, in 1890, Louis D. Brandeis and Samuel D. Warren were aroused by this lack of full protection to the privacy of the individual. In a beautifully written, well-considered article, which was first published in the *Harvard Law Review,* they pointed out that instantaneous photographs and newspapers had invaded the sacred precincts of private and domestic life and said:

> Of the desirability—indeed of the necessity—of some such protection, there can, it is believed, be no doubt. The press is over-stepping in every direction the obvious bounds of propriety and of decency. Gossip is no longer the resource of the idle and of the vicious, but has become a trade, which is pursued with industry as well as effrontery. To satisfy a purient taste the details of sexual relations are spread broadcast in the columns of the daily papers. To occupy the indolent, column upon column is filled with idle gossip, which can only be procured by intrusion upon the domestic circle. The intensity and complexity of life, attendant

upon advancing civilization, have rendered necessary some retreat from the world, and man, under the refining influence of culture, has become more sensitive to publicity, so that solitude and privacy have become more essential to the individual; but modern enterprise and invention have, through invasions upon his privacy, subjected him to mental pain and distress, far greater than could be inflicted by mere bodily injury.

In the article, "The Right of Privacy", they argued for a new conception of law which would protect the individual against gossip and against violation of his right to be let alone. Some minor courts thereafter attempted to grant relief. The doctrine was definitely rejected by the Court of Appeals in New York, in a case in which a beautiful young woman's picture had been used to advertise flour, both in posters and magazine advertisements, with a slogan "Flour of the Family." She sued, alleging that she had been caused to suffer mental distress, but the court felt that in view of the fact that there was no prior common law on the subject that it ought not, through the instrumentality of judicial legislation, incorporate a new doctrine into the body of law. The court feared, among other things, that such doctrine would bring about a large amount of litigation.

Immediately following this case, in 1903, the New York State Legislature adopted a law incorporating the doctrine of the Right of Privacy, which granted to an aggrieved individual the right to sue for an injunction and damages when his name or portrait was used for purposes of trade or advertising. The right is expanding. In New York, Utah, and Virginia it is statutory. It is in some form a creature of judicial decision in other states, including Alabama, Arizona, California, Colorado, Florida, Georgia, Illinois, Indiana, Kansas, Kentucky, Louisiana, Michigan, Missouri, Montana, New Jersey, North Carolina, Ohio, Oregon, Pennsylvania, South Carolina, and Alaska and in the District of Columbia.

The flood of litigation which the court had feared developed. The courts were obliged to restrict the extension of the doctrine. "Use," they said, was not the same as "publish." The sections of the law were limited to the precise dangers which were sought to be covered, that is, the commercial exploitation of personality. The laws have been held not to apply to the dissemination of current news and matters of information and general interest. The right of privacy statutes applied only to the unauthorized use of a name or picture to sell a collateral commodity.

Current thinking would establish some exceptions to the usual law of privacy. Prominent among such exceptions are biographies and persons who have been thrust into the category of public characters or newsworthy personalities. Among more recent cases have been those involving Koussevitzky, Ernest Hemingway, Howard Hughes, Bob Dylan and Warren Spahn.

In the cases involving these persons the proceedings for an injunction were denied. In one of the earliest of these cases it was stated:

> . . . there may be no recovery under the statute for use of a person's name or photograph "in connection with an article of current news or immediate public interest" and that, as a general rule, articles which are not strictly news, but which "are used to satisfy an ever-present educational need" such as "stories of distant places, tales of historic personages and events, the reproduction of items of past news," are not within the ban of the statute.

Bob Dylan, singer, poet, and musician, sued to restrain the publication of a book of photographs of himself. The court stated, among its grounds for denying the injunction, that

> . . . it is not shown that the proposed publication in any way places plaintiff in an unfavorable light or contains any matter detrimental to his professional standing. In fact, it would appear that plaintiff's professional standing and career will be enhanced by the publication of the photographs in this biographical book.

When Random House published the biographical study of Ernest Hemingway entitled *Papa Hemingway* by A. E. Hotch-

ner, Mrs. Hemingway sued because of the claimed invasion
of her privacy, as to which the court said that:

> [her] status as the wife and widow of a man of celebrated promi-
> nence who was the recipient of both the Nobel and Pulitzer
> Prizes during his lifetime and her own activities incidental to
> such position have thrust her into the category of a newsworthy
> personality who, as a figure of public interest, is dehors the pro-
> tection of the statute.

In 1966 Random House published *Howard Hughes—a
Biography* by John Keats. Random House had obtained the
services of the author who worked on a manuscript previously
prepared for the publisher by Thomas Thompson, a member
of the staff of *Life* Magazine. Apparently Howard Hughes
learned of the forthcoming publication by Random House, and
through his attorneys warned the publisher that Hughes was
opposed to the biography and "would make trouble if the book
was published." The Circuit Court of Appeals to which the
case came considered the question of the public interest in the
book and said:

> The Keats biography is laudatory and where critical is critical in
> an understanding fashion. Judging by the accounts in the *Look* arti-
> cles and the biography, Hughes has almost an obsession as to
> his privacy and his right thereto. However, when one enters the
> public arena to the extent that he has, the right of privacy must
> be tempered by a countervailing privilege that the public have
> some information concerning important public figures. . . .
> Everyone will agree that at some point the public interest in
> obtaining information becomes dominant over the individual's
> desire for privacy.

The Circuit Court of Appeals reversed the decision of a lower
court and denied an injunction to Hughes.

The right to recovery has been denied for the use of a name
and picture in a motion picture of current events; for the use
of a name once in a novel of about four hundred pages; the

use of the name and picture of an alleged strikebreaker, together with the names and likenesses of eight others on the frontispiece and the mention of his name four times in a book of approximately three hundred and fourteen pages dealing with strikebreaking.

The rules with regard to unauthorized publication of photographs in a single issue of a newspaper have been summarized as follows:

1. Recovery may be had under the statute if the photograph is published in or as part of an advertisement, or for advertising purposes.

2. The statute is violated if the photograph is used in connection with an article of fiction in any part of the newspaper.

3. There may be no recovery under the statute for publication of a photograph in connection with an article of current news or immediate public interest.

4. Newspapers publish articles which are neither strictly news items nor strictly fictional in character. They are not the responses to an event of peculiarly immediate interest, but, though based on fact, are used to satisfy an ever-present educational need. Such articles include, among others, travel stories, stories of distant places, tales of historic personages and events, the reproduction of items of past news, and surveys of social conditions. These are articles educational and informative in character. As a general rule, such cases are not within the purview of the statute.

The use in nonfiction was upheld in a striking case growing out of the publication of a profile in *The New Yorker*. In 1937 it published a biographical sketch of William Sidis, who in 1910 was a famous child prodigy. The profile complained of described the early accomplishments of Sidis and his subsequent development over the years. Although Sidis had since the time of prodigality sought private life, he was held to have the status of a "public figure" and the article was held to be within the scope of a legitimate dissemination on a matter of public interest. The fact that reference was made on the wrapper-band of the magazine to the article within was held not to bring it within the statutory meaning of use for purposes of trade or advertising.

In the course of the opinion in the Sidis case, the court said:

> In defining the term "purposes of trade," however, the courts have drawn certain distinctions. In the following types of cases recovery was denied: The use of plaintiff's name and picture in a motion picture of current events . . . ; the use of a name once in a novel of almost 400 pages . . . ; the portrayal of plaintiff's factory on which his firm name clearly appeared, in a motion picture dealing with the white slave traffic . . . ; the use of the name and picture of an alleged strikebreaker together with the names and likenesses of eight others on the frontispiece, and the mention of his name four times in 314 pages of a book dealing with strikebreaking . . . ; and the attributing of the authorship of an absurd adventure story purporting to be true, to a well-recognized and reputable writer. . . ."

Nor does the right of privacy extend to biographical works, as is illustrated by the case brought by Serge Koussevitzky, who had been an important public figure in the musical world. He sued to prevent the publication of a biography and it was held that his stature as a conductor brought him within the orbit of public interest and scrutiny. The Koussevitzky case established that the right of privacy does not apply to an unauthorized biography of a public figure, unless the biography is fictional or novelized in character. But the fact that a biography may contain untrue statements of fact and error of fact does not make it fictional. Where there is the right to publish biography, advertisement of the biography is also permitted, since it is merely incidental to the right to publish.

On the other hand, where a novel relates to events and acts of a person, but does not contain his name or portrait, this does not constitute a portrayal violative of the right of privacy. In John Hersey's *A Bell for Adano* the events narrated the story of Major Victor Joppolo, described in the book as the senior civil affairs officer of the Allied Military Government in a town in Sicily which was called Adano. Frank E. Toscani had been the senior civil affairs officer of the Allied Military Government in the town of Licata, Sicily, during its occupation by the Allied armies of World War II. Mr. Toscani claimed that this narration by Hersey was a portrayal of himself and an exploitation of his acts, life and personality. Since he was not directly named, nor was any likeness of him used, it was held that the mere portrayal of acts and events concerning a person designated fictitiously in a novel or play does not bring it within the law giving action for an invasion of privacy. The court said:

> Where a name is used, it, like a portrait or picture, must, upon meeting the eye or ear, be unequivocally identified as that of the complainant. In the case of a name having no public recognition, this can be established only by a clear showing that the details surrounding the fictional character portrayed are such as to identify the complainant as the person of that name in that particular setting. If they do not, then, taken with the statement of the author that all characters portrayed are wholly fictional, the identity of name must be set down as pure coincidence, since there always will be persons with similar names and writers of fiction could not give names to their characters without violating the statute. Such result was clearly never intended by the Legislature and is not within the contemplation of the statute. Otherwise, the writing of fiction would always be susceptible to the hidden and virtually unavoidable peril of making authors and publishers criminal perpetrators.

Suit was brought by Miss Zelma Cason alleging that Marjorie Kinnan Rawlings had portrayed her in the novel *Cross Creek*, which was a Book-of-the-Month Club selection. The characterization was favorable. The court found that Miss Cason had a cause of action, but had suffered no damage.

In the course of limiting the right of privacy it has been held that the law protects the true name of a person from use for purposes of advertising or trade. It does not protect a nickname known to a few intimates any more than it protects a business name, or a partnership name, or an assumed name. Nor does it apply to stage names.

Claire H. Davis, who was also known as Cassandra, sued when R.K.O. Pictures produced a motion picture, *Bunker Bean,* in which there was a character designated as Countess Casandra, who was a psychic. Claire Davis alleged that she was a psychic and had practiced her profession throughout the United States, had achieved a great reputation and prominence, and that she was entitled to have her name protected under the Civil Rights Law. The court held that only a legal name could be protected and that stage names were not protectible. On the other hand, if she had legally changed her name to Cassandra, she might then have been protected.

The right to sue is personal. It dies with the person whose name is used. His survivors have no cause of action, nor do the descendants of a person whose name is used have such a cause of action, even though the use of the name may reflect in some way on them.

The grandchildren of the famous German composer Robert Schumann sought damages for the exhibition of a motion picture depicting his life. They objected particularly to the fact that the picture showed that he had become mentally ill before his death and had died in that condition. No recovery was allowed.

In all states, of course, the use of a person's name or likeness with his consent in writing will bar the maintenance of any action. Oral consent under the statutes is inadmissible, but where the matter rests upon judicial recognition of the doctrine then oral consent under special circumstances may be sufficient.

The dangers which were foreseen by Brandeis and Warren have never been met by the law. The gossip columnists still continue to violate the privacy of the individual and of the home. Only where the use of the name or picture is for trade or advertising does the law protect.

Ultimately the right to recover for invasion of privacy reached the Supreme Court of the United States in the case of *James J. Hill* v. *Time.* For the first time the constitutional limitations on enjoining invasions of the right of privacy in books was considered.

In the spring of 1953 James Hayes' novel *The Desperate Hours* was published. It told the story of a family of four held hostage by three escaped convicts in the family's suburban home. The family was released unharmed, but in the novel the family suffered violence at the hands of the convicts; the father and son were beaten and the daughter subjected to a verbal sexual insult. The book was made into a play and *Life* published an article about the play. The defense by *Life* was that the subject of the article was "a subject of legitimate news interest" and of general interest to the public. The ultimate finding was that the factual reporting of newsworthy persons and events is in the public interest and is protected, and following in part the opinion of the Supreme Court in the *New York Times* case, the court said:

> The guarantees for speech and press are not the preserve of political expression or comment upon public affairs, essential as those are to healthy government. One need only pick up any newspaper or magazine to comprehend the vast range of published matter which exposes persons to public view, both private citizens and public officials. Exposure of the self to others in varying degrees is a concomitant of life in a civilized community. The risk of this exposure is an essential incident of life in a society which places a primary value on freedom of speech and of press. "Freedom of discussion, if it would fulfill its historic function in this nation, must embrace all issues about which information is needed or appropriate to enable the members of society to cope with the exigencies of their period."

Going back into history we find James Madison in the debates on the Federal Constitution saying:

> Some degree of abuse is inseparable from the proper use of everything and in no instance is this more true than of the press.

Following which the Supreme Court held:

We create grave risk of serious impairment of the indispensable service of a free press in a free society if we saddle the press with the impossible burden of verifying to a certainty the facts associated in news articles with a person's name, picture or portrait, particularly as related to nondefamatory matter.

Publishing with serious doubt as to the truth of the publication or with reckless disregard for truth and falsity demonstrates actual malice. Liability may follow.

The case of Warren Spahn against the publishing house of Julian Messner, Inc. followed *Hill* in the Supreme Court. Warren Spahn was the well-known professional baseball pitcher. The biography which was published of him was a so-called juvenile biography intended for teen-age readers. In order to accentuate the telling and to emphasize the dramatic, situations were described in dialogue rather than in narrative form. The dialogue was, of course, invented or "fictionalized." After a long litigation in the state courts this case finally got to the Supreme Court of the United States which followed its previous ruling and sent the case back for determination as to whether or not there had been actual malice or a reckless falsity. That would seem to be the present rule with regard to biography.

Chapter 11

LITERATURE AND CENSORSHIP

Censorship is one of the plagues of those who write and publish. The censor is not only official, he is unofficial, for it is not the courts and judges who are alone the determiners of what shall and shall not pass.

Official censorship is exercised under the penal laws of the several states, and in addition thereto there are the laws of the United States, which act principally through the Post Office and the Customs Department. In addition to the penal laws there are the various state regulatory laws which apply principally in the field of motion pictures. But there are also laws which enable semiofficial bodies, such as boards of regents, library boards, school boards, etc., to ban literary material. In addition to the official bodies charged specifically with censorship there are the extralegal bodies, such as commissioners having the right to license theatres, who utilize their licensing power as a means of censorship. There are also, in addition to the official bodies, volunteer organizations, under one name or another, to police writing and see that it remains virtuous; there are church organizations which effectively, down to the parochial level, use their parishioners as volunteer overseers of what may or may not be sold in their localities, or who notify their parishioners of what books or motion pictures they may buy or see.

It is somewhat paradoxical that the machinery for censorship helped the notion of property in literature to come into being. The history of legal protection for literary works springs originally from the wish to restrain blasphemy, libel, and sedition. Obscenity, in which censorship is most firmly entrenched today, was historically of no importance. Authors always wrote at the peril of those in high places, who were in a position to say: "Off with his head!" because it was those in high places who suffered most from the widespread seditious and blasphemous attacks which the printing press made possible.

The duplication of copies in manuscript form was, at best, a tedious job, and even though one city in France boasted ten thousand copyists, distribution was not so wide as to be in any sense public. The rapid duplication which the printing press inaugurated brought the lively pamphleteer with his scurrilous attacks upon the established Church and State. For the coming of printing coincided with the coming of the new learning and the Reformation, and the new has always been disliked by those ensconced in comfortable vested interests.

To discourage these attacks, a new social weapon was invented. Since obviously it was printing which enabled the attack to be made, the dissemination of learning to the public was attacked at its source, and printing was licensed. There was a double aspect to this, since not only could a book do a wrong, it could also make profits. Licensing the printer, therefore, served not only as a means whereby one could control the product of the press, it also created a master guild of printers who profited by their control over authors.

Henry VIII took as his own prerogative printing of the laws of the country and all the books of the rites of the Church of England, Bibles, testaments, educational works, and Latin grammars. In 1534 Henry granted, by letters patent, to the University of Cambridge a license to appoint three printers who might, within the university, print and put on sale all manner of books which might be approved by the chancellor and three doctors. Henry's letters of patent were later confirmed by the Statute of Elizabeth. These letters of patent were not always general in terms. Sometimes they were granted to a bookseller for a particular book. In rare circumstances they were granted to the author. But the intention was always to keep a monopoly of the right to print under the Crown and Church, so that the text might be limited to that which was pleasant to them. The hunting of heresy, the suppression of blasphemy, and the interdiction of libel against the persons of the great were the objects of the creators of the monopoly.

The Star Chamber with its machinery was admirably adapted to the purposes of secret investigation, quick and obliging trial, and immediate execution of sentence. Its secret interrogatories and its use of the right to put to the torture persons whom it adjudged guilty of contempt for refusing to answer questions gave to the Star Chamber just such powers as censors lust for, and it was able to bring the peace of the Crown to those who disagreed with it. Its decrees upon the subject of licensing and printing of books were codified in 1637, and, although the Star Chamber was wiped out shortly thereafter, its decrees survived in a statute of Charles II. Among the provisions of the code set up by the Star Chamber was one providing that the duty of the licensees was to testify that the book contained nothing that was contrary to the Christian faith and the doctrine and discipline of the Church of England, nor against the state or government, nor contrary to the good life or good manners or otherwise. In 1643 the House of Commons established a committee to search for printing presses where scandalous and lying pamphlets were printed, and to destroy them, and to commit to prison the printers and vendors thereof. In June of the same year Parliament published a new order to establish the rights between the members of the Stationers' Company and those others who had been infringing, which brought forth the famous attack by Milton contained in his *Areopagitica*.

In 1662 the Licensing Act of Charles II was passed, carrying on the spirit of the Star Chamber decrees. It ordered that no person shall presume to print "any heretical, seditious, schismatical, or offensive books or pamphlets, wherein any doctrine or opinion shall be asserted or maintained which is contrary to the Christian faith, or the doctrine or discipline of the Church of England, or which shall or may tend or be to the scandal of religion or the Church or the government or governors of the Church, State or Commonwealth or of any corporation or particular person or persons whatever," and further provided that the masters and wardens of the Stationers' Company were to seize books suspected of containing matter hostile to the Church or government. It further provided that it should be necessary to print at the beginning of every licensed book the certificate of the licenser to the effect that the book contained nothing "contrary to the Christian faith or the doctrine or discipline of the Church of England or against the State and Government of this realm or contrary to good life or good manners or otherwise." These licensing acts continued by various acts of Parliament until 1694.

The control of the printer, and thus of the author, whether by licensing act or by decrees or ordinances of the Star Chamber, or by Parliament, had as their principal object the regulation of the press and the suppression of all writings deemed libelous or obnoxious to the government or the Church. That purpose is apparent in every document governing the right to print until 1694. From that year until 1709, when the Statute of Anne was passed, there was a hiatus.

When copyright was established in the author instead of in the bookseller by that statute, it carried over the tradition that there could be no property in that which was blasphemous, seditious, or immoral. The argument, as advanced by Lord Eldon, was that since anything which attacked the Church or State was obviously evil, there could be no property in such instrumentality of evil-doing. Where there was no property there could be no right, and, accordingly, for a long period of time, English judges refused protection to works where the defense was astute enough to raise the issue of immorality, blasphemy, or sedition.

Until about the mid-nineteenth century, censorship concerned itself mainly with politics and religion. In the nineteenth century the lusty vitality of the eighteenth century was forgotten, and with the coming of Victorianism sex joined treason and blasphemy and came to the fore as an avowed object of censorship. With the coming of the bowdlerized version of Shakespeare, and the purified version of the Bible by our own Noah Webster, censorship changed its incidence toward repressing what was called sexual impurity. In 1857 Lord Campbell's Act was passed, which was designed to apply to works written for the purpose of corrupting the morals of youth and of a nature to shock the common feeling of decency in any well-regulated mind. At least that was the purpose ascribed to it by Lord Campbell. Unfortunately, the first test of the Act came in a case where both religion and sex were involved. (*Regina* v. *Hicklin,* L.R. 3, Q. B. 360 [1868].) The Hicklin case arose out of a pamphlet containing a diatribe against the Catholic Church. Its purpose was to show the depravity of the priesthood and the character of questions put to women in the confessional. The famous but now abandoned rule of the Hicklin case was:

> I think the test of obscenity is this, whether the tendency of the matter charged as obscenity is to deprave and corrupt those whose minds are open to such immoral influence and into whose hands a publication of this sort may fall.

For many years the courts struggled with the vague language of most statutes which were designed to suppress works which were obscene, lewd, lascivious, indecent, filthy, or vile. They were seeking a rationale for words whose content was obviously vague and transitory. So we find in the decisions an attempt to define and make certain the statutory language. It led to the use of still vaguer language, which left the definition of the crime as variable as the judge before whom a particular case might come on to be tried. Among the words employed by the courts to describe their distaste for the works before them, and which would enable them to condemn the work, we find "arouse," "chastity," "corrupt," "debasing," "debauch," "decency," "depravity," "desires," "disgusting," "dissolute," "immodesty," "immorality," "impurity," "lascivious," "lewd," "lust," "morality," "nasty," "purity," "salacity," "sensuality," "shame," "stimulation," "tendency," "unchaste," "vulgar."

Since the courts could not agree upon what came within the exact language of the law, they hit upon the notion that the collocation of terms, "obscene, lewd, lascivious, indecent, filthy, and vile", had a historic, accepted meaning, sufficiently "well understood through long use in the criminal law" to satisfy the constitutional requirements of definiteness and certainty, and that therefore works which could be brought within the collocation were not within the protection of the guarantee of freedom of the press. The courts were further bothered by the fact that many a book which, read on the whole, did not come within the statutory combination, nevertheless contained parts which were objectionable, and convictions were had on parts of books, even though it was conceded that the books in their entirety were valuable. For many years Massachusetts stood as the leader of this partial doctrine, but today in the federal courts and in most of the states the notion prevails that the entire book must fall within condemnation and that it cannot rest on parts alone.

In the state courts most of the interpretation of the law was at the police-court level, and the result has been many weird and contradictory proscriptions. In the welter of politics, occasionally a good judge slips in, and it is the fortunate author who finds his book judged by his literary peer. Among the books which have been the basis of prosecution are the *Satyricon* of Petronius, Schnitzler's *Casanova's Homecoming*, D. H. Lawrence's *Young Girl's Diary, God's Little*

Acre by Erskine Caldwell, Gautier's *Mademoiselle de Maupin* and *Madeleine, Decameron* of Boccaccio, the *Heptameron* of Margaret of Navarre, *Jurgen* by James Branch Cabell, *The Well of Loneliness* by Radclyffe Hall, *Pay Day* by Nathan Asch, and *A World I Never Made* by James T. Farrell. The publishers or distributors of these books fought and were victorious. Hemingway's *A Farewell to Arms* and *The Sun Also Rises*, Eugene O'Neill's *Strange Interlude*, Sinclair Lewis's *Elmer Gantry*, Herbert Asbury's *Hatrack*, Upton Sinclair's *Oil*, among others, were attacked in Boston, which then still applied the punitive law under which a book could be attacked not as a whole but on parts. Several of our states still have laws prohibiting the publication of works which *contain* matter alleged to be obscene, thus still continuing the notion that a book may be judged not as a whole. The problem of censorship is no mere academic problem, but a real one involving each practicing writer. No one can tell where the ax will fall and when the sale of the work of months or years will be destroyed by the actions of the censorious. Here, too, queer happenings sometimes occur. So when Eugene O'Neill's *Strange Interlude* was forbidden production in Boston, the Theatre Guild, which produced it, transferred the production to the nearby city of Quincy, where it was permitted. Herbert Asbury's *Hatrack,* which appeared in the *American Mercury,* brought both the publisher and the editor of the *American Mercury* into court. The editor was acquitted, but a bookseller was fined for selling it.

In the *Ulysses* case, Judge Woolsey appreciated the difficulty of finding a standard by which one could test obscenity, other than that which was personal and subjective to the court, and attempted to check on himself by inviting the cooperation of two of his friends to act as reagents. He said:

> Whether a particular book would tend to excite such impulses and thoughts must be tested by the court's opinion as to its effect on a person with average sex instincts—what the French would

call *l'homme moyen sensuel*—who plays, in this branch of legal inquiry, the same role of hypothetical reagent as does the "reasonable man" in the law of torts and "the man learned in the art" on questions of invention in patent law.

The risk involved in the use of such a reagent arises from the inherent tendency of the trier of facts, however fair he may intend to be, to make his reagent too much subservient to his own idiosyncrasies.

Of course, so much character and delicacy are not found in the average city magistrate, who sits ostensibly as one to determine criminal guilt, but who, in fact, acts as a censor of society. In New York the Court of Appeals has laid down a rule much like that of Judge Woolsey, but it is honored as much in the breach as in the behavior of the lower courts. In considering the dramatization of *Frankie and Johnnie*, the court said:

> Perhaps in an age of innocence the facts of life should be withheld from the young, but a theatergoer could not give his approval to the modern stage as "spokesman of the thought and sentiment" of Broadway and at the same time silence this rough and profane representation of scenes which repel rather than seduce. . . .

Although the mind of the child and the feeble mind have been eliminated as devices for measuring the impact of a book, difficulties still arise, and contemporaneous literature has erected its own standards. Samuel Seabury, when on the bench, said:

> Contemporaneous literature must, of course, be judged by current opinion; . . . It is not at all inconceivable, and has frequently been the case, that the works which receive the condemnation of one generation are the objects of veneration and praise in another.

Dreiser, Erskine Caldwell, with his *God's Little Acre*, and James T. Farrell, in his *Studs Lonigan* trilogy, have all been accused of indecency in sex, when their works lay in the realistic description of people whose principal habitat was not the drawing room. In so doing, and in attempting literally to transcribe the speech and conversation of their characters, they have used the words of the street and farm. Joyce in *Ulysses* used many of the four-letter words which are commonly called Anglo-Saxon. Judge Woolsey, in his memorable opinion, said, with regard to Joyce's language:

> For his attempt sincerely and honestly to realize his objective has required him incidentally to use certain words which are generally considered dirty words and has led at times to what many think is a too poignant preoccupation with sex in the thoughts of his characters.
>
> The words which are criticized as dirty are old Saxon words known to almost all men and, I venture, to many women, and are such words as would be naturally and habitually used, I believe, by the types of folk whose life, physical and mental, Joyce is seeking to describe. In respect of the recurrent emergence of the theme of sex in the minds of his characters, it must always be remembered that his locale was Celtic and his season Spring. . . .
>
> In many places it seems to me to be disgusting, but although it contains, as I have mentioned above, many words usually considered dirty, I have not found anything that I consider to be dirt for dirt's sake. . . .
>
> If one does not wish to associate with such folk as Joyce describes, that is one's own choice. In order to avoid indirect contact with them one may not wish to read *Ulysses;* that is quite understandable. . . .
>
> I am quite aware that owing to some of its scenes *Ulysses* is a rather strong draught to ask some sensitive, though normal persons to take. But my considered opinion, after long reflection, is that whilst in many places the effect of *Ulysses* on the reader undoubtedly is somewhat emetic, nowhere does it tend to be an aphrodisiac.

Regarding the case of *Frankie and Johnnie,* the play was for strong stomachs. Graphically, indeed, were set forth the adventures of the country lad, Johnnie, in a setting designed for drinking, gambling, and prostitution in the middle of the last century. With regard to it the Court of Appeals said:

The language of the play is coarse, vulgar and profane; the plot cheap and tawdry. As a dramatic composition it serves to degrade the stage where vice is thought by some to lose "half its evil by losing all its grossness." That it is "indecent" from every consideration of propriety is entirely clear; but the court is not a censor of plays and does not attempt to regulate manners. One may call a spade a spade without offending decency, although modesty may be shocked thereby. The question is not whether the scene is laid in a low dive where refined people are not found or whether the language is that of the barroom rather than the parlor. The question is whether the tendency of the play is to excite lustful and lecherous desire.

In the Post Office there is a long history of law which bars from the mail so-called obscene literature within the collocation of terms. Although a former solicitor of the Post Office Department testified before a congressional committee that if five of his assistant censors should attempt to determine what is obscene, "you will get five different results, because in some cases it is just one of those things that depends upon your own personal ideas and your own bringing up", nevertheless, the Post Office has not hesitated to bar works written by Caldwell, Dumas, Freud, O'Hara, Hemingway, Steinbeck, and others. Similarly, the Customs Service barred Abélard's *Letters*, Boccaccio's *Decameron*, Voltaire's *Candide*, Rousseau's *Confessions*, Balzac's *Droll Stories*, George Moore's *A Story-Teller's Holiday*, and Joyce's *Ulysses*.

Some of the restrictions of the Customs House are faintly amusing. For instance, *Mademoiselle de Maupin* by Gautier was forbidden in Spanish but permitted in French and English. Aretino, the sixteenth-century Italian writer, was permitted in Italian or English but not in Spanish. But the humors of the Customs House are too numerous to give each its mention. Only recently has the Customs House adopted a more enlightened policy and appointed a literate gentleman to pass upon what is, and what is not, permissible for the citizens of this country to read from abroad.

Out of this welter of vague and contradictory opinions there has come a search for some definitive standard to guide the author and publisher and to safeguard also the rights of readers. Since Lord Campbell's day we have recalled that the First Amendment to the Constitution provides that Congress shall make

> no law . . . abridging the freedom of speech, or of the press; . . .

In the hubbub of the chase after impurity and indecency, constitutional rights have been forgotten. With the embarrassment of a century of confusion there is now an attempt to find a rationale in the law of censorship. This embodies a recognition of the constitutional limitation and of the limitation placed upon the amendment by the "clear and present danger" doctrine, under which the press may be censored, providing that publication presents a clear and present danger of a substantive evil. This was stated by Mr. Justice Rutledge of the Supreme Court in a case involving *Memoirs of Hecate County,* by Edmund Wilson. He said:

> Before we get to the question of clear and present danger, we've got to have something which the state can forbid as dangerous. We are talking in a vacuum until we can establish that there is some occasion for the exercise of the state's power.
>
> Yes, you must first ascertain the substantive evil at which the statute is aimed, and then determine whether the publication of this book constitutes a clear and present danger.
>
> It is up to the state to demonstrate that there was a danger, and until they demonstrate that, plus the clarity and imminence of the danger, the constitutional prohibition would seem to apply.

The necessity for finding antisocial conduct resulting from alleged obscenity in literature is stated by Judge Jerome Frank in *Roth* v. *Goldman:*

> I think that no sane man thinks socially dangerous the arousing of normal sexual desires. Consequently, if reading obscene books has merely that consequence, Congress, it would seem, can con-

stitutionally no more suppress such books than it can prevent the mailing of many other objects, such as perfumes, for example, which notoriously produce that result. But the constitutional power to suppress obscene publications might well exist if there were ample reason to believe that reading them conduces to socially harmful sexual conduct on the part of normal human beings.

Writing and publishing would be protected and censorship would prevail only in obscenity cases where it could be found that there was incitement to evil, to antisocial conduct, and to lustful and lecherous desire which might tend to antisocial conduct. It has been said that the matter charged to be obscene must:

> "deprave and corrupt," which describes dissolute and unchaste acts . . . calculated to excite lustful and sensual desires; . . .
> corrupt the morals . . . with respect to sexual indulgences, invite . . . lewd, obscene and lascivious . . . conduct; . . .
> appealing to the animal passion, stimulating it; . . .
> exciting sensual desires and libidinous thoughts; . . .
> tend to promote lust; . . .
> arouse the salacity of the reader; . . .

These, too, do not set up a too-definite standard, but at least we get from this an attempt toward an objective, rather than a purely subjective, standard of judgment. It does not mean that police courts will thereby be rendered wise. It does mean that resort to the higher courts may bring about a better level of censorship. The dangers, however, still lurk.

The censorship involved in cases before the courts has been punitive.

Judge Curtis Bok, in a brilliant reflective opinion, directly attacked the validity of any such punitive legislation. In *Commonwealth* v. *Gordon* (1949), he said:

> A book, however sexually impure and pornographic . . . cannot be a present danger unless its reader closes it, lays it aside, and transmutes its erotic allurement into overt action. That such action must inevitably follow as a direct consequence of reading the book does not bear analysis, nor is it borne out by general

human experience; too much can intervene and too many diversions take place. . . . The only clear and present danger . . . that will satisfy . . . the Constitution . . . is the commission or the imminence of the commission of criminal behavior resulting from the reading of a book. Publication alone can have no such automatic effect.

The constitutional operation of "the statute," Judge Bok continued, thus

> rests on narrow ground . . . I hold that [the statute] may constitutionally be applied . . . only where there is a reasonable and demonstrable cause to believe that a crime or misdemeanor has been committed or is about to be committed as the perceptible result of the publication and distribution of the writing in question: the opinion of anyone that a tendency thereto exists or that such a result is self-evident is insufficient and irrelevant. The causal connection between the book and the criminal behavior must appear beyond a reasonable doubt.

The Supreme Court of the United States is the final arbiter. In the *Roth* case it examined the collocation of terms defining obscenity and added to all of the words which we have herein quoted a standard:

> Whether to the average person, applying contemporary community standards, the dominant theme of the material taken as a whole appeals to prurient interest.

Since the *Roth* decision it was obvious that merely adding the word "prurient" to the twenty-six odd words which had theretofore been used did not lay to rest the question of what was obscene. There has not been a single unanimous opinion by the Court and despite many, many pages of opinion judges cannot agree on what is to be protected under the First Amendment. In the *Roth* case the Court held "obscenity is not within the area of constitutionality, protected speech or press." It characterized as obscenity that which is utterly without redeeming social importance and which "deals with sex in a manner appealing to prurient interest."

Justice Stewart of the Supreme Court attempted to set forth a definition of what is hard-core pornography. He accepted as a definition the following:

> . . . Such materials include photographs, both still and motion picture, and no pretense of artistic value, graphically depicting acts of sexual intercourse, including various acts of sodomy and sadism, and sometimes involving several participants in scenes of orgy-like character. They also include strips of drawings in comic-book format grossly depicting similar activities in an exaggerated fashion. There are, in addition, pamphlets and booklets, sometimes with photographic illustrations, verbally describing such activities in a bizarre manner with no attempt whatsoever to afford portrayals of character or situation and with no pretense to literary value. All of this material . . . cannot conceivably be characterized as embodying communication of ideas or artistic values inviolate under the First Amendment. . . .

At least in New York the Court of Appeals has agreed in a notable opinion that the prohibitions of the Penal Law should apply only to what may properly be termed "hard-core pornography." But the court set forth no definitions from which one could decide what would be considered hard-core pornography. In fact, it conceded: "The one point of universal agreement is that a precise definition is impossible."

But no matter how often the cases come up, there can be no agreement amongst the judges as to what is obscene. In *Roth* (1957) there were four written opinions. In the case involving *Memoirs of A Woman of Pleasure* (commonly known as *Fanny Hill*), written by John Cleland in about 1750, four of the seven judges of the Massachusetts Supreme Judicial Court concluded that *Fanny Hill* was obscene. Four of the seven judges of the New York Court of Appeals concluded that it was not obscene. When it came to the Supreme Court on appeal from the Massachusetts Court, six of the judges voted for reversal, but they could not agree upon an opinion. One joined in the reversal on the ground that the book

250 THE PROTECTION OF LITERARY PROPERTY

need not be "unqualifiedly worthless before it can be deemed obscene." One concurred on the reversal on the ground that in his opinion the court was without power to censor speech or press. One concurred on the ground that the Federal Constitution leaves no power in government over expression of ideas. One concurred on the ground that the book was not hard-core pornography.

The courts are really not, and never can be, other than a given man making judgments in specific cases and without any standards which can be called judicially determinative. Like obscenity itself, judgment becomes a matter of personal involvement.

Since 1957 the only agreement as a matter of law has been the further establishment of the principle that obscenity is not protected by the free speech provision of the First Amendment. It must have been obvious even to the members of the court that all they were doing in their opinions was to disagree acrimoniously on what constituted obscenity.

Ten years after *Roth*, in 1967, three cases came before the Supreme Court which have been reported under the general title of *Redrup* v. *New York*. In one case Redrup was a clerk at a New York City newsstand. He was approached by a plainclothesman, who asked for two paperback books by name. Redrup handed him the books and received the price. He was thereafter charged in the New York City Criminal Court with violating a state criminal law and was convicted.

William Austin owned and operated a bookstore in Paducah, Kentucky. A woman residing there purchased two magazines from a salesgirl, after asking for them by name. Whereupon Austin was convicted for violating a criminal law of the State.

In *Gent* v. *Arkansas*, the third case, the prosecuting attorney of the Eleventh Judicial District of Arkansas brought a civil proceeding to have certain issues of various magazines declared obscene, to enjoin their distribution and to obtain a judgment ordering their surrender and destruction. The magazines proceeded against were: *Gent, Swank, Bachelor, Modern Man, Cavalcade, Gentleman, Ace* and *Sir*. The County Chancery Court entered a judgment against the storekeeper.

Thereupon in its opinion the court said, referring to previous decisions:

> In none of the cases was there a claim that the statute in question reflected a specific and limited state concern for juveniles. . . . In none was there any suggestion of an assault upon individual privacy by publication in a manner so obtrusive as to make it impossible for an unwilling individual to avoid exposure to it. . . . And in none was there evidence of the sort of "pandering". . . .

The court said:

> We have concluded, in short, that the distribution of the publications in each of these cases is protected by the First and Fourteenth Amendments from governmental Suppression, whether criminal or civil, in personam or in rem.

And further described as among its reasons:

> Others [courts] have subscribed to a not dissimilar standard, holding that a State may not constitutionally inhibit the distribution of literary material as obscene unless "(a) the dominant theme of the material taken as a whole appeals to a prurient interest in sex; (b) the material is patently offensive because it affronts contemporary community standards relating to the description or representation of sexual matters; and (c) the material is utterly without redeeming social value," emphasizing that the "three elements must coalesce," and that no such material can "be proscribed unless it is found to be utterly without redeeming social value." . . . Another Justice has not viewed the "social value" element as an independent factor in the judgment of obscenity.

In the aftermath of *Redrup*, the court, whenever a majority could be obtained, adopted the policy of reversing state obscenity convictions without issuing a written opinion—a frank admission of the justices' inability to agree on a workable obscenity standard, but a practice which also left the state and federal courts in the dark as to the standards they should follow.

The first hint of a departure from this practice came when the court, in a short opinion, upheld the conviction of Ralph Ginzberg, publisher of *Eros*, on a charge of purveying smut in his advertising. Although this decision was limited to advertising and did not apply to authors per se, the advent of the Burger Court signalled the end of the more liberal *Redrup* approach, and in 1973 in *Miller* v. *California* and three accompanying cases, the Supreme Court, in a series of five to four opinions, once more found itself in the business of fashioning an obscenity standard which has had a marked impact on state obscenity prosecutions.

In its broad outlines, the *Miller* decision reaffirmed *Roth*'s holding that the First Amendment does not protect obscene materials and held that such material could be regulated by the states without a showing that the material was utterly without redeeming social value—a retreat from the court's stance in the *Fanny Hill* or *Memoirs* case that positive proof of the utter absence of redeeming social value would be required before a work could be prosecuted as obscene.

More specifically, Chief Justice Burger, writing for the majority, held that state statutes establishing criminal penalties for obscenity could be applied to works depicting or describing sexual conduct. Such state-created offenses, the court said, "must be limited to works which, taken as a whole, appeal to a prurient interest, which portray sexual conduct in a patently offensive way, and which taken as a whole do not have serious literary, artistic, political, or scientific use." The decision as to whether a work was or was not obscene, the court stated, would be up to the jury which should consider three factors in reaching its decision: (a) whether "the average person, applying contemporary community standards would find that the work taken as a whole, appeals to the prurient interest, (b) whether the work depicts or describes, in a patently offensive way, sexual conduct specifically defined by the applicable state law, and (c) whether the work taken as a whole lacks serious literary, artistic, political, or scientific value."

To aid the states in formulating their obscenity statutes, and to attempt to overcome the vagueness inherent in the term "patently offensive," the court specified the type of material at which state laws could constitutionally be aimed without violating the First Amendment as material containing "representations or descriptions of ultimate sexual acts, normal and perverted, actual or simulated, and representations or descriptions of masturbatory, excretory functions, and lewd exhibitions of the genitals."

In the accompanying cases, the court held that state criminal prosecutions for a movie shown in an "adult" theatre in Atlanta, Georgia, for an 8 mm film seized by customs agents, and for a plain cover book, which repetitively, and with only the most tenuous plot, described varieties of sexual conduct, were constitutionally permissible provided that the state laws fell within the guidelines set forth in *Miller*.

Following the *Miller* decision, the court by a similar five to four majority upheld a conviction under a federal statute for mailing and conspiring to mail a brochure advertising an illustrated version of the report of the Presidential Commission on Obscenity and Pornography, even though the original, albeit unillustrated text, had been an official government publication. In so doing, the court affirmed that local community standards were to be applied even when the prosecution was brought under federal law. However, in the case of *Jenkins* v. *Georgia*, the court struck down a state prosecution involving the film *Carnal Knowledge*, and held that occasional scenes of nudity and sexual conduct do not fall within the categories proscribed in *Miller*.

As a result of its decision in *Miller*, the Supreme Court has provided the states with authority and guidelines for local obscenity prosecutions and has once more opened the door to such prosecutions as long as the statutes under which the indictments are obtained conform to the *Miller* criteria. The court's recent tendency to deny rehearings for such state convictions is in direct contrast to its earlier tendency, following *Redrup*, of reversing such convictions and indicates how far the court has swung from its more liberal approach before *Miller*.

PRIOR RESTRAINT AND FREEDOM OF THE PRESS

Censorship by prior restraint, which had been the rule under the Star Chamber, grew obnoxious to the people of England and the American Colonies. This was probably foremost among the reasons for the strict injunction of the First Amendment that Congress should make no law abridging the freedom of speech or of the press.

In his report on the Virginia Resolutions, Madison emphasized the difference between our constitutional system with respect to censorship and that which had been enjoyed in England. He wrote: "The great and essential rights of the people are secured against legislative as well as against executive ambition. They are secured, not by laws paramount to prerogative, but by constitutions paramount to laws. This security of the freedom of the press requires that it should be exempt not only from previous restraint by the executive, as in Great Britain, but from legislative restraint also."

In 1925 a law was passed in Minnesota making anyone guilty of a nuisance who published

(a) an obscene, lewd, and lascivious newspaper, magazine, or other periodical, or
(b) a malicious, scandalous, and defamatory newspaper, magazine, or other periodical

and provided that a perpetual injunction might be obtained restraining the commission of such nuisance.

An action was commenced under this statute against one J. M. Near, in Hennepin County, Minnesota, and a permanent injunction was granted against him from publishing a newspaper known as the *Saturday Press*. He appealed to the Supreme Court of the United States, which court held that liberty of the press meant primarily immunity from prior restraints or censorship. Accordingly, it struck down the statute. This decision was to have a tremendous impact upon the motion picture industry.

In 1915 the Supreme Court had held that the exhibition of moving pictures was a business pure and simple, originated and conducted for profit and not to be regarded as part of the press of the country, or as organs of public opinion, which came under the protection of the First Amendment. It had, therefore, refused to enjoin a board of censors which had been set up to license, by prior approval, moving pictures. Acts establishing similar boards of motion picture censors had been passed in most of the states of the Union.

In 1951 the Supreme Court had occasion again to pass upon the subject of licensing motion pictures after prior review by a board of censorship. There had been imported into this country from Italy a film trilogy called *Three Ways of Love,* of which *The Miracle* was a part. The license to distribute the film had been rescinded on the ground that the picture was "sacrilegious." The Vatican censorship agency, the Catholic Cinematographic Centre, had declared that the picture constituted an abominable profanation, and His Eminence, Francis Cardinal Spellman, had condemned the picture. The Supreme Court thereupon was asked to review its previous holding that motion picture films were not within the protection of the First and Fourteenth Amendments, and also to decide whether or not a picture could be barred as "sacrilegious." In a great and carefully studied series of opinions the court held that the mere fact that motion pictures were produced as large-scale business for private profit did not remove them from the protection of the

Constitution, pointing out that books, newspapers, and magazines are also sold for profit. The court then held that the state had no legitimate interest in protecting any or all religions from views distasteful to them, saying it is not the business of government in our nation to suppress real or imagined attacks upon a particular religious doctrine, whether they appear in publications, speeches, or pictures. Insofar as the statute under consideration set up the term "sacrilegious" as the standard, the court held that under the First and Fourteenth Amendments a state could not ban the film. The decision left open the question whether a state might censor motion pictures under clearly drawn statutes designed to prevent the showing of obscene films. Since that time other state statutes providing for prior licensing of films have been refused judicial sanction by the Supreme Court. It is noteworthy that we have come a long way from the original notion of censorship, which had been designed to protect the hierarchy of the Church, to the position taken by the Supreme Court.

As Judge Frank said in *United States of America* v. *Roth*:

> For a long time, much was made of the distinction between a statute calling for "prior restraint" and one providing subsequent criminal punishment; the former alone, it was said, raised any question of constitutionality vis-à-vis the First Amendment. Although it may still be true that more is required to justify legislation providing "preventive" rather than "punitive" censorship, this distinction has been substantially eroded.

In the State of New York a law was passed amending the Penal Law by providing an additional civil remedy in the Supreme Court by way of an action for an injunction against the sale and distribution of written or printed matter found, after trial, to be obscene. The definitions of obscenity were the same as those of the Penal Law. The statute provided that an action might be brought against anyone who "sells or distributes or has in his possession with intent to sell or distribute any such matter." If an injunction was granted, then it would be required of the defendant that he "surrender" the offending matter to the sheriff who "shall be directed to seize and destroy the same."

Thereupon the Corporation Counsel of the City of New York brought an action against the distributors of a series of paperbound booklets, collectively entitled *Nights of Horror*. The defendant conceded that the book was pornographic, but contended that the remedy by injunction constituted an unconstitutional "prior restraint" interfering with the rights of freedom of speech and press under the Constitution. Three of the Judges of the Court of Appeals concurring in an opinion said:

> We hold on most ample authority that the First Amendment does not protect obscene books against prior restraint.

This decision of the Supreme Court was affirmed by the United States Court of Appeals. However, in the *Redrup* opinion, one of the cases involved such a civil proceeding under a state statute of Arkansas under which a judgment was entered declaring various magazines obscene, enjoining their distribution and ordering their surrender and destruction. The Supreme Court reversed the judgment without reference to its previous opinion. The opinion in *Redrup* was in 1967, ten years after the appeal in *Kingsley*, in which Chief Justice Warren dissented on the ground that the application of the statute imposed a prior restraint. The confusion is evident.

With the change in judicial definition of obscenity and the realization that hard-core obscenity would probably be the borderline of enforcement, Rhode Island tried a new tactic. It created the "Rhode Island Commission to Encourage Morality in Youth." The Commission set up a practice of notifying a distributor on official Commission stationery that certain designated books and magazines distributed by him had been reviewed and declared by the majority of the members on the Commission to be objectionable for sale, distribution or display, to youths under eighteen years of age. The local police officers would thereafter visit the distributor for the purpose of learning what action the distributor had taken following the receipt of the notice. It was argued in the Supreme Court that the Commission's activities amounted to a scheme of governmental censorship devoid of statutory safeguards and would thus abridge the First Amendment liberties. It was the Commission's suggestion that it did not regulate or suppress obscenity but simply exhorted booksellers. The court said that though the Commission was limited to informal sanctions—the threat of invoking legal sanctions and other means of coercion, persuasion, and intimidation—that nevertheless the Commission did by its act deliberately set up to achieve the suppression of publications deemed "objectionable." It also found that such conduct on the part of the Commission clearly intimidated the distributors and caused them to refuse to take orders for books, to stop selling books, to withdraw unsold copies from retailers, to return unsold copies to the publishers. This form of government by intimidation in the field of obscenity and literature was held unconstitutional.

In its more recent decisions, the Supreme Court, in specifying which state actions do, and do not, constitute prior restraint, has looked with disfavor on the prior restraint of allegedly obscene matter. Generally these decisions have held seizures or injunctions directed at allegedly obscene material to be unconstitutional when there is an absence of adequate judicial scrutiny prior to seizure or the issuance of an injunction. For such prior judicial scrutiny to be adequate, the Court has required more than a police officer's opinions to support the issuance of a warrant to seize allegedly obscene material. However, in the case of *Heller* v. *New York*, the Court did hold that a seizure would be permissible, without a previous judicial hearing, where the warrant for seizure was issued by a judge who had personally viewed the allegedly obscene film at a local theatre.

Generally, then, there is no prior restraint when the seizure of materials is pursuant to a warrant, when the warrant issues on a finding of probable cause by an impartial magistrate, when a prompt adversary proceeding follows the seizure and when the exhibitor of the seized film may make a copy he can show pending final judicial determination.

The criteria established by the court for prior restraint involving injunctions, as opposed to seizure, are, however, somewhat less stringent, at least where city-owned facilities are involved, and there may be some limited restraint before a judicial hearing, provided that such restraint is only temporary. That this is so was decided in litigation to prevent a municipal city board in Chattanooga, Tennessee, from restraining a production of the musical, *Hair*. The board refused to allow the production in a city-owned auditorium to go forward because it felt that the play was not in the best interests of the community. The Supreme Court, in holding that the proper procedural safeguards had not been employed, set forth three guidelines that government officials must meet before they can impose any restraint. These are (1) that the burden of instituting judicial proceedings and of proving that the material is obscene must rest with the censor; (2) that any restraint prior to judicial review can be imposed only for a specified brief period and only for the purpose of preserving the status quo; and (3) that a prompt, final judicial determination must be assured.

Since these decisions, the Supreme Court has not made any definitive pronouncements on prior restraint. However, several state and lower federal cases indicate a general drift. Thus in *Sanders* v. *Georgia*, the Georgia Supreme Court struck down a nuisance statute which authorized the shutdown of an entire business if it could be proved that a single obscene publication had been sold there. The presence of only one publication, the court said, should not be a basis for a blanket finding that the entire business was engaged in selling obscene materials. And, in *Grove Press* v. *City of Philadelphia*, a Circuit Court held that public nuisance concepts may not be used to define standards of protected speech and to serve as a vehicle for its restraint.

However, many jurisdictions have permitted the use of public nuisance proceedings to control material regarded by some as objectionable, and people and institutions which seek to curtail the rights of free speech and free press will remain active. Although the Supreme Court, at least in the field of prior restraint, has discouraged some of these activities, the decision in *Miller* has provided local authorities with a license to draft and enforce statutes aimed at what the court has for the present, at least, determined to be obscene.

Chapter 12

✺ CONTRACTS FOR PUBLICATION IN BOOK FORM

The objections, refusals and wishes of the plaintiff (author) after parting with the title in the property may betray the eccentricities of the author; but they have no greater weight in law than the wishes of a stranger to the transaction after it was consummated.

This short excerpt from the opinion of the court in *Clemens* v. *Press Publishing Co.* should be taken to heart by every author when he undertakes to sign a contract for the disposition of his works in any form. The signed contract is binding, and afterthoughts and wishes can play no part in the transaction between the author and his publisher. Too often authors have complained of their treatment at the hands of publishers when they were receiving everything that the contract between them provided for. The grievance may be just, but remedy there is none. The time to think about what the author wants is before, not after, he has made his engagements.

It is true that the usual lengthy printed form offered by most publishers tends to intimidate. But so does any document unless it is broken down and analyzed in terms of what is being disposed of, to whom it is being given and what the term or time of the proposed grant is, what natural benefits in terms of money accrue to each of the parties and what additional legal liabilities they incur by reason of the publication of the work. A printed contract tends to have a persuasive effect, particularly when it is accompanied by a statement that it is a standard form used by the publisher. Most authors, particularly young ones, do not have any standard form to which they can make reference as containing the clauses which they need and desire.

There is no such thing as a standard form. There are as many forms in use as there are publishing houses, since each one of them endeavors to get a contract corresponding to their prior experience in the business.

Undue desire for change in a proffered contract is unnecessary and sometimes disastrous. Change should be made only where an understood and urgent need for change arises. Language is only objectionable when it tends to take from the author rights which he ought to enjoy. It is frivolous to waste time on language. The end result is what should be the subject of negotiation.

In examining the contract the first step ought be a quick rundown or analysis to see if the contract contains or does not contain the essential parts of a contract for publication in book form.

The following outline discloses all the necessary parts of a grant of book rights. Each of them is discussed more fully and explained below.

1. The parties, to wit, the author and publisher.
2. The grant of the right to publish.
3. Copyright—in whose name to be taken, where and how.
4. Covenant by the author that the work is original, does not infringe, and will not subject the publisher to danger by reason of libel or other illegality.
5. Delivery date of the manuscript.
6. Agreement by publisher to publish, covering price of volume, form of volume, publication date.
7. Delivery of publisher of galley and page proof and provision for charges for revision.

8. Provision for royalty, including basis of computation of percentages and advances, if any, against them.
9. Accounting by the publisher.
10. Accounting for rights sold in gross.
11. Free copies to the author.
12. Obligation on publisher to keep work in print. Reversion to author for failure thereof.
13. Termination by bankruptcy.
14. Reservation of rights other than those specifically granted.
15. Termination of contract for breach at author's option.
16. Option for next work.
17. Subsidiary rights.
18. Miscellaneous provisions: property in manuscript; conflicting option; author's property in and the return of manuscript; deduction of sums due from author; law applicable; assignment; complete agreement.

The clauses which are included in the above analysis afford a complete contract for the author. Publishers, however, add other clauses thereto, including subsidiary rights covering:

1. Reprint in book form including full-length, condensed or abridged versions
2. Book clubs or similar organizations or royalties from mail order organizations
3. Anthology
4. Second serial and syndication, including full-length, condensed or abridged version in one part in magazines and newspapers (after publication in book form)
5. Pictorial versions of the work, or any part thereof, including books, strips, toy books and any other pictorial adaptations and pictorial or illustrative material contained therein
6. Commercial rights, i.e., the exploitation of the author's name in connection with the work and all material contained therein through their use, simulation or graphic exploitation on or in connection with merchandise
7. Full-length, condensed or abridged versions in one part in newspapers or periodicals before book publication
8. First serial publication in newspapers or periodicals (before publication in book form)

9. Dramatic rights (with or without music, public readings and other non-dramatic performing rights)
10. Motion picture rights
11. Radio and television rights
12. Mechanical reproduction and audio-visual rights, including all forms of reproduction, electronic or mechanical, including photocopy, recording, or any information storage and retrieval system by any method now known or hereafter devised regardless of the nature of the material objects in which the works are embodied.
13. Sole and exclusive rights of publication in
    (a) The United Kingdom
    (b) The British Empire and/or the British Commonwealth of Nations as now constituted
    (c) Other foreign countries
14. Translation

These rights will be discussed further hereinbelow, but insofar as possible the author should remember that the skinnier his contract, and the more he reserves to himself, the better his trading position. He should be chary of giving up any of his rights, and with regard to some of them should refuse absolutely so to do.

No author can be expected to know all the intricacies of legal draftmanship. It would be well to bear in mind that there is an Authors League of America, Inc., and that there is the Authors Guild thereof, which stands ready at all times to aid the author in the adaptation and improvement, for his own protection, of the clauses, and if such cooperation cannot be availed of by the author at the time of preparing his contract, he should avail himself of such expert advice as he has access to.

In discussing the special terms of an agreement we set forth the terms of the current Random House contract. The reason for setting forth this contract is that the Authors Guild Contract Committee negotiated with Random House in the preparation of that agreement. The inclusion of the terms of that agreement here is for example only. Individual examination of each contract proffered is essential to know whether or not it correctly embodies the specific situation between author and publisher in each particular case. The discussion following each clause takes into account the varying forms of contract which will be proffered to the author by the publisher.

1. *The parties, to wit, the author and publisher.*

> AGREEMENT made this   day of
>
> 19   between
>
> of
>
> (referred to as the Publisher), and
>
> whose address is:
>
> who is a citizen of
>
> and resident of (state)   (referred to as the Author and designated by the masculine singular pronoun).

This clause assumes a single author. There are however many situations in which the author is a plurality of persons:

(a) A collaboration between two or more authors.
(b) The author is an editor and compiler.
(c) There may be an author and illustrator.
(d) In some cases of biography there may be the biographee and the writer or biographer.
(e) A work written by one man based upon material in the possession of another.

These are only a few of the instances in which the word "author" needs further thought and definition.

So in the case of collaborators, they may wish to state the separate terms of their collaboration and the conditions that follow a breach or failure of the terms between them. It should be borne in mind that under our copyright law any person who is designated as an author and is a copyright proprietor, even though joint, may have the right to dispose of the entire copyrighted material.

Sometimes the joint effort is not even one sought by the author, as in the case of an author and illustrator, or biographee and biographer. Here the publisher may have selected the illustrator or the subject of the biography. There may be differences between the persons designated as author which arise subsequent to the entry of the contract. The question of whether there should be independent contracts or joint contracts becomes important and somewhere in the agreement provision should be made for the solution of such differences.

Since the situations which arise are not always foreseeable, it is impossible to discuss all such situations. Nevertheless, in entering into the contract the preliminary definition of "author" may be important.

This clause should not be enlarged by the inclusion therein of words of grant to the publishers' "heirs, executors, administrators or assigns" or "successors and assigns." It is desirable from the standpoint of the author that his contract should be with the publisher in whom he has placed confidence, and such rights should not, by operation of law, as for instance, through bankruptcy or death, or through private assignment, without the written consent of the author, be transferred to another.

2. *The grant of the right to publish.*

The Author grants to the Publisher during the term of copyright, including renewals and extensions thereof:

a. Exclusive right in the English language, in the United States of America, the Philippine Republic, and Canada, and non-exclusive right in all other countries except the British Commonwealth (other than Canada), the Republic of South Africa, and the Irish Republic, to:

i. Print, publish and sell the work in book form;

ii. License publication of the work (in complete, condensed or abridged versions) by book clubs, including subsidiaries of the Publisher;

iii. License publication of a reprint edition by another publisher with the consent of the Author. The Author shall be deemed to have given consent if within twenty (20) days after the forwarding of written request he fails to notify the Publisher in writing of his refusal to consent;

iv. License publication of the work (in complete, condensed, adapted or abridged versions) or selections from the work in anthologies and other publications, in mail-order and schoolbook editions, as premiums and other special editions and through microfilm and with the Author's consent Xerox or other forms of copying;

v. License periodical publication including magazines, newspapers and digests prior to book publication;

vi. License periodical publication after book publication to the extent that any such right is available;

vii. License, subject to the approval of the Author, adaptation of the work for filmstrips, printed cartoon versions and mechanical reproduction;

viii. License, without charge, transcription or publication of the work in Braille or in other forms, for the physically handicapped;

ix. For publicity purposes, publish or permit others to publish or broadcast (but not dramatize) by radio or television, without charge, such selections from the work as in the opinion of the Publisher may benefit its sale.

b. Exclusive right to license in the English language throughout the British Commonwealth (other than Canada), the Republic of South Africa, and the Irish Republic, the rights granted in subdivision a. above, revocable by the Author with respect to any country for which no license or option has been given within eighteen (18) months after first publication in the United States.

c. Exclusive right to license in all foreign languages and all countries, the rights granted in subdivision a. above, revocable by the Author with respect to each language or country for which no license or option has been given within three (3) years after first publication in the United States.

d. Exclusive right to use or license others to use, subject to the approval of the Author, the name and likeness of the Author, the work and the title of the work, in whole or in part, or any adaptation thereof as the basis for trademark or trade name for other products or for any other commercial use in connection with such other products.

The grant clause should first be examined both as to territory and time. There are some publishing houses which are equipped to handle Great Britain and the rest of the world through direct contact or through agents with whom they regularly do business. In such cases it is best to permit the publisher to have the widest possible territory, since it is better equipped than most authors to handle such sales and may even have a proper right to a more extensive territorial grant because of the nature of its initial publication in the United States and Canada. Unless dealing with such a house the author should reserve as much territory as is possible, particularly where the author has an agent whose foreign contacts may equal or be better than the publisher's. It should be noted that the clause contains many of the subsidiary rights. Such clause should be read in connection with the royalty clause and the grant should not be made unless a satisfactory royalty is agreed upon.

3. *Copyright—in whose name to be taken, where and how.*

The Publisher shall copyright the work in the name of the Author, in the United States, in compliance with the Universal Copyright Convention, and apply for renewals of such copyright. If copyright should be in the name of the Publisher, it shall assign such copyright upon request of the Author. The Publisher agrees to arrange for the sale of the work in Canada. If the Publisher adds illustrations or other material, and if copyright is in the Author's name, he agrees, upon request, to assign the copyright of such material. If the Author retains the right to periodical or foreign publication before publication by the Publisher, he shall notify the Publisher promptly of any arrangement of such publication or any postponement thereof. In the event of a periodical publication, if the copyright shall be in the name of any person other than the Author, he shall promptly deliver to the Publisher a legally recordable assignment of such copyright or of the rights granted. In the event of a publication outside the United States, promptly thereafter, he shall furnish to the Publisher three copies of the first published work and the date of such publication.

The copyright clause should contain language authorizing and binding the publisher to take out copyright in all countries covered by the agreement and specifically to print the notice in the form required by the Universal Copyright Convention, and to require that whenever a grant is made by the publisher of rights in territory other than the United States and Canada that the contract will contain an appropriate clause requiring the foreign publisher to take out copyright in each edition, particularly where translation is involved. All copyrights should be taken in the name of the author. This cannot be too strongly stressed. Cases frequently arise where due to time or circumstance the relationship terminates between the author and publisher and in those cases it becomes essential that the author should be the copyright proprietor.

4. *Covenant by the author covering warranties and indemnities.*

a. The Author warrants that he is the sole author of the work; that he is the sole owner of all the rights granted to the Publisher; that he has not previously assigned, pledged or otherwise encumbered the same; that he has full power to enter into this agreement; that except for the material obtained pursuant to Paragraph 3 the work is original, has not been published before, and is not in the public domain; that it does not violate any right of privacy; that it is not libelous or obscene; that it does not infringe upon any statutory or common-law copyright; and that any recipe, formula or instruction contained in the work is not injurious to the user.

b. In the event of any claim, action or proceeding based upon an alleged violation of any of these warranties (i) the Publisher shall have the right to defend the same through counsel of its own choosing, and (ii) no settlement shall be effected without the prior written consent of the Author, which consent shall not unreasonably be withheld, and (iii) the Author shall hold harmless the Publisher, any seller of the work, and any licensee of a subsidiary right in the work, against any damages finally sustained. If such claim, action or proceeding is successfully defended or settled, the Author's indemnity hereunder shall be limited to fifty per cent (50%) of the expense (including reasonable counsel fees) attributable to such defense or settlement; however, such limitation of liability shall not apply if the claim, action or proceeding is based on copyright infringement.

c. If any such claim, action or proceeding is instituted, the Publisher shall promptly notify the Author, who shall fully cooperate in the defense thereof, and the Publisher may withhold payments of reasonable amounts due him under this or any other agreement between the parties.

d. These warranties and indemnities shall survive the termination of this agreement.

The clause covering warranties and indemnities is included in every contract and of course differs in each. It is proper for an author to give a covenant that a work is original and that he owns the rights which he is granting. If the book is published with editorial changes made by publisher, or if the publisher supplies a jacket with a blurb or description, the author ought not be held accountable under this warranty for material supplied by the publisher. Some place in the covenant clause there should be an express statement that the author is liable only for material contained in the manuscript. Libel, obscenity or other unlawful matter covers so much in law and so much in territory that it should be carefully considered. Under our law there are fifty states which each have separate jurisdiction of cases arising under these categories. Because the publisher necessarily must sell in a number of states the courts of these states may severally obtain jurisdiction and suits may have to be defended all over the United States. In addition, obscenity cases may arise under the postal laws. The costs of such suits are onerous since counsel may (in jurisdictions other than the publisher's) and probably will be counsel not usually employed by the publisher but counsel who are employed for the specific case. Counsel fees tend therefore to be heavy and onerous. It is best that the author request a clause giving him the right to approve or designate counsel.

The author also should not be liable for settlements made by the publisher without the author's consent, nor should he be liable for costs and expenses where the suit is terminated in favor of the author. Any number of actions are brought for which the author is in no way responsible. There are crank suits of all kinds. Just as the author profits from the publication of the book so does the publisher, and it is a reasonable business risk for the publisher to assume the defense of these suits to which the work of the author has not contributed.

The author should also not be liable for any judgment unless there is a final judgment by a court having the highest appellate jurisdiction, at least certainly in the state in which the action is brought. While an author would have a right to waive such appeal, he ought not be liable until he has the assurance that a court other than the trial court has examined the case.

Of great importance to the author is the right of the publisher to withhold royalties and payments due the author pending such litigation. Not only are there crank cases but even legitimate cases may be unduly extended and an author may be deprived of royalty and payment for years. The money liability in any given cause cannot frequently be appraised by counsel, since amounts sued for are usually grossly disproportionate to the actual recovery. Since the publisher can utilize the money while the cause is proceeding, it is sometimes to the publisher's advantage to aggrandize the dangers of any particular suit. To guard against this the author's royalties and payments should at least be deposited in an escrow account for the benefit of the author, subject to liability, and the author should have the right to arbitrate the amount of money withheld, unless he can reach an agreement with the publisher. The importance of this cannot be too much stressed. This concerns the total moneys due to the author. There are and have been publishers who have withheld too much and too long.

5. *Delivery date of the manuscript.*

The Author agrees to deliver two complete copies (original and clean copy) of the manuscript of the work in the English language of approximately words in length, in content and form satisfactory to the Publisher, together with any permission required pursuant to Paragraph 3, and all photographs, illustrations, drawings, charts, maps and indexes suitable for reproduction and necessary to the completion of the manuscript not later than If he fails to do so the Publisher shall have the right to supply them and charge the cost against any sums accruing to the Author. The complete manuscript shall include the following additional items:

If the Author fails to deliver the manuscript within ninety (90) days after the above date the Publisher may terminate this agreement by giving written notice, whereupon the Author agrees to repay forthwith all amounts which may have been advanced hereunder.

One of the most frequent causes of difficulty between author and publisher arises from non-delivery of material on time. Since failure on the part of the author to deliver on his agreed date constitutes a breach on his part, the author should consider carefully the amount of work involved and the possibility of delivery on the due date. It is best to play on the safe side and take more time than may ultimately prove to have been necessary, rather than to make rash promises and find oneself in default. From the publisher's standpoint this is desirable, since he will not be misled into placing the book on a list or advertising it for sale to the trade prior to completion, thus embarrassing him. In fixing this date, the author should also take into account the type of work and the publisher's seasonal list best suited to the book's sale.

A deadline is a deadline and it is reasonable to require that the author either deliver or pay back. On the other hand, the deadline for the publisher is subject to delay for many reasons beyond his control. Certainly the author is entitled to a similar delay for causes beyond his control and including illness.

6. *Delivery by publisher of galley proof and page proof.*

The Author agrees to read, revise, correct and return promptly all proofs of the work and to pay in cash or, at the option of the Publisher, to have charged against him, the cost of alterations, in type or in plates, required by the Author, other than those due to printer's errors, in excess of ten per cent (10%) of the cost of setting type, provided a statement of these charges is sent to the Author within thirty (30) days of the receipt of the printer's bills and the corrected proofs are presented on request for his inspection.

It is extremely difficult to determine what are printer's errors and what are author's corrections, and the author may find himself presented with a bill for proof corrections far beyond that which was contemplated by him. Since he is to bear the cost of such corrections, it is absolutely essential that the clause contain the distinction between author's changes and additions and correction of printer's or publisher's errors. The author should, whenever possible, insist upon getting proof which has already been proofread by the publisher and corrected, so that there can be as little confusion as possible between corrections made necessary by his additions or corrections, and the publisher's or printer's.

Even though this be done, there will still be corrections which will be made by the author, but which are due to the printer or publisher. In proofreading and revising, the author would do well for himself to make a note, therefore, of which is which.

Many publishers' contracts set ten percent as a basis for the cost of revisions. It is important to notice the percentage and to bargain with regard thereto, for it must be remembered that the author's corrections are valuable to the publisher. The afterthought may be an improvement on the original manuscript, and insofar as the author's corrections enhance the value of the script submitted, mere manufacturing costs become insignificant. For that reason the publisher might well allow the author more than even the ten percent suggested without charge. But that ten percent minimum seems to be a satisfactory minimum. It will be noticed that the liability of the author to pay is in the disjunctive, that is to say, that the author may either pay the charges or they may be charged against his royalties. From the author's standpoint it is usually advisable to permit the amount to stand as a charge against royalties, and perhaps even to enlarge the clause so as to wipe out the alternative specific obligations to pay, since there is no reason why the author should suffer a loss on account of the production of the book, as he might, if the royalties were insufficient to meet the additional manufacturing costs. Of course, the author may be loath to think, at the time of making his contract, that the book will not earn enough royalties to pay even for corrections, but unfortunately publishing experience has proven that that may often happen, and the author may find himself in the position of owing money to his publisher. Guard against it wherever possible by providing that the overcharge for corrections shall be a charge against royalties only.

Proofreading is a publisher's job and the author should not be liable at all for changes from the text or for typographical errors made by the printer. These may arise from copy submitted by the publisher. Publishers sometimes make their own copy for the use of the printer, including editorial changes from the manuscript as submitted. Since the author will suffer from any excess of correction costs, he should examine this clause carefully and insist on the protective changes.

7. *The agreement by the publisher to publish.*

Within one year after the Author has delivered the manuscript in conformity with Paragraph 2, the Publisher shall publish the work at its own expense, in such style and manner, under such imprint and at such price as it deems suitable. The Publisher shall not be responsible for delays caused by any circumstance beyond its control. No changes in the manuscript or the provisional title shall be made without the consent of the Author. However, in no event shall the Publisher be obligated to publish a work which in its opinion violates the common law or statutory copyright or the right of privacy of any person or contains libelous or obscene matter.

The author would do well, if he can, to procure the insertion therein of a minimum first edition. This is omitted from the suggested clause only because it never has been a usual practice in the publishing trade to guarantee to the author a minimum royalty based upon a minimum edition. There is no reason why the publisher's engagement should not be stated specifically. Editions vary in size, and sales vary. The author must remember that his percentage is computed upon sales. Sales may be low. The fault may lie in the book, or it may lie in the salesmanship. The publisher's function is to sell. If a burden is imposed upon him to meet a minimum demand, there would be much less of the usual feeling on the part of the author that the book has been advertised inadequately or insufficiently pushed. Take for example a book published at $5, having a minimum edition of two thousand copies at ten percent. Two thousand at five dollars is $10,000, and ten percent would be $1,000. The figures are given so that the writer may have some idea as to what his royalties actually amount to. Using that figure as a basis, find that reasonable sum which would compensate for the writing, and, if possible, insist upon its inclusion in the contract. This can be done either by providing for the minimum edition suggested, or by providing for an advance royalty to be charged against earned royalties, but which is in no event to be returned to the publisher or chargeable on future works of the author.

The suggested clause provides for a minimum retail price. In fixing that retail price, the author should take into account the type of book, its probable market, and should fix a price as high as possible as its minimum retail price. For contract purposes, in determining the amount of advance royalties, this is much better than setting a low price. If the high price should prove impractical, the condition could be met when it arose, and the price lowered.

With regard to the date of publication, the author should consider this in connection with the clause requiring him to deliver the manuscript, and should fix a date which would make it reasonably certain that the manuscript can be delivered, corrected, and manufactured and then meet a sales date which coincides with a good selling period in the trade.

8. *Provision for royalty, including basis of computation of percentages and advances, if any, against them.*

The Publisher shall pay to the Author as an advance against and on account of all moneys accruing to him under this agreement, the sum of dollars ($), payable

Any such advance shall not be repayable, provided that the Author has delivered the manuscript in conformity with Paragraph 2 and is not otherwise in default under this agreement.

The Publisher shall pay to the Author a royalty on the retail price of every copy sold by the Publisher, less returns (except as set forth below):

a.   per cent (%) up to and including   copies; per cent (%) in excess of   copies up to and including copies; and   per cent (%) in excess of   copies. Where the discount in the United States is forty-eight per cent (48%) or more from the retail price, the rate provided in this subdivision a. shall be reduced by one-half the difference between forty-four per cent (44%) and the discount granted. In no event, however, shall such royalty be less than one-half the rate provided herein. If the semiannual sales aggregate fewer than 400 copies, the royalty shall be two-thirds (2/3) of the rate provided in this subdivision a. if such copies are sold from a second or subsequent printing. Copies covered by any other subdivision of this Paragraph shall not be included in such computation.

b. Five per cent (5%) of the amount received for copies sold directly to the consumer through the medium of mail-order or coupon advertising, or radio or television advertising.

c. Five per cent (5%) of the amount received for copies sold by the Publisher's Premium or Subscription Books Wholesale Department.

d. Ten per cent (10%) for hard-cover copies and five per cent (5%) for soft-cover copies sold with a lower retail price as college textbooks.

e. For a School edition the royalty provided in subdivision a. of this Paragraph but no more than:

   i. Ten per cent (10%) of the amount received for a Senior High School edition;

   ii. Eight per cent (8%) of the amount received for a Junior High School edition;

   iii. Six per cent (6%) of the amount received for an Elementary School edition.

f. Five per cent (5%) for an edition published at a lower retail price or for an edition in the Modern Library (regular or giant size) or in Vintage Books; and two per cent (2%) or two cents (2¢) per copy, whichever is greater, for an edition in the Modern Library College Editions.

g. Ten per cent (10%) of the amount received for the original edition and five per cent (5%) of the amount received for any lower-price edition for copies sold for export.

h. For copies sold outside normal wholesale and retail trade channels, ten per cent (10%) of the amount received for the original edition and five per cent (5%) of the amount received for any lower-price edition for copies sold at a discount between fifty per cent (50%) and sixty per cent (60%) from the retail price and five per cent (5%) of the amount received for copies sold at a discount of sixty per cent (60%) or more from the retail price, or for the use of the plates by any governmental agency.

i. No royalty shall be paid on copies sold below or at cost including expenses incurred, or furnished gratis to the Author, or for review, advertising, sample or like purposes.

j. Fifty per cent (50%) of the amount received from the disposition of licenses granted pursuant to Paragraph 1, subdivisions a., ii, iii, iv, vi and vii. At the Author's request his share from book club and reprint licensing, less any unearned advances, shall be paid to him within two weeks after the receipt thereof by the Publisher. If the Publisher rebates to booksellers for unsold copies due to the publication of a lower-price or reprint edition, the royalty on such copies shall be the same as for such lower-price edition.

k. Ninety per cent (90%) of the amount received from the disposition of licenses in the United States and Canada granted pursuant to Paragraph 1, subdivision a., v.

l. Eighty per cent (80%) of the amount received from the disposition of licenses granted pursuant to Paragraph 1, subdivision b.

m. Seventy-five per cent (75%) of the amount received from the disposition of licenses granted pursuant to Paragraph 1, subdivision c.

n. Fifty per cent (50%) of the amount received from the disposition of licenses granted pursuant to Paragraph 1, subdivision d., provided that all expenses in connection therewith shall be borne by the Publisher.

o. If any license granted by the Publisher pursuant to Paragraph 1 shall include material of others, the amount payable to the Author shall be inclusive of royalty to other authors.

Consideration should first be given to the advance royalty. The factors that enter into it are the amount of research, cost of procuring data and information, the checking which the author must do, and other elements which enter into the time required to produce, and the specific nature of the work. Scientific, historical or other work calling for research, and the expenditures of moneys for obtaining the material, may call for specific advances for that purpose. Other than that, the author's reputation, previous sales, etc., enter into the computation of the advance.

As to the royalties themselves, that is entirely a bargaining matter. Make the first percentage as high as possible, and the first number of books as low as possible and keep that rule for each step in the gradation. Ten percent on the first five thousand, twelve and one-half percent of the next twenty-five hundred, fifteen percent on all over seventy-five hundred, would be a fair royalty for an author of moderate standing.

There has been a recent innovation in computation of royalties whereby the basis of calculation is made the net price received by the publisher instead of the catalogue retail price. There is a wide spread between the price at which the publisher sells and the price to the public at retail. The catalogue retail price includes jobbers' and retailers' profits and also the author's royalty. The publisher does not receive from the dealer a standard price. His price-making is subject to fluctuation caused by varying discounts, in sales of large quantities and to jobbers. Since the price received by the publisher varies while the retail price does not vary, a royalty percentage based upon the retail price may make it difficult for the publisher and author to exploit the sales possibilities of the work. The practice has therefore grown by fixing the percentage to the author on the price received by the publisher. This need not necessarily work hardship on the author. By calculating his percentage upon the net price received by the publisher the author may obtain the same amount. It is entirely a matter of computation and foresight. The publisher's average discount is between 40 and and 45 percent. Applying this to a $5 book the author can, by asking for a slightly less than double royalty on the retail price, obtain the same emolument while permitting the publisher the greater elasticity in dealing which the net price allows him. Publishers take the gamble when the author has something to sell. Weigh what you have in your basket, and sell at the market—not less.

Most publishers use as a basis the retail catalogue price. They then proceed to lessen this percentage in a wide variety of sales. So, for instance, there may be varying royalties depending upon the discounts granted by the publisher. The publisher's rationale is that he widens the distribution of the book by utilizing as many varied sources of income as he can find. There is no real reason for the author's lessening his royalty for the wider market, since it is to be assumed that when a book sells many copies the cost of producing each copy goes down and the proportionate profit is greater. Nevertheless, it is a general trade custom to take and permit such discounts. The author should study this to make sure that in no event is his royalty ever less than half of his agreed royalty. Publishers ask for reduced royalties in cases where they grant discounts greater than the usual trade discount; on sheets where the book is sold in sheets instead of in bound copies; on copies sold for export; through mail order; school editions, lending libraries, school depositories, reading circles and educational associations, and remainders. Publishers also ask for a reduced royalty from reprintings of less than a stipulated number. With regard to such reprintings for a limited number of copies the author should provide that where such reprintings aggregate more than the limited number the higher royalties shall then apply. Publishers have been known to reprint a smaller number than required in successive reprintings in order to obtain the benefit of a reduced royalty. Therefore the total reprinting in the course of a year should be the basis of royalty, not any single reprinting.

9. *Accounting by the publisher.*

The Publisher shall render semi-annual statements of account to the first day of April and the first day of October, and shall mail such statements during the July and January following, together with checks in payment of the amounts due thereon.

Should the Author receive an overpayment of royalty arising from copies reported sold but subsequently returned, the Publisher may deduct such overpayment from any further sums due the Author.

Upon his written request, the Author may examine or cause to be examined through certified public accountants the books of account of the Publisher in so far as they relate to the sale or licensing of the work.

Notwithstanding anything to the contrary in this or any prior agreement between the parties, the Author shall in no event be entitled to receive under this and all prior agreements with the Publisher more than $
during any one calendar year. If in any one calendar year the total of the sums accruing to the Author under this and all prior agreements with the Publisher shall exceed such amount, he shall be entitled to receive the excess amount in any succeeding calendar year in which the sums accruing to him under this and all prior agreements with the Publisher do not exceed the maximum herein stated, provided that the total amount to which the Author may be entitled under this and all prior agreements with the Publisher in any succeeding calendar year shall not exceed the maximum herein stated.

A typical publisher's statement of account will include a list of Domestic Regular, Domestic Wholesalers at varying discounts, Domestic in Sheets, Export, Canadian and Remaindered Below Cost of the varying items above set forth, and in addition other earnings. This may be mystifying to the author who receives the statement. He should compare it with his contract to find out whether or not the statement correctly reflects the contractual agreement.

The fourth paragraph of the above clause on payment provides for a stipulated sum to be paid by the publisher to the author during any one calendar year. The object of this clause is frankly for the benefit of the author, since his tax position may be such that he wishes to spread income from the book over a long period of time. If this clause is used, the author is well advised who first consults with a tax expert to find out how much of the tax resulting from the book he may spread over prior years. He may then consider the future and determine whether he wants his royalties withheld and paid to him over a period of years.

A word of caution ought to be given in connection with this clause. Royalties paid may be utilized for the author for further income by way of dividends or interest. If he postpones payment in this fashion his money is idle. He spreads his taxes but he delays income, and income on income. For an author in the very high brackets such a spread may be warranted, but otherwise it should be the subject of close calculation.

10. *Accounting for rights sold in gross.*

The subsidiary rights which we have referred to are frequently sold for a gross amount less agent's commissions or an advance against royalties. Where this occurs the publisher will receive a considerable sum of money on the signing of the contract. There is no reason why the author should not receive his share of such subsidiary sales forthwith and at the same time that the publisher receives them. The contract should contain a clause providing for this. This may be done by providing for payment to be made to the author of his share by the payer or by the publisher within a reasonable period, not more than ten days after the receipt by the publisher of any moneys for subsidiary rights.

11. *Free copies to the author.*

On publication the Publisher shall give ten (10) free copies to the Author, who may purchase further copies for personal use at a discount of forty percent (40%) from the retail price.

Ten free copies is usual, as is the forty percent discount. Provision might be made that such purchases be against royalties due rather than for cash, since if the book sells at all the publisher always has accrued royalties payable to the author, the author might well be permitted to charge against them.

12. *Obligation of the publisher to keep the work in print. Reversion to the author for failure thereof.*

The usual grant is for the term of copyright and renewals, which may turn out to be for life plus seventy-five years, and is even now fifty-six years. Within the grant there is included not only the first or hardcover publication, but there are paperback rights and all of the enumerated subsidiaries, including mechanical, motion picture, etc. All of these rights have varying times during which they are valuable, as well as contractual terms. A book may go out of print, but contracts for specific subsidiaries may or may not have been entered into which are still in force. The usual clauses in publishers' contracts do not offer adequate protection in a modern framework and in any consideration of the author's and the work's lifetime. All too frequently an author may have a good use for a work years after its first publication. He may have an opportunity to rewrite and reissue. He may have demands for reprint rights. There may be demands for modernized motion picture versions or television. All of these instances have arisen. All too frequently the author finds that having granted the rights he cannot recapture them without considerable delay and trouble. The contract should make adequate provision for the future.

In the case of hardcover the onus should be on the publisher to notify the author when it ceases to keep the book in print. The author can then determine whether he wants to make a demand on the publisher to keep it in print or whether he then elects to terminate. Whether a work is in print can easily be determined. When the sales of a work fall below a minimum of fifty copies a year the author ought to have the right to terminate the contract. This fact can be established by the royalty statement and therefore is determinable.

The situation is clouded by the fact that the publisher has the right under most contracts to grant subsidiary rights. Without question all subsidiary rights not granted prior to termination should revert to the author. Where subsidiary rights have been granted there should be a limit in each contract on the time for the exploitation of such rights. This falls within a pattern of each of the industries involved in subsidiary rights, for it has long been usual to put a limitation on the term of motion picture grants and television grants, and there is no reason why subsidiary book rights, such as reprint and paperback, should not contain a like covenant. Where there has been a sale for a single sum there should be a period of years. Where there has been a payment for a single year plus royalties the contract should terminate whenever the royalties do not reach a minimum amount per annum. The rights of reversion to the author should not be subject to licenses previously granted unless such licenses have the limitations suggested.

Many contracts require the author to repurchase the plates from the publisher on termination. This ought never be necessary. The publisher has used the plates for its purposes. The author may provide for an option in him to purchase the plates, but it should never be compulsory.

13. *Termination by bankruptcy.*

If (a) a petition in bankruptcy is filed by the Publisher, or (b) a petition in bankruptcy is filed against the Publisher and such petition is finally sustained, or (c) a petition for arrangement is filed by the Publisher or a petition for reorganization is filed by or against the Publisher, and an order is entered directing the liquidation of the Publisher as in bankruptcy, or (d) the Publisher makes an assignment for the benefit of creditors, or (e) the Publisher liquidates its business for any cause whatever, the Author may terminate this agreement by written notice and thereupon all rights granted by him hereunder shall revert to him. Upon such termination, the Author, at his option, may purchase the plates as provided in Paragraph 12 and the remaining copies at one-half of the manufacturing cost, exclusive of overhead. If he fails to exercise such option within sixty (60) days after the happening of any one of the events above referred to, the Trustee, Receiver, or Assignee may destroy the plates and sell the copies remaining on hand, subject to the royalty provisions of Paragraph 8.

The clause covering recapture in the event of bankruptcy of the publisher has unfortunately become of great importance, due to the number of publishing houses which spring up and disappear. In the event of bankruptcy or reorganization by involuntary sale through the courts, the author may find that he has been sold down the river to a publisher little interested in his works, and with whom the author does not desire to have business relationships. It has been held by at least one court that the author's contract does not terminate with bankruptcy. This is most unfortunate, for undoubtedly the relationship existing between the author and the publisher, while essentially a business relationship, has in it many elements of personal relationship. The clause as printed is fair.

14. *Reservation of rights other than those specifically granted.*

With the author's rights covering a wide variety of methods of exploitation, it is essential that in the publishing contract he should reserve to himself all rights other than those which he has specifically granted. The following language is suggested for that purpose:

All rights, now existent or which may hereafter come into existence, except those hereinbefore specifically granted to the Publishers, are hereby reserved to the Author, which rights he may exercise at any time.

15. *Termination of contract for breach at author's option.*

The suggested clause reads as follows:

If the Publishers should at any time during the existence of this agreement fail to comply with, or fulfill, any of the terms or conditions thereof, it being expressly agreed that time is of the essence of this agreement, then or in any of these events, this agreement shall terminate at the option of the Author, said option to be exercised by the Author in writing and by registered mail and thereupon all rights granted by the Author to the Publishers shall forthwith terminate and revert to him and any payment which may have been made to the Author under this agreement shall remain his absolute property, all, however, without prejudice to any other remedies which the Author may have as against the Publishers.

The above clause is self-explanatory.

16. *Option for next work.*

The Author agrees to submit to the Publisher his next book-length work before submitting the same to any other publisher. The Publisher shall be entitled to a period of six weeks after the submission of the completed manuscript, which period shall not commence to run prior to one month after the publication of the work covered by this agreement, within which to notify the Author of its decision. If within that time the Publisher shall notify the Author of its desire to publish the manuscript, it shall thereupon negotiate with him with respect to the terms of such publication. If within thirty (30) days thereafter the parties are unable in good faith to arrive at a mutually satisfactory agreement for such publication, the Author shall be free to submit his manuscript elsewhere, provided, however, that he shall not enter into a contract for the publication of such manuscript with any other publisher upon terms less favorable than those offered by the Publisher.

Most publishers' contracts provide for an option in the publisher to acquire one or more of the next works of the author. The publisher urges, for the justification of this practice, that he may, by the publication of the first book, create the author as a potential seller, and that he is entitled to the benefit of the advertising and exploitation of the author's works by acquiring the right to sell his subsequent works. Very little can be said for this, since the publisher's efforts are directed toward the sale of the particular work which he acquires. If he sells, the advertising and publicity costs have been recompensed. If the work does not sell, it has answered the publisher's statement that he has created a demand for the author's works. If the relationship between the publisher and the author has been pleasant, no question usually arises, and the author usually is pleased to continue. It is only where there has been trouble that the clause becomes effective, and then it operates to bind the unwilling author to an undesirable publisher. Such inharmonious relationship should not be the creature of the author's contract. The author should endeavor at all times to have as complete a control over his subsequent works as possible, and should refuse to contract for his as yet unborn or unpublished work.

Most of the option clauses are troublesome for the further reason that they are drawn upon the basis of future agreement between the parties. These options are so vague and indefinite that the courts cannot enforce them. It is a rule that the courts cannot make contracts for the parties, and where the contract lacks definiteness and certainty there is no enforceable option. Enforcible or no such clauses make for trouble, since their mere inclusion in the contract may have some kind of compulsion in them, even though it is an imperfect obligation. It is therefore better practice to leave it out. The parties can always negotiate for a second work if their relations have been harmonious.

17. *Subsidiary rights.*

Hereinabove there were enumerated some fourteen classifications of subsidiary rights. These rights range through first serial, second serial, reprint, mechanical, etc. In the usual instance all of these rights to the publisher flow merely from an agreement by the publisher to publish the work in hardcover. Modern packaging arrangements have made it possible for a publisher on making his first contract, and even before he has sold a single copy of the book contemplated as the basis of the contract, to sell subsidiary rights for large sums. What the publisher is doing in effect is trading on his contract, which he sometimes does not even prepare until preliminary investigation has proven that subsidiary rights will be sold.

Agreements are made by the publisher for the sale of paperback, serial, one shot, motion picture, TV rights, sometimes singly and sometimes in combination. Negotiations advance to a point of acceptance. Then and only then does the publisher make his contract with the author. It is evident that it is the author's work which is commanding this money. The publisher has made no contribution, except that of an intermediary. The publisher is then in a position to publish the work knowing that no matter what he does with the hardcover edition he is in the black.

There should be no right in the publisher in and to any subsidiary right unless he fulfills his primary function of publishing the book. His share of subsidiary rights should be governed by his work in promoting the sale of that book. For instance, it has already been established in the work of the dramatist that the producer of the play does not obtain motion picture and television rights unless the play is produced for a minimum number of performances in first-class theatres in first-class cities. So in the case of the book there should be an agreement that no subsidiary rights should go to the publisher from the author unless certain publication requirements have first been met.

Since it may be advisable from the author's standpoint to enter into preliminary packaging agreements, the ingenuity of counsel should be called in to make provision for payment to the publisher of moneys obtained through such package deals or through single preliminary sales of subsidiaries providing that the publisher publishes the work. Such contracts could well contain clauses already used providing for percentages based upon volume of sales.

The same reasoning applies to all sales of subsidiary rights. Unless the publisher has so published the work and so promoted it as to create a market for subsidiary sales, there is no reason why he should profit, and a ceiling might well be imposed on the publisher's right to receive moneys from subsidiaries, except based upon sales of the hardcover work. There are instances in the contract where the publisher receives and retains royalties of the author for various purposes. There is no reason why the publisher's share of subsidiaries should not be deposited in an escrow account to be paid out only upon compliance by the publisher of his primary obligation.

In connection with all subsidiary rights the author should remember the primary copyright and insist in all cases copyright should be taken in his name no matter what the use.

18. *Some miscellaneous provisions.*

Property in manuscript.

If the Author incorporates in the work any copyrighted material, he shall procure, at his expense, written permission to reprint it.

Some works require many permissions. In fact, most publishing firms have a Permissions Editor for that purpose. An anthology may consist in large part of copyright material, so may works of scholarship and research. Each manuscript must stand on its own and the author should approximate the amount of money which will be required for permissions and negotiate with the publisher either to pay the permissions or to increase the advance to the author so as to provide the funds for obtaining permission. When permission is obtained, it is important to obtain the permission for use in the book, its reprints, and translations, territorially throughout the world.

Conflicting option.

The Author agrees that during the term of this agreement he will not, without the written permission of the Publisher, publish or permit to be published any material, in book or pamphlet form, based on material in the work.

This clause is troublemaking. In the case of fiction there are situations, locations, characters, etc., who may appear and reappear in the author's work. He may follow a family through seven generations. He may follow the peoples of a country in numerous works. The author may have hit upon a picturesque locale. What is material in the work as contained in this clause above is altogether too inclusive. We have seen recently a best seller, *Peyton Place* followed by *Return to Peyton Place,* followed by its use in motion pictures. Every subsequent use contained some part of the material in the original book. An author should not be asked to give up such rights to future work.

In the case of nonfiction an even more onerous condition exists. Specialists must write on their specialty. Each subsequent work may utilize some of the past work. Some special works become outdated. New scholarship may make a new work essential. Under our law, and indeed under the proposed new copyright law, anyone may make fair use of previous work. Surely an author should not be prohibited by a contract from making less use of his prior works than others have a right to.

There may be special occasions where a competitive work ought to be provided against. If the publisher insists on such clause it should be limited to the use of such material as would be held to be an infringement of the original work.

Author's property in and the return of the manuscript.

Except for loss or damage due to its own negligence, the Publisher shall not be responsible for loss of or damage to any property of the Author.

In the absence of written request from the Author prior to publication for their return, the Publisher, after publication of the work, may dispose of the original manuscript and proofs.

The author should require the publisher to return all manuscripts and proofs as corrected by the author. They are his property and have value, monetary as well as sentimental. The disposition should be his and not the publisher's.

Deduction of sums due from the author.

Any sums due and owing from the Author to the Publisher, whether or not arising out of this agreement, may be deducted from any sum due or to become due from the Publisher to the Author pursuant to this agreement. For the purposes of this Paragraph a non-repayable unearned advance made to the Author pursuant to another agreement shall not be construed as being a sum due and owing, unless the Author is in default under such other agreement.

This clause or a variant of it is appearing in most publishing contracts. Under the covenants given by the author to the publisher it has been noted that the publisher claims the right to withhold payments due to the author pending the defense of claims, actions or proceedings. The publisher could withhold under this clause not only moneys due from the book in litigation, but all moneys due the author. Where an author has written more than one book for a publisher and royalties are due him, he may find that all of his income is tied up because of litigation on one book. This can be a real hardship, and if possible should be avoided by limiting the right in the publisher to withhold sums due only on each specific contract and to delete the words "whether or not arising out of this agreement."

Law applicable.

This agreement shall be interpreted according to the law of the State of New York.

If, in fact, the contract has been entered into in the State of New York this clause is not objectionable, but if the author resides other than in the State of New York and wishes to have his contract governed, for instance, by the law of California, this clause calls for consideration. It is usually not questioned.

Assignment.

This agreement shall be binding upon the heirs, executors, adminstrators and assigns of the Author, and upon the successors and assigns of the Publisher, but no assignment shall be binding on either of the parties without the written consent of the other.

Complete agreement.

This agreement constitutes the complete understanding of the parties. No modification or waiver of any provision shall be valid unless in writing and signed by both parties.

There may be and usually are special clauses in every agreement providing for the requirements of each contract. For the very reason that each contract ought be separately considered there can be no standard contract. There is none. What has been printed above and what has been commented upon are equally only suggestions.

❧ INDEX